The Grass Never Grew Greener!

The life and labour for the Lord

of George Leith Shivas

1884 - 1963

based on his diaries

Edited by

Murray D. Regis

The Grass Never Grew Greener!

The Diaries of George L. Shivas

Published by
Murray D. Regis
80 Ontario St. N. Apt. 809
Milton, Ontario L9T 4Z6

ISBN 0-9696715-0-4

Publishing co-ordination by Jim Dills, 419 Campbell Ave. Milton Ont. L9T 1C1
Front Cover by Ruth Mudge, Campbellville, Ont.
Printed by Stan Brown Printers Limited, Owen Sound Ont.
First Printing January 1993.

I Have A Goodly Heritage,
Psalm 16.6.

What lessons from my father can be learned
From what he said, and by his life discerned.
He loved and gladly served his Father, God,
And for His glory were his footsteps trod;
He said "Thank God" so many times each day,
A thankful spirit garrisoned his way.
"No matter what your circumstance may be,
Something to be thankful for you'll always see."
This was his motto, and he thanked the Lord
For all His tender mercies on him poured.

He loved to tell how happy was the day
When Jesus washed his many sins away;
A Bible on the kitchen table lay
That God through it the Gospel might convey;
"For God so loved the world, His Son He gave,
That Everlasting Life his soul might have."
The grass grew greener, with a brighter hue,
The birds sang sweeter, blue skies seemed more blue.

He loved the Saviour, loved to tell of Him
Who died to save lost sinners from their sin.
This was his great desire, to faithful be
In warning all about Eternity,
And of a hell to shun, a heaven to gain:
He loved to tell of all the Saviour's pain,
The thorny crown which on His head He wore,
The awful Cross on which our sins He bore.

4

He loved the Word of God, its sacred page
Did many times each day his thoughts engage.
No morning's work without it was begun,
At noon a Proverb read — the thirty one
Marked off the month; the golden verse each day
Was thought upon to help us on our way.
No evening closed without a fresh delight
From God's own Word to think upon at night.

———————————

He loved to raise his voice in fervent prayer
That all might in the Saviour's knowledge share,
That saints might be refreshed and onward go
To love and serve the Lord while here below.
He loved the place where those who gather there
Show forth the Saviour's death, together share
The bread, His body, and the wine, His blood,
In symbol taken, thankful for His love.

———————————

What better heritage could he bestow
On those who follow after him below?
"The memory of the just is blessed" we read,
"They rest, their works do follow them" indeed,
And though he's been in heaven for many a year,
My father's voice in prayer I still can hear.

E. A. R.

George L. Shivas

Foreword

It is one of the happy, though sometimes confusing, characteristics of a family with a plurality of children, that each one is uniquely different. In time we come to appreciate each other's uniqueness. If happily that family is a Christian family, then we also are able to acknowledge the sovereignty and wisdom of our God in designing each one's distinctiveness. So it is, and much more also, in the family of God. We thank God for each and every one of His children, for they are also our brothers and sisters. Occasionally one of the children of God has been given a distinctiveness that excels in a certain way, which to us is outstanding because of the impact it makes on our normal way of thinking. It breaks that general mould in which the most of us see ourselves cast.

This was the reason why the people of God enjoyed the refreshing and attractive uniqueness of the servant of the Lord, Mr. George Shivas. His ability to surprise us, and shock us betimes, was the quality that kept us on the edge of our seats, fearing we might miss some little quip he would throw in to see if we were listening. The element of surprise has always been one of the special tools that men have used to hold the attention of the audience. In this, Mr. Shivas was a natural master of the art. Acknowledging that he was a gift of God to the church, one never needed to have envied his gift. This should be comforting to every one of us when we acknowledge that each one of God's children is a gift to the church of Christ, for the blessing and edification of all the members.

This book therefore, which has been compiled by his son-in-law, is in response to the wishes of many, that somewhat of Mr. Shivas' happy style and uniqueness might be preserved for many of us who knew him so well. Many others have heard about him, and have been compelled to recognize that the memory of so many of his sayings and ways should be kept available in print for us all.

The apostle Paul's words to the Corinthians in the first epistle, chapter 14, verse 12, "Seek that ye may excel," are very carefully and wisely qualified by the injunction "to the edifying of the church." It is inherent in the nature of us all to want to excel in some field. Members in a living body have only to fulfil the function that they find natural to them. If they are living members in the body of Christ, then a further quality is a vital necessity. That quality is a constant recognition of those member's devotedness to the Head of the body. This will direct them for the wellbeing of the whole body.

As indicated in my father's letter, a few pages over in this book, Mr. Shivas held me in his arms when I was ten days old, and called me a "poor little sinner" which offended my dear mother, and she wouldn't speak to him for weeks. Of course mother soon discovered to her dismay that he was correct in his assessment of her firstborn. Shortly after my wife and I were married in 1938, we had the great honour of entertaining Mr. Shivas in our home, while he had gospel meetings in "Pape," just around the corner from where we lived. It was at that time that I became very much aware that here was a man that as a member in the body of Christ was in constant and happy communication with the Head of the body. He didn't consider it necessary to bring the Lord into every situation, but he lived rather in the enjoyment of the fact that the Lord was already IN all his situations. One morning when he came down for breakfast I said, "Mr. Shivas, you would like to be home." "Oh no, I wouldn't, Arnold." "You wouldn't like to be home?" I asked. "No, because I am convinced that I am right where the Lord wants me to be, and that's where I want to be. As soon as these meetings are ended, I will be happy to head home." This was a lesson that has helped much in moulding my general thinking.

I would say that the conscious awareness of the nearness of his God, that we all can develop, contributed to the godly character of his unique gift. If all of us, who are vital members in the body of Christ, would set our minds and hearts to be more God-conscious, we also would excel, not only to the edifying of the church, but also to the blessing of all those with whom we live, and whom we meet day by day, along life's way.

Arnold Adams, Orillia, Ontario, January 1993

Introduction

There must be many of us who recall being at a Toronto Conference, under the following circumstances:

It is a Saturday or Sunday afternoon, and the weather has been exceptionally mild. The ministry has been excellent, and we have endeavoured to follow attentively the intent of the messages. There have been three speakers, possibly four. Our minds are loaded, and overloaded, attempting to retain the rich ministry of able brethren. Our bodies are protesting the close quarters, and the warmth of the afternoon. Beside all this, the time has drifted around to 4:42 pm, and there really is not time for another speaker before the supper hour.

In the midst of this dilemma a brother rises and proceeds to the platform. But rather than an inaudible groan rising from the company, the Lord's people seem to be instantly revived, attentive, and even smiling, obviously ready to listen.

Who could engender such a transformation in this congregation, and utilize the remaining minutes to profit? None other than Mr. George Shivas, a well-known servant of the Lord.

Many remember him as he looked over his glasses, opened his Bible, and began in his slow, measured tones:

"Now we'll read from John's gospel,
chapter three, verse sixteen,

For.... God.... so..... loved.... the world,
dear friends, that.. he.. gave... his.......
only... begotten...**Son**.., that.. **whosoever**..
believeth.. in **him**... should not perish.....
but.. have... everlasting LIFE. THANK GOD!"

Then would follow a few pithy remarks, a common theme running through them, leaving us with something to take home from the conference, for our further meditation. It would be a rarity if he did not pause somewhere in his message, and say;

"Did I ever tell you how God saved my poor soul? I was standing by the table, in the kitchen, in a house on St. George Street, reading John three, verse sixteen. Some people call it blue Monday, but I say,

The grass never grew **greener**,
and the sun never shone **brighter**,
and the birds never sang **sweeter**,
than they did that happy Monday afternoon,
when God saved my soul!"

One of his habits was to keep a diary, and these diaries are the basis of this book. The earlier years are incomplete. From 1915 on he kept a diary regularly, with the exception of the year 1921. These diaries are a valuable record of the work of the Lord in the early 1900's.

What is written of the labours of Mr. Shivas is representative of the work of all the brethren who went forth in faith to proclaim the gospel of the grace of our Lord Jesus Christ. In those times their labours were as much physical as spiritual, as they worked, and walked, and preached from place to place. At the end of this book is an alphabetical list of all the Lord's servants who were contemporaries of Mr. Shivas, and whose names appeared in his diaries. Precious memories are recalled of those whom we knew personally, as well as those of whom we have only heard.

Some years ago, Mr. Ross Clark, a grand-nephew of Mr. Shivas, collected letters from some of the Lord's servants who wrote their impressions of him. Most of these brethren, in their turn, have gone to be with the Lord. Their letters are included in this book.

Mr. Shivas enjoyed writing poetry. We recall his searching for a brown paper grocery bag, sharpening a lead pencil, smoothing out the bag, and committing to paper his latest inspiration. These poems are also included in this book.

As Mr. Shivas was a man of variety, so is this book. We trust it will be an encouragement to the Lord's people who knew him, and provide for younger believers a fresh view of pioneer gospel work.

"How.. When and Where"

The year was eighteen eighty four,
On April twenty seven,
That I was born on distant shore,
But not a child of Heaven.

'Twas in old England's favoured land,
Manchester's smoky town,
That I in sin first took a hand,
The Broad Road hurrying down.

By Christian parents well brought up,
God's word was often read,
Was taught it e'er I scarce could sup,
'Twas crammed into my head.

Though outwardly a sinner fair,
To others all seemed well,
In God's eyes all was clear and bare,
A sinner bound for hell!

For pleasures, joys, and sports, and sin,
Forgetting God and home,
Lured on by all earth's whirl and din,
I far away did roam.

And still my heart was empty yet,
With many an ache and pain,
For lasting joy is hard to get,
And riches hard to gain.

God's Holy Spirit oft did make
Me feel my load of sin,
At times I felt my heart would break,
And darkness reigned within.

And then there dawned one happy day,
The brightest e'er was seen,
The year nineteen and six I say,
The month April sixteen.

The Grass Never Grew Greener!

'Twas on a Monday afternoon,
The clock had just struck two,
I never could forget so soon,
If you were saved, could you?

Toronto means "a place to meet,"
'Twas there I met the Lord;
At number forty St. George Street
I heard His blessed Word.

'Twas in John's Gospel, chapter three,
Sixteen, that blessed verse,
I saw so plain He died for me,
And bore my sin and curse.

God's wondrous love, Christ's precious blood,
I rested here my soul,
Believed at once the Word of God,
His stripes had made me whole.

That "whosoever" took me in,
I ceased from all my strife;
I should not perish for my sin,
I had eternal life.

The tears of joy o'erflowed my eyes,
I now could read it true -
My title clear beyond the skies,
My soul was born anew.

For over forty happy years
I live and love to tell
Of Christ Whose blood and toil and tears,
Can save the soul from hell.

To you who still God's grace will spurn,
In love we speak it plain,
In hell's dark lake your soul will burn,
Unless you're born again.

G. L. S. 1946

Early Days

As the poem has informed us, George Leith Shivas was born on April 27th, 1884, in Manchester, England. His parents were Samuel and Annie Shivas of Aberdeen. Her maiden name was Henderson. He had an older brother, Jim, and a younger sister, Evelyn.

Samuel Shivas was a banker in Aberdeen, and was moved temporarily to Manchester, England, where George was born. In 1893 he came to Canada from Scotland with his family, and settled in Orillia, Ontario. He made a fresh start in this country, and turned from banking to market gardening. He obtained some land on West Street, which was at the edge of town in those days. His business was to supply storekeepers and citizens with fresh produce.

Young George went to Pinegrove Public school, which was on West Street, further out of town. One thing he developed in school was a keen interest in the English language and grammar, and had an ear for "the turn of a phrase." He had one illustrious schoolmate, Mr. LeTourneau, who became a Christian, and was well-known for his development of the articulated hitch.

When George was twenty years old, he and his brother Jim signed on to a cattle boat going to the British Isles, and tended cattle for their passage.

Evidently these years in his life were accompanied by an increasing conviction of his need as a sinner, and on April 16, 1906, at 22 years of age, while attending Toronto Conference, he trusted the Lord Jesus Christ as his personal Saviour. Thereby the course of his life was changed.

This brings us to the first diary, 1907, which begins on Tuesday, January 1. "First happy New Year. Psalm 23. Thanks be unto God for His unspeakable gift." There are only a few months of diary in 1907, but there are two things to note.

The first is a developing romance between George and Maude Robena Holditch of South River, Ontario. The Holditchs were a pioneer family who opened up the towns of Bracebridge, Magnetawan, South River, Sudbury, and other towns in Ontario further north. They established post offices, general stores, and bakeries. Maude and her parents and many of her brothers and sisters were in fellowship in the assembly at South River. It is apparent that both George and Maude approached their relationship with the utmost care and tenderness and with much waiting upon God for guidance.

The second is the hard work associated with market gardening in the early spring, as the excerpts from May reveal.

Box 390, Orillia, Ont.
April 17, 1906.

Dear Mary,

I must write and tell you, I'm saved. How wonderful!
I hardly know what to say about it.
It happened in the kitchen of the house where Annie Cleavely works, with no one present but Cecil and me.
I came quite to an end of myself, and saw I could do nothing. Then I took God's word to whosoever! Praise God, I know you will.
It was the last thing I could do. I got past preachers, and trying to believe, and everything else.
Then I saw I had nothing to do, God had done it all.
What a time I had to give up everything, but I was in earnest.
It's almost too good to be true, but God says so.
Have quite a few to write to, so I won't write more now.
Yours by the Grace of God.

(Sgd) George L. Shivas

The original of this letter was among Mr. Shivas' papers.

We believe it was sent to Miss Mary Cossey, his Sunday School teacher, who must have returned it to him in later years.

Jim, Evelyn, & George Shivas, Cecil Clark,
Samuel & Annie Shivas.
The homestead on West Street, Orillia, Ont. 1905.

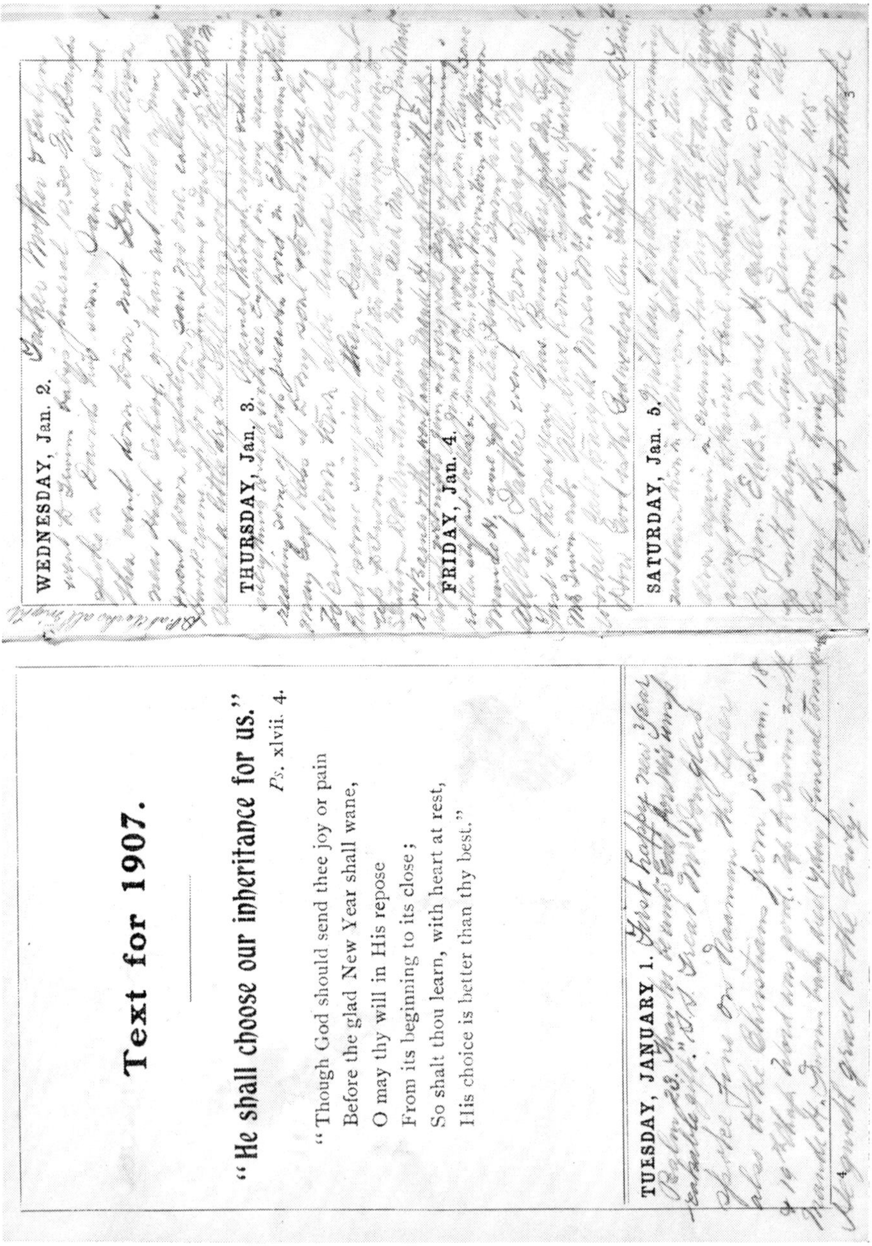
Text for 1907.

"He shall choose our inheritance for us."

Ps. xlvii. 4.

" Though God should send thee joy or pain
Before the glad New Year shall wane,
O may thy will in His repose
From its beginning to its close;
So shalt thou learn, with heart at rest,
His choice is better than thy best."

TUESDAY, JANUARY 1.

WEDNESDAY, Jan. 2.

THURSDAY, Jan. 3.

FRIDAY, Jan. 4.

SATURDAY, Jan. 5.

First page of diary for 1907

1907

Tue. Jan. 01 First happy New Year. Psalm 23. Thanks be unto God for His unspeakable gift. Sunday school treat, Mr. Douglas spoke fine on Naaman the leper also to the Christians from 1st Sam., 18th and 19th chapters, word was good. Up to Irwin's with Maude H. Irwin's baby died yesterday, funeral tomorrow - He giveth grace to the lowly.

Wed. Jan. 02 Father and mother and Evelyn went to Irwin's baby's funeral 10.30. Mr. Douglas spoke on David's two sons. Sawed some wood then went down town, met David Patterson near high school, got hair cut, called on Jim and went down to station, saw no one. Called at Clark's. Dave Patterson came up for tea. Jim, Dave, and I went to Young Men's Prayer Meeting. Seemed a little dry but still it was good to be there. D.P. at Clark's.

Thu. Jan. 03 Rained through night and still raining. Everything covered with ice. Enjoyed in some measure reading some of God's precious word in Ephesians and Philippians, may God bless it to my soul and to grow thereby. Went downtown after dinner to Clark's, had some singing, then Dave Patterson and I to Irwin's.

Fri. Jan. 04 Maude H. came up for tea. I stayed at Irwin's for a while. All but father went down to prayer meeting, first in the new year. Charles Benner there with Mr. S.W.B., Mr. Irwin out. All drove home together. How good is the God we adore, Our faithful unchangeable Friend.

Sat. Jan. 05 Maude H. at Irwin's. Stayed at Irwin's pretty late, enjoyed the time, got home about 11.15, had to get up between 12 and 1 with toothache.

Sun. Jan. 06 Beautiful day. All went down to remember Him who remembered us when far from God. Did enjoy the meeting, and saw the Lord in some measure. Cecil, Harold, Moses McC, and self went to **Foxmead** 3.30, had a little word on Naaman the leper, and at Warminster, Teskey's for tea. Meeting at 7.30 - Spoke from John 4. Left about 9.00, had a good time. Called at Irwin's on way home about 10 oclock. Stayed late, but enjoyed the little time very much. Benners were all at Irwin's. Maude perhaps going to stay till Thursday.

Mon. Jan. 07 Rather dull day - washing. Drew out 3 loads of manure from stable in morning, broke trace. Went downtown in afternoon, called at Irwin's. Maude not going. Left horse at Bailey's. Horse's teeth filed. Took Bob Adams' milk down. Went up to Irwin's, stayed till about 10, called at Hall for father - business meeting.

Tue. Jan. 08 All went to meeting, Mr. Douglas, John 15, 'twas very good, may God bring all things to our remembrance, abide in Me. Went up with Maude - had long talk, rather serious, but God knows the way, He holds the key. May God Himself guide us and keep us, for His own Name's sake, and bless each one of us. 2nd Sam. 24.14, Ps. 34 & 37, Isaiah 60.19, Romans 4.21.

Wed. Jan. 09 Rather stormy and windy but clear. All at meeting, Mr.Douglas, I am thine. Went up with Maude and Mr. Irwin. Mrs. I. disappointed at my staying so late last night, not much said. He leadeth, Isaiah 55.12, 58.2, may I know something of this.

Thu. Jan. 10 Cold day out - fine. Drove J. C. Beattie down town, went up to Irwin's, had it out with Mrs. Irwin. All at meeting. Oh that I might feed upon His precious word and grow thereby, Ps.145. Went up with Maude and had a little talk but would both leave it with the Lord - may He Himself guide and bless us. Mr. Douglas and Beattie here all night. Their bed broke down!

Fri. Jan. 11 Nice morn, J.C.B. left for Foxmead. Cleaned cabbage etc. Mr.Douglas here, had nice talk after dinner at table. I went to Irwin's and drove Maude to station - saw Maude off. God watch between us and bless us for Jesus' sake.

Sat. Jan. 12 Rather rough day, calmed at noon. Drove Mr. Douglas and father over to Hart's, found Mr. Hart in a bad way, Mr. D. had prayer. Went over to Armstrong's, found Mrs. A. very ill - Flora home at noon, the rest all sent for, God bless them.

Sun. Jan. 13 A fine day, a day in His courts. Remembered Him according to His own blessed word, who died for me. At Clark's for dinner, had a little prayer after. Mr.Orton at Bible Class, Rom. 8. Mr. Douglas' meeting after, very solemn and searching about conscience - may God help me to keep a good conscience, void of offence. Home for tea, down at 6.30 for prayer. Good gospel meeting - Mr.D. on 20th Joshua, a good meeting, but God giveth the increase. How good is the God we adore, our faithful unchangeable Friend, He is precious.

Mon. Jan. 14 Nice morn, mild and quiet. Men came to wire the house, finished about 11 oc. Mother and I drove over to Armstrong's, found that Mrs. A. had departed to be with Christ, which is very far better - so sudden - took sick Friday morning. God bless the rest, and save those who are still out of Christ.

Tue. Jan. 15 Men connected the wires at home all day.

Wed. Jan. 16 Wrote a few more lines to Maude - Jim posted this am with what I wrote Mon. night, may God bless and guide.

Wed. Jan. 23 Rec'd PPC from Maude. Went to Young Men's Prayer Meeting - 9 there, had a good time. 'Twas good to be there.

Thu. Jan. 24 Fine morning but very cold. Cistern pump frozen this morning. Went to Warminster Cafe for mtg - Mr. D. spoke on Jacob's name being changed, and things accompanying salvation, was very good, and glad to be there, home about 10.30.

Fri. Jan. 25 Rather stormy day, chores, got cistern pump thawed out and working. Wrote to Auntie Lyd. All but mother at mtg tonight. Rec'd letter from Maude, South River. Seems all OK. May God Himself have His own blessed way with us both, and guide for His own honour and glory. Had a good mtg, quite a number took part. Hymns, 'O for a faith,' 'Behold the throne of grace,' 'Grace 'tis a charming sound.'

Mon. Jan. 28 Went to Warminster at night. Evelyn and I drove our own horse, 17 of us came home in one load. Father and mother drove home with our own horse.

Wed. Jan. 30 Cold but fine today. At Young Men's Prayer meeting tonight, 10 present, truly 'twas good to be there.

Sat. Feb. 02 Soft day like a thaw. Mr. D. gone down town. I went to Irwin's. Mrs. I. had letter from Maude, saw part of it. Bless our heavenly Father, may He give grace to wait on Him. May He guide day by day, and make us to know His way is perfect.

Sun. Feb. 03 What a privilege to be in His presence Who died for me - a wonderful meeting, in some measure saw Jesus only.

Wed. Feb. 06 Went down town with mother, got buckle rubbers at Northway's $1.25, rec'd letter from Maude, trust the Lord has guided so far, we being in the way, may the Lord still guide us for His Name's sake and bless us. Went with S. W. Benner to Rama - about 100 Indians, spoke a little word from Heb. 9. May God bless His own precious word. Give Him the glory, great things He hath done.

Thu. Feb. 07 Did chores, then father and mother and I left for Rankin's about 3.30, got there safe about 5 oc, had tea, then a good sing, then to mtg. Spoke little word from Isa. 55, The word of God, which liveth and abideth forever. Mr. Douglas spoke from 1st Sam. 30 - folks staying over Sunday.

Sun. Feb. 10 Very stormy, not at Rama in afternoon. Large morning meeting, blessed privilege, Oh how sweet to be there. Mr.Morrison at Bible Class. At Adams' for tea.

Mon. Feb. 11 Very cold clear day. At McClelland's at night singing, nice crowd there, had a nice time. Cecil Clark read Ps. 118, had prayer, got home about 11 oc.

Tue. Feb. 12 Called at McClelland's while horse being shod. Had nice talk with Dave etc, met folks at 4.30 train, rec'd letter from Maude, at evening time it shall be light.

Wed. Feb. 13 10 at Young Men's Prayer Mtg. All took part. Mr. Morrison spoke a good word from Psalm 17.

Thu. Feb. 14 Went out to Teskey's, **Warminster** 32. Had good time singing, reading and prayer, supper. Got home 1.50 am, trust God may get something out of it for His Name's sake.

Fri. Feb. 15 Called at Irwin's, rec'd letter from Maude enc. with Mrs. I's. Wrote letter to M. and posted. Good prayer meeting.

Wed. Feb. 20 Rec'd letter from Maude, decided to go up to South River. Went up to Irwin's after dinner, Mrs. I. made me some lunch, went down town, wired Maude at 4.00, left on 4.40, arrived at S.R. about 9.00, Maude met me. Was glad to see her, as also the rest.

Thu. Feb. 21 Don't remember but with Maude most of time, OK cold day, car frozen, also Jack Murdock's. Went to Fisher's in eve.

Fri. Feb. 22 Still very cold. Brn. Watson and Lyon arrived at South River today, out in evening.

Sun. Feb. 24 Good morning meeting, about 12 present at South River. All took part. Watson and Lyon spoke. Maude and I went to station after night mtg. Train late, had tea and a little talk, left S.R. 1 am.

Sat. Mar. 02 Wild stormy day, March lion a day late. Went down town, rec'd letter from Maude, just like her dear self, posted mine to her. Called up at Irwin's, stayed a wee while, had nice talk with Mrs. I. Another word from dear Maude at 4.40.

Sun. Mar. 03 The Lord's day, blessed day, a large gathering to remember the Lord, by His grace in some measure saw the Lord, was made glad. Mr. Stack spoke at 3.30, a large meeting at night, the word was good from Rom.1. Mr. Stack spoke up at Irwin's after mtg. Wrote Maude after coming home. Smoked out!

Sun. Mar. 10 Goodness and mercy. Up at Irwin's for a sing after meeting.

Mon. Mar. 11 Goodness and mercy, rec'd letter from Maude.

Wed. Mar. 13 6 out at Young Men's Prayer Mtg, grand!

Fri. Mar. 15 Rec'd letter from M. in forenoon.

Wed. May 01 Scuffled rhubarb. Put wood in shed. Ploughed piece for onions. Father sowed onions. Filled some boxes for tomatoes.

Thu. May 02 Filling more boxes. Ploughed land for potatoes (old onion patch). Planted onions, potatoes.

Fri. May 03 Cutting potatoes in am. Planting potatoes in pm. Filling boxes and sowing cabbage seed after tea.

Sat. May 04 Filling boxes for tomatoes in am. Drawing out manure, 6 loads. Finished planting potatoes in onion ground.

Mon. May 06 Working in greenhouse in am. Drew out two loads of manure and ploughing behind barn in afternoon.

Tue. May 07 Cutting brush along north fence. Finished ploughing behind barn. Harrowing after tea.

Wed. May 08 Finished harrowing and rolling part of land behind barn. Filling flats in greenhouse part of afternoon.

Fri. May 10 Working in greenhouse and planting hotbed in am. Planting beans and mangels.

Sat. May 11 Made up hotbed and planted with tomatoes, over 1000. Finished planting tomatoes in hotbed.

Mon. May 13 Working in greenhouse etc. Discing strawberry ground with Joe Stubb's horse and ours. Hauled out manure in afternoon.

Tue. May 14 Harrowed and rolled strawberry ground and planted corn and filled tomato boxes before dinner.

Thu. May 16 Working in greenhouse all day again. Wet and cold. 14 dozen lettuce, 2 dozen tomatoes.

Fri. May 17 Working in greenhouse in am. Dug some strawberry plants and planted them after dinner. Fixed floor in stable.

Sat. May 18 Digging strawberry plants in am. Ploughing and discing old potato ground for corn in pm. Finished after tea.

The Grass Never Grew Greener!

Niagara Falls, Ontario,
March 2nd, 1975.

Dear brother Ross,

"He was a good man and full of the Holy Ghost," was said of Barnabas, and I am sure it could be said also of our esteemed brother George Shivas. He was a man that stood alone in his sayings, his actions, and while several have tried, yet he couldn't be copied. Many of his little quips don't sound the same when repeated or written, without his little quizzical smile that accompanied them.

I remember on New Year's Day some place, as he walked down the aisle, before he had reached the platform, he began to say, "I've got a brand new sermon today, never been used before," and it was too, and everbody enjoyed it.

He seldom missed an opportunity when on the platform to tell the story of his conversion. No matter what his subject matter was, he would work it in, introduced by a remark like, "Oh, by the way, have I ever told you how I got saved?" And even though everyone in the audience knew it almost by heart, he would proceed to tell how the grass never grew greener, and the birds never sang sweeter, and the sun never shone brighter, than it did that Monday afternoon in April, 1906.

When our first baby was only a few weeks old, I took my wife and son up to Orillia, to show off our first son and heir to my brother Robert and his wife. George was there and he asked if he might hold the baby in his arms, and, looking down at it he remarked, "The dear little sinner." This was typical of him, but the baby's mother was horrified at him calling her baby "a sinner". Events soon proved he was right, yet that same "little sinner" is now a servant of Christ, preaching to little and big, saved and lost, sinners.

In those early days, back in 1910, when I first knew George, we used to go down to the main street corner in Orillia on a Saturday night for a street meeting. There would be about a dozen of us, most had good voices, and one of the favourite hymns was the Infidel's Hymn, "I've tried in vain a thousand ways, my fears to quell, my hopes to raise." Dear brother George's rich tenor would never fail to draw a crowd. As far as I can remember, I am the only one left of that group of Orillia young men who occupied the street corner in 1910, the others are all "Home."

Yours in Him,
(Sgd) Frank Adams

Collingwood, Ontario,
May 5, 1975.

Dear brother Ross,

Yes, I enjoyed so very much, hearing Mr. Shivas at conferences, and at Strongville.

I'm pretty sure it was the fall of 1913 or 1914, he and brother Silvester had a series of meetings here in Collingwood. I was on the farm at home at Strongville, but he was staying at Ruth's father and mother's place. As she listened to the melting story, from such a young man, and saw the love they had for her soul, and others accepting Christ, she thought there was no hope for her.

She was working about 2 miles or more from home, and one of them would get the horse and buggy and drive her to work, as they could see how troubled she was.

On the last night of the meetings, she trusted the Saviour for herself, and Mr. Shivas didn't even ask her if she had gotten saved. He just said, "Well, what do you feel like now?" He saw what a change had taken place.

Some time after we were married, he and Mrs. Shivas were at our place having a few meetings at Strongville when the man we had working for us got saved out in the field. That was the summer of 1924. He was Robert McMillan's brother, Hugh, shortly out from Ireland.

I asked Mr. Shivas once about that verse, "A man's life consisteth not in the abundance of the things which he possesseth." I never forgot his answer. "You're not coveting something some one else has, are you?" That little word has been a stay to me all the years, just to be satisfied with what He has seen fit to trust me with.

One morning when at breakfast I remarked that he was awake early. "Yes," he said, "but the devil was awake earlier."

Often at the close of a conference he would have a little word. One of them was when Joseph sent his brethren away with the wagons, "and see that ye fall not out by the way."

With Christian love and greetings,
(Sgd) George E. Johnston

*George and Maude Shivas
on their wedding day,
April 8, 1909*

1908- 1912

During 1908 the friendship between George Shivas and Maude Holditch blossomed into mutual trust and commitment.

They were married on April 8th, 1909, in the bride's home in South River, and went to Toronto Conference on their honeymoon.

They took up residence in Orillia, and he continued to work with his father at the market garden. His exercise in spiritual matters continued to develop, both in the local assembly, and in preaching the gospel with the Lord's servants.

He once recounted to us an experience concerning his exercise about the Lord's work. He and Mrs. Shivas were living in a rented house in Orillia, and they had some chickens, and a bicycle. He was convinced that if the Lord wanted him in His work, He would meet his temporal needs. If not, he could always sell the chickens, or the bicycle, to pay the rent. "Well," he said with a chuckle, "the Lord let me sell both the bicycle and the chickens."

At that time he was helping brother James Lyon in gospel meetings in a tent. On the last night of the meetings, in the home where they were staying, Mr. Lyon lined up on the dresser five sets of four quarters each. Mr. Shivas had a burden - the rent of $3.50 was due, and he was looking to the Lord for guidance. The thought flashed into his mind that Mr. Lyon might give him two of the piles of coins, or even half of all the coins, but even that wouldn't be enough to pay the rent. Mr. Lyon calmly began to speak to Mr. Shivas, about how he could see he was an exercised young man, (and slid one pile of quarters over toward him), and that he was putting more and more time into the Lord's work, (and slid another set over), and that he was glad to have him help him in the meetings, (and slid a third set over), and that he wanted to share with him the fellowship he had received, (and took 2 quarters off the next pile), and slid them over! Mr. Shivas said that his heart leaped up in rejoicing to God, not only that the need was exactly met, but that his exercise about the Lord's work was being confirmed.

In 1911 he was commended to the Lord's work by the assembly of Christians meeting at Dominion Street Gospel Hall, Orillia, Ontario.

Early in 1912 he had gospel meetings with his brother-in-law, Mr. Ed Steen, in a schoolhouse in a country community (now disappeared) called Hartfell, which was east of Lake Bernard, near Sundridge, Ontario,

Some of the diary record of those meetings follows.

Tue. Feb. 20 Left home at 4.28 pm, arrived South River at 8.

Sun. Feb. 25 Stayed in **South River** over Sunday, to remember Him in am, meeting in Brennan's school in afternoon - Let us alone. At hall in S.R. in evening - In no wise. Ernie and mother out.

Mon. Feb. 26 Went to **Sundridge** at 8 oc, hired rig and drove to **Hartfell**, $1.50. Reached there safely. Snow storm very bad, the rest of the day. No one at meeting at schoolhouse on Monday.

Tue. Feb. 27 Snow storm continuing this morning. About 15 out to meeting tonight, some help to tell of His grace and His gospel.

Wed. Feb. 28 A little word with Mrs. W. Trust to see her and her husband led to Christ. Rec'd $2.50 from mother Holditch Monday.

Thu. Feb. 29 Went down to school about 4 oclock. Filled and cleaned lamps, swept floor, etc, sang a little, prayed a little. A nice number out at night, about 25, stayed till nearly 10 oclock. Tommy Stewart, a young fellow from Glasgow professed to receive the Lord Jesus as his own Saviour according as it is written. May he go on for God and His glory.

Fri. Mar. 01 About 30 out to meeting. Visited Hendersons. Sang, read and prayed, and had tea with Mr. Hannsford, good number out, young man Dobbs somewhat concerned.

Sat. Mar. 02 Paid $4.20 for board, walked to Sundridge. Rec'd letter from dear Maude. Walked to South River, reached there about 12.30, had dinner, fixed pants. Mr. Fisher called and gave us $2. fellowship in the gospel.

Sun. Mar. 03 Walked to Sundridge to remember Him, had a good time, Jesus only, had a little word - Four forths. After meeting, Bro. Harrison gave us $3. fellowship from the little assembly. Had Bible reading after dinner, John 15. The true vine in contrast to Israel. Started to walk to Hartfell. Dukes caught up with us, and gave us a ride half way, thank God. Had tea, walked to school, got fire lit, etc. No man came to meeting, all at church but every word of God is good.

Wed. Mar. 06 A few out to meeting, some help and interest. Ed spoke from Acts 8, the eunuch. Had straight talk with a couple about the new birth, and God's way of saving a soul, through the Spirit, and the Word. Job said, "My righteousness will I hold fast, and I will not let it go."

Thu. Mar. 7 Ed and I helped Mr. D. load his logs. Nice few out to mtg in evening.

Fri. Mar. 8 Left almanac and tracts at mailman's, and called at McArthur's. Tommy Stewart and brother and an Englishman, had a good preach to them, left almanac and tracts. Called at John Hannsford's, left A. and T. At Whittington's for tea. Sang, 'Take a' your care to Jesus,' left A. and T. Just Mr. Henderson to mtg. After dinner today we were asked to find other lodging and etc. They thought it not advisable to continue. "Rich and increased with goods, and have need of nothing." "Joined to their idols." Trust our leaving and our going is of God.

Sat. Mar. 09 Walked into Sundridge this morning, lovely day. At Harrison's. After tea went to phone office and after long wait spoke to Maude, also mother and Willie - 80c. I was encouraged by hearing of Maude feeling better, spoke 7 mins.

Sun. Mar. 10 At Sundridge for morning meeting. Hired team and Ash Harrison drove us to Hartfell. Large crowd, some help in preaching. Invited back to our boarding house after meeting, Jehovah-jirah.

Tue. Mar. 12 Left after dinner for Hartfell, reached here about 4 oc. Nice few men out, also Mr. and Mrs. Weaver and daughter to mtg, spoke on pleasures of sin etc, Ed from the axehead. Trust God may bless and honour His own word. Everything nice here, Charlie H. very kind. God over all, blessed forever. Written from McDonald Camp No.3, on Wednesday.

Wed. Mar. 13 Had tea at Weaver's at camp. Nice few out to mtg after tea. Our God gave help and some joy in speaking His word. Thank God for all His goodness. May He bless His word. Slept real well. Said goodbye to the Weavers, and Charlie. He gave me $2. as from the Lord. We walked out to Sundridge, rode first 2 miles. Went to Post Office first. Rec'd letter from Maude, all well at home, thank God, Maude some better. God is faithful. Why should we distrust or fear Him, Oh how He loves. Trust God may guide further.

Fri. Mar. 15 Very stormy today. Purposed going to Bloomfield to see about a few meetings, looks as if it would be too stormy, but my Father knows, in His love I rest.

Sat. Mar. 16 Beautiful bright day. "The goodness of God endureth continually." Phoned home last night .50c. Spoke to Maude, and father and mother, for Maude to come up today, D.V. Trust she will be brought along safely in His fear and love, to His own praise and glory. Purpose visiting Bloomfield today, this am. Trust God will open the way for the gospel if it be His will at this time. Hired horse in afternoon, Mrs. Harrison, Ed and I drove out to Mrs. Adams'. Called on O'Brien and Cunningham, trustees of schoolhouse, but the way not open for the gospel. Mrs. Adams very kind. Willing for us to have meetings in her house and board there. Met dear Maude on 8 oc train. Went to S.R. together, found all well.

Mon. Mar. 18 Came down to Harrison's, Sundridge, on noon train. Ash H. drove us out to Pinkerton's in afternoon, with their horse. People willing to receive the gospel, but roads not fit for mtgs. Got names of some to send almanacs, and left tracts.

Tue. Mar. 19 Visiting a little today, and on to S.R. in afternoon. Hitherto hath the Lord helped us. He giveth more grace.

Mr. George Shivas and Mr. Edmund Steen
Arnstein, Ontario. June 1913

1915

The diary for this year lists the preachers present at Toronto Conference in March. They are as follows; Beattie, Binch, Bradford, Dobbin, Douglas, Goodfellow, Johnson, Livingstone, Lyon, Martin, McCartney, McClintock, McCracken, McCrory, McGeachy, Muir, Oliver, Pearson, Pinches, Shivas, Stack, Steen, Telfer, Touzeau, Watson, Waugh.

During May of 1915, Mr. Shivas had gospel meetings with the assembly in Warminster, a community 12 kms west of Orillia.

He reached there using various means of transportation — walking, wheeling, by horse and buggy, and even in an automobile!

Tue. May 25 Went to Warminster at night in Mac Clark's <u>automobile</u>
His goodness endureth continually!

On Friday, July 16, he left Orillia for Trout Creek by train.

On Saturday, July 17, he travelled from Trout Creek to **Arnstein** by stage, and arrived at 5 pm, to join brother Ed Steen.

Sun. Jul. 18 Rather good morning meeting. Baptism at 2.30 pm. Ed baptized 4 brethren and 5 sisters. Good gospel meeting.

Visits to the assembly at **Sundridge**, and gospel meetings at **South River**, are detailed in the diary from October 9 onwards.

Sat. Oct. 09 South River. Visited Brennan's. Ed and Ena and Margaret came at 4, mtg on street at night.

Sun. Oct. 10 Went to Sundridge to remember Him. Ed and Maude and I at Brennan's school in aft - Walk and please God, 4 I AM's. Hall at night - Great.

Sat. Oct. 16 Maude and I visited Roland Peacock, street meeting.

Sun. Oct. 17 Ena, Ed and I went to Sundridge, mtg in afternoon for children - Bartimaeus. Small meeting at night.

Wed. Oct. 20 Took walk in am. Gave away a few tracts. M & I visited in pm, nice few out to mtg.

Sat. Oct. 23 At Sage's and Brennan's.

Sun. Oct. 24 At Sundridge, Brennan's school, and South River 7pm.

Thu. Oct. 28 Mr. Herald, Sundridge, died at 10 pm.

Sun. Nov. 07 Maude and Ed and I went to Sundridge for am.

Mon. Nov. 08 Maude and I visited Mrs. McCrea, long walk. Mtg.

Wed. Nov. 10 M & I had tea with Mrs. Wood who professed to be saved, trust it's real. Nice few out at night.

Thu. Nov. 11 Rainy day, Brennan's horse hurt last night.

Fri. Nov. 12 Visited Mrs. Campbell and Watties. Mtg at night.

Sun. Nov. 14 Ed, Maude and I walked to Sundridge. Drove back to Brennan's school - So great a sin. South River at night.

Mon. Nov. 15 M & I visited Campbells and McLeans.

Sat. Nov. 20 Oiled all chairs in hall. Talk with mother in afternoon. M&I visited Noicks and Woods.

Sun. Nov. 21 Ed, Ena and I at Sundridge - Call to remembrance.

Wed. Nov. 24 Ed and I visited Murdocks and Mrs. Garner. Peacock's for dinner, Sage's for tea. Walked about 9 miles. Meeting.

Thu. Nov. 25 Lovely day. Visited Boadways, and Mrs. Furlong.

Sun. Nov. 28 Ed, Ena and I went to Sundridge in am with Peacocks. Brennan's school in aft, Lev. 15 - Portion. Hall at night <u>full</u>.

Thu. Dec. 02 Lots of snow <u>sleighing</u>.

Sun. Dec. 05 Breaking of Bread in South River. Brennan's school in aft - Whosoever. Hall at night, Mark 5 - Often.

Mon. Dec. 06 Alcinda Harrison and Ash stayed all night. Walked out to McCrea's, Ed and I. Mtg at night - Lift up eyes, Gen. 22.

Tue. Dec. 07 Wrote Fred Simms, Cecil, and R. McClintock. Ed and I saw Mrs. Sage, sought to instruct in God's ways. At Brennan's, had talk with Jimmie and Boadways, tried to act for God.

Thu. Dec. 09 More snow. Alcinda H. <u>saved</u> this am. Went home on 8 train. Wrote the Rankins and Mrs. Clark Sr. <u>Stormy day</u>. Ed and I visited Murdocks. No meeting, all at home.

Mr. Shivas must have been impressed with Alcinda Harrison's request to the brethren for baptism, for he wrote it out in a separate notebook. "I expect you have been told about God saving me. This is my stand... The devil says I am not saved. I say I am because I believe the report God gave of His Son and God's word says in Acts 16, Believe on the Lord Jesus Christ and thou shalt be saved. Therefore if I am not saved God must have told a lie, and God cannot lie. Therefore I am saved. I see from God's word that the second step is baptism. I would like very much to follow His command, and then the third step, to be accepted into fellowship with His people. This will be my last chance to obey God in baptism until the summer so I would like to do His will when I can, seeing He has done so much for me."

Fri. Dec. 10 Was to have gone to Arnstein today. Stormy — love that grants and love denies.

Sat. Dec. 11 Bright morning, but cold, below zero. Cleaned hall, put in wood. Maude and I had walk in evening.

Sun. Dec. 12 Remembered the Lord's death at South River. Gave word on Consider. Brennan's school at 3 - Joined. Hall at night.

Mon. Dec. 20 Maude and I left S.R. on train, came as far as Huntsville safely, thank God. Met Ed at station from Deer Lake and then visited Mrs. Watson, Mrs. Widdifield and sons,McCalls. Spent evening at Ed and Ena's.

Tue. Dec. 21 Left Huntsville at 9.15 am for Orillia. Arr'd safely at noon. Father met us at station with Harold Clark's horse.

Going Out and Coming In

It seems to me our little stay
In this dark world of self and sin
Is just made up from day to day
Of going out and coming in.

It is not long since we went out
Our little race down here to win;
And scarce we know what it's about
Our time has come to enter in.

Thrice happy we who saved by grace,
Have entered in through Christ the door;
Soon we shall find in heaven a place
To dwell with Him for ever more.

How sad for those who scorn and doubt,
Reject the gospel known so well,
From heaven's glory now shut out,
Eternity to spend in hell!

G. L. S.

Calvary Never Grows Old.

I read in God's word of Christ Jesus my Lord,
Who by Judas for silver was sold,
How His visage was marred, and His form rudely scarred,
But Calvary never grows old.

Chorus
It will never grow old, it will never grow old,
'Twill always precious be;
Blest cross where He died, Heaven's King crucified,
To save a poor sinner like me.

Though the years come and go as I journey below,
And there's nothing that's new to behold,
The poor world's empty show fades and dies, that I know,
But Calvary never grows old.

Heaven and earth pass away for there's nothing can stay,
To corruption 'twill go I am told,
Poor things made of clay, born for but a brief day,
But Calvary never grows old.

In the glory I see One who died on the tree,
As a Lamb newly slain from the fold,
How He suffered for me, and to set sinners free,
But Calvary never grows old.

In that day we shall sing, and our sheaves gladly bring,
Far more precious than silver and gold,
Then His praises shall ring - Priest, Prophet, and King,
For Calvary never grows old.

Tune: They crucified Him.   G. L. S.

1916

The diary of this year shows visits further afield, with two series of gospel meetings in Chapman Valley, Ont., two in Sault Ste. Marie, Ont., and one in Duluth, Minn. Selections from the diary follow.

It is interesting and encouraging to note the family names of so many years ago, some of which are still familiar in these local assemblies.

Sun. Jan. 02 **Midland** Conference.

Mon. Jan. 03 Returned at 3 oc from Midland.

Tue. Jan. 04 **Orillia** S.S. treat, Pearson and Telfer spoke.

Wed. Jan. 05 At **Severn** S.S. treat, McMullen and McClintock spoke.

Sat. Jan. 15 Left at 3.47, CPR, for Glenarm. John Truman met us.

Sun. Jan. 16 Mtg at **Glenarm** in am to remember Him. Spoke word from Rev. 3 - Remain. Truman's for dinner. Called at Hargrave's. McLeod's for tea. Mtg at 8 oc - How long.

Mon. Jan. 17 Truman's all night. Mrs. Truman came home. Hargrave's for tea. Mtg at night, Jer. 3 - How. At McLeod's all night.

Tue. Jan. 18 Had reading etc in morning. Came to J. Brentnell's for dinner. Stormy day. Visited Wm. Kennedys. Meeting.

Wed. Jan. 19 Dinner at Neil Parrington's, also visited Wm. P.'s and the store. Tea at D. Bell's. Meeting, good crowd.

Fri. Jan. 28 Left at 4.30 for **Huntsville**, Ena met us. Prayer mtg.

Sat. Jan. 29 M & I called at Sommacal's and had tea with Mr. and Mrs. Widdifield.

Sun. Jan. 30 Mtg in am, rather good.

Sun. Feb. 06 Drove down to **Chapman Valley** with Ash and Mrs. Harrison with McCabe's livery, $1.50 each. Mtg in am, gospel at night. At Mumford's all night.

Mon. Feb. 07 Visited Kings who are sick. Back to Mumford's for tea. Mtg at night - Without.

Tue. Feb. 08 Visited W. Harrisons and for tea. Mtg at night.

Wed. Feb. 09 Stormy day and snowing. Fixed blackboard and made notice of mtgs.

Fri. Feb. 11 Feeling rather "grippy." Took walk before dinner. Wrote Cecil. Visited Harrisons and for tea. Mtg at night - Come down. Mrs. McLaughlin professed last night.

Sat. Feb. 12 Feeling some better, thank God. Visited T. Hicks', Kings, Tarrants and J. Hicks'.

Sun. Feb. 13 "Sweet feast of love divine" in am, also Bible class Rom. 8. Ed and I went home with Bobbie Hicks for dinner.

Fri. Feb. 18 Very stormy day. Went down to Tom Hicks' for tea. About a dozen out at night. Had Bible Rdg, 1 Thess. 1.

Sun. Feb. 20 Good day. Nice mtg in am. Bible Rdg Rom. 8.9-18. Hugh H.'s for dinner. Mrs. House told us she was saved Sat. am. Good mtg at night - Must be saved.

Wed. Feb. 23 Cleaned stove pipes at hall etc after dinner.

Thu. Feb. 24 Came up to Henry Barton's last night. Visited Whites, Mr. W. and Ellen, tried to bring eternity before them. Back to Barton's for tea. Drove with them to meeting.

Sat. Feb. 26 Drove down to Robertson's with Alex R. in am. Visiting Robertsons all day. Read and sang in eve.

Sun. Feb. 27 Stormy day. Mr. R., Ed and I drove with the team to the Valley. Spoke word in am, 2 Cor. 5 - Always. Bible class Rom. 8. Gospel 7.30, Ps. 142 - Cared.

Fri. Mar. 03 After dinner called at Boyce's, and at Tarrant's. Tea at T. Hicks'. Mtg, Lev. 13 - In no wise.

Sat. Mar. 04 Drove to Cliff Miller's with King's horse. Had dinner there. Came back to King's for tea. Home in evening, had walk.

Sun. Mar. 05 Nice mtg in am. Last gospel meeting, good crowd.

Mon. Mar. 06 Wrote out 'I have Christ' for Mrs. Tarrant. Packed our grips etc. Had rdg and prayer. Wes Mumford drove us to Castell's for dinner and Sandy C. drove us to Sundridge. Arr'd South River 4.30, Maude and Ena met us.

Sat. Mar. 11 Left at 3.30 am with Ed for Soo. Arrived about 6 pm. A. West met us where we stayed all night. God is faithful.

On March 10th, a son was born into the James Clark family and was named Edmund George after the two preachers who had just arrived, Edmund Steen, and George Shivas!

Sun. Mar. 12 Kept the feast at **Cdn. Soo.** Across the river to baptism in pm. Met bro. McGeachy and Leo Sheldrake.

Tue. Mar. 14 Tea at Welling's. Talked with Mrs. Strachan. Meeting.

Thu. Mar. 16 Visited Mrs. Grothe in pm. Wright's for tea. Meeting.

Wed. Mar. 22 Called at Mrs. Graham's & Mrs. Weatherhead's. Tea at Barker's. Meeting, Ps. 116 - Trouble.

Thu. Mar. 23 Went out to Smith's before dinner. Walked to mtg.

Sun. Mar. 26 Remembered the Lord Jesus in His own way. Dinner with Mrs. Groath. Bro. Wright and I went over river to baptism. Bro. McG. & Dickson came back with us to Wright's for tea.

Tue. Mar. 28 Helped pile wood etc in am. After dinner called on Mrs. Lively near hall, Mrs. Gallanger. Tea at Alton's, prayer, walked to mtg, bought new rubbers. Spoke from Mark 10.

Wed. Mar. 29 Through steel plant with R. H. Davis. Visited Mrs. Hogg and had tea there. Mtg at night, Luke 13 - Bound.

Thu. Mar. 30 Called on Mrs. McGorby, Mrs. Hunter, Mrs. McIntyre and for tea at Bro. Clark's. Mtg.

Sat. Apr. 01 Tea at Gallinger's, Mr. G. professed to be saved. Went over to Mich. Soo about 12 midnight, to McRorie's.

Sun. Apr. 02 Remembered the Lord's death once more till He come.

Thu. Apr. 06 About 1 foot of snow fell last night.

Mon. Apr. 10 Called on Mrs. Davis, Weatherheads, Murrays, Mrs. Graham. Bro. Barker and Italian brethren over river for meeting.

Sat. July 22 Left at 1.12 for Sundridge. Prudie Harrison drove us to **Chapman Valley**. At Will Harrison's.

Mon. July 24 to Fri. July 28 Helping with the hay and gospel meetings at night. Mrs. King told us she was saved. Some interest and help.

Sat. July 29 At the hay all day till 9 pm. Letter from Maude.

Sun. July 30 Very warm day. Warmest in 11 years in Mag. 96 degrees in shade. Nice morning meeting.

Mon. Jul. 31 Went to town with Will Harrisons. Visited Kings and Mrs. Hicks. Ash Harrison came this morning. Hughs' for tea. Meeting, Prov. 14 - Away.

Tue. Aug. 01 Haying and preaching again this week.

Sat. Aug. 05 Ed left for S.R. after mtg last night. Finished haying at Willie's about 5 oc.

Sun. Aug. 06 Remembered the Lord's death. Spoke word from 1 Cor. 3 - Increase. Bible class, 1 Cor. 10. Mtg in Mag. in evening.

Tue. Aug. 08 Visited Mrs. McLaughlin with bro. Barton.

Wed. Aug. 09 Went to Willie Harrison's last night. Picking huckleberries all day. Home about 6. Willie drove us to mtg.

Fri. Aug. 11 Came to Hugh H.'s with Birdie Robertson last night. Visited Alexanders for dinner, Mag. for tea. Meeting, Job 3.

Sat. Aug. 12 Came to Barton's last night. Visited Wilsons and Whites in pm.

Sun. Aug. 13 Walked to hall to remember Him. Precious privilege!

Mon. Aug. 14 Helped "Pa" cut a bit of barley. Wrote Maude. Had rest after dinner. Repainted sign. Meeting at night.

Tue. Aug. 15 Helped a little in barley. Put new peg in rake. Helped Mr. Edwards down with boxes etc. Visited Mrs. King and Snyders.

Thu. Aug. 17 Helped with barley in am. Visited in pm, McLaughlins, Osbornes, Snyders, Kings, Morris'. Mtg at night.

Fri. Aug. 18 Helped draw in barley in am. Visited Mrs. J. Mills and painted on the rocks in pm.

Sun. Aug. 20 Ed and I walked to the Valley. Very warm. Sweet the feast of love divine, till He come. Spoke from John 11 - Come forth. Mtg at 3, Baptism, Mrs. House, Mrs. H. King, Ethel and Martha Hicks. Walked back to Mag. Spoke at close of mtg - Honest.

Tue. Aug. 22 Helped "Pa" put up barley. Ed and I helped draw in.

Wed. Aug. 23 Drove to Tarrant's for dinner. Visited T. Hicks' and Kings after dinner. Repainted texts on rocks. Brought King's horse to blacksmith. Meeting, 2 Peter 3 - Willing.

Thu. Aug. 24 Repainted texts and a new one on rock near hall.

Fri. Aug. 25 Visited Cliff Millers. Painted texts on rocks and gave away tracts at houses in Mag. before tea. Meeting, Acts 4 - Saved.

Sat. Aug. 26 Went to Robertson's, Dunchurch. Visited all day. Read and sang in evening. Stayed all night.

Sun. Aug. 27 Drove to Chapman Valley to remember the Lord's death once more till He come. Geo. Osborne baptized in afternoon.

Sat. Oct. 21 Arr'd Soo about 6. Leo Sheldrake met us. Went to Wright's, stayed there all night.

Sun. Oct. 22 Kept the feast at **Cdn. Soo**. Rather nice soft mtg.

Sun. Oct. 29 Cdn. Soo. Kept the feast among the children. Geo. Duncan spoke before B.B.

Fri. Nov. 03 Left at 5.30 pm for **Duluth**, Minn.

Sun. Dec. 03 Remembered the Lord Jesus at West Duluth. Spoke word from Deut. 33 - Precious. Home for dinner. Sam Hamilton, Willie Gould and I gave away cards of invitation. At Gould's for tea. A few out to first mtg in firehall.

Tue. Dec. 05 Out again in pm with invitation cards. Nice lot out to mtg, 12 from West Duluth, 6 strangers.

Sun. Dec. 10 Math. 18.20, Till He come. Calling at houses in aft.

Wed. Dec. 13 Visiting in pm, Mrs. Wood, Mrs. Liske & Smiths.

Sun. Dec. 17 At W. Duluth all day. At Brown's for dinner and tea. Meeting, Luke 11 - Strong. Good number in.

Detroit, Mich.
January 4, 1976.

Dear brother in Christ,

I do recall an incident or two regarding brother Shivas.

Mr. Sheldrake sang well, and when Mr. Shivas was with us he supplied the bass, and my, it went well. On one occasion, as the three of us came from Sault Ste. Marie, crossing by ship to Mackinac, we went into a restaurant to eat.

We gave our order for the food and while waiting to be served we sang, not too loudly, but so that all could hear. Our wait was rather long. Finally I called the waitress and in a kind way asked her if they had difficulty in killing the calf.

She answered that the boss was in the kitchen and she would ask him. She returned and told us that the boss said if we would sing one more hymn out loud he would serve us. We did so with gusto.

I recall on one visit when we lived in Detroit, he came to us at old Central Hall, and was asked to take the service. After announcing his subject he said, "It seems to me I spoke on this the last time I was here. If you remember it, it must have done some good; perhaps someone else will be helped this time; and if you don't remember it, it is time we were getting it again." And like himself, he gave us a good message.

In any event, George added much to our song.

Yours in our Lord Jesus Christ.
(Sgd) F. W. Mehl

Only A Tract

Only a tract that someone had written,
Telling of Jesus Who died on the Tree,
Bearing our sins, was wounded and smitten,
Paying our debt and setting us free.

Only a tract that someone had printed,
Printed and folded so neat and so white,
Telling of Jesus, His love so unstinted,
Leaving His home in the Glory so bright.

Only a tract but someone had bought it,
Paid it in full by the work of his hand;
But it told of the sheep, how the Shepherd had sought it,
Found it and brought it to Heaven's happy land.

Only a tract but somebody gave it,
Gave it in prayer, and in hope, and in love,
Telling the lost soul of One who could save it,
Save the poor sinner for glory above.

Only a tract but somebody mailed it,
Sent it away across land or the sea;
Someone received and read and then hailed it,
Hailed it as bringing Glad Tidings so free.

Only a tract, but he still tells the story,
How God in grace saved him, as he read it through,
Saved him through somebody giving God glory
Telling of Christ. Was that somebody YOU?

God bless the tracts, and all those that give them.
Give them because of the message they bring.
May they have courage to look up above them,
Soon in the Glory His praises we'll sing.

G. L. S.

1917

The outstanding feature of this year was fourteen weeks of pioneer gospel work with brother Leo Sheldrake, in Cheboygan, Michigan. The diary reveals the day-by-day mundane activities of lighting the fire, sweeping the floor, setting the chairs, shovelling the walk, in order to provide a presentable place in which the people could hear the gospel. As well, they were deprived of the privilege of remembering the Lord for those fourteen weeks. The Lord honoured their stedfastness, and souls were saved.

In November of 1917 they had three weeks of gospel meetings in Pickford, Michigan. The Grand Theatre was rented for a meeting place. Portions of the diary follow.

Sun. Jan. 14 In Amer. Soo today. Good crowd to the gospel mtg.

Tue. Jan. 16 Left at 6.35 for **Cheboygan**. Arr'd safely according to the good hand of God upon us about noon. Carried our grips to Mr. Greenlees'. Seeing about hall, cards, stove, etc.

Wed. Jan. 17 Got stove and 70 ft of pipes up, chairs, lights. Swept floor etc. Fixed chairs. Chas. Greenlees making sign.

Thu. Jan. 18 Down to hall in am. Got cards. Made sign for windows. Home for dinner. Put up sign outside hall. Delivering cards to the houses in aft. inviting the people. Stormy evening. First mtg, 8 all told. Read Gen. 7 - Come.

Fri. Jan. 19 At the houses with cards of invitation. Nice lot out to mtg, about 23. God is faithful. Spoke from Math. 12.

Sat. Jan. 20 Went down town and to mail. Dinner at Elliott's restaurant. Tried to speak to the people there. Put up sign in window. Peddling cards to the houses. Visited Mrs. Greenlees Sr. Home for tea. Down town in eve. Had little mtg on street.

Sun. Jan. 21 Had quiet time in am. Read Mark 14, 15 & 16. My meditation of Him shall be sweet. Terrible stormy day. Mr. G., Leo and I went down to hall about 4 oc, got fire lit etc. Had prayer, a few came in. Prov. 26, 3 R's.

Mon. Jan. 22 Home for dinner. Out in pm again with cards, speaking a word as we had opportunity. Went to hall and lit fire. Nice lot out to mtg. Talk with Lutheran preacher.

Wed. Jan. 24 Mrs. Campbell told us last night that she got saved the night before. Trust it is of God. Lot out to mtg, Ps. 142.

Thu. Jan. 25 Out in pm with cards to houses and to Mrs. Metivier's for tea. Others there. Nice few, over 20, to meeting.

Sun. Jan. 28 Spent the morning quietly in our room. Read last three chapters of Matthew and prayed a little. Tried to think of Him who remembered us. Went to hall early, got fire lit etc, had prayer. About 30 out. Good meeting, God gave help.

Mon. Jan. 29 About 30 out, and some help from God. Mrs. Metivier said she was saved. Meeting, Mark 10 - Called.

Wed. Jan. 31 Visited Mrs. Bannister and Mrs. Harrington. Had contention with a relative about the certainty of eternal punishment. Cold and very stormy, 13 out all told.

Fri. Feb. 02 Cold bright day. Visited McDonalds. Enjoyed bringing God's word before them, also Mrs. Hopkins. They came out to mtg last night. 10 all told. Mrs. Bannister saved.

Sun. Feb. 04 Still cold. Came over to hall at 10.30. Read last 3 chapters of Luke and tried to praise and think of Him. Chilblains very bad. Mrs. Campbell and daughter and son-in-law in to mtg at 2.30. Mrs. B. Jance out at night, also Mrs. Dodd and Mrs. Porter.

Wed. Feb. 07 After dinner visited Martinos and for tea. Mr. Martino may have gotten saved.

Tue. Feb. 13 In home in the morning. After dinner Leo and I visited Mrs. Keyes and had good word with them. Called on Greenwoods and Mrs. Harrington who was out, also Mrs. Dodd and tried to speak for God. Paid rent. Lit fire in hall. Home for tea. 20 out to mtg. Contention with 'no hell' man.

Thu. Feb. 15 After dinner Leo and I called and had talk with Dr. Kelsden. Also called at Smith's, then to hall. Lit fire. Mtg.

Sun. Feb. 25 Read together Pss. 22,23,24, Cross, Crook, Crown. Good Shepherd, Great S., Chief S. Tried to think of Him and praise God. Not many in to mtg in afternoon, yet God gave help.

Tue. Feb. 27 Out with 'Eternal Punishment' booklets to houses before dinner. Meeting encouraging, Prov. 6 - How long.

Wed. Feb. 28 Nice bright day. Cleaned stove pipes first thing, 6.30, before breakfast. Cleaned off sidewalk at hall.

Thu. Mar. 01 Mr. Warwick told us last night that he got saved night before. Trust it is of God.

Fri. Mar. 02 Visited Mr. Jodway, had talk with him about eternity. Also called at C. Greenlees'. Good crowd to mtg. Mrs. Warwick saved night before.

Sat. Mar. 03 Chas. G. called and told us his wife got saved.

Wed. Mar. 14 Very stormy night, regular blizzard. 12 out to mtg.
Sun. Mar. 18 Nice day. Went to hall and lit fire about 11. Read Ps. 69, sung hymn 210 and prayed. Lot out at 2.30.
Mon. Mar. 19 Mrs. Hopkins came and we spoke with her till 5.30. Mrs. H. professed to get saved some time before night.
Fri. Mar. 23 Wet day. Wet all day. Leo at Kelsden's all pm, getting treatment, speaking with Mr. Kelsden.
Sat. Mar. 31 Thunder, lightning, and rain. Looking at hall down town. Moved partition etc. Had street mtg at night. Good number listened, gave out tracts.
Sun. Apr. 01 Charles Kelsden called after tea. Spoke with him. He professed faith in Christ.
Sat. Apr. 07 Split kindling at hall. After dinner gave away some tracts. Put some in farmer's rigs.
Sun. Apr. 08 Lovely bright day. Read Ps. 136. Leo lit fire in hall. Mtg together in hall at 10.30, sang and sought to thank God for all His love in His Son. Read 'In the midst.' S.S. in afternoon and B. Class, Acts 1. Mtg at night, Heb. 9.27.
Mon. Apr. 23 Packing up etc. Left Cheboygan at 11.54, safe journey, thank God, to Standish.
Sun. Apr. 29 Dull morning and cold. Remembered the Lord's death once more after those 14 weeks at Cheboygan. "God is faithful!"
Sun. Oct. 14 Kept the feast at **Cheboygan** for first time. Twelve broke bread. Nice few in at night, some help, thank God.
Wed. Nov. 07 Left Soo for **Pickford** at 2.45 pm. Stayed all night in hotel. Meals 2.00. Visited Smiths.
Thu. Nov. 08 Secured Grand Theatre for two weeks for mtgs. Visited Smiths and there for tea and all night.
Fri. Nov. 09 Walked out to Leach's, 6&qtr miles and back over very muddy road. Read and preached and prayed and sang. Back at 4 oc, 13 miles. Got invitation cards for meetings.
Sat. Nov. 10 Got cards and put in stores and on posts etc. Swept out hall in pm and gave cards to all the houses. Sang and preached on street in evening.
Sun. Nov. 11 Read together in the home - Mark 15, and prayed. Went over to hall and got fire going. Read Ps. 69 and tried to think of Him, the blessed Lord Jesus Christ. About 15 to mtg at 3. Gen. 7 - Come, and about 30 at night, with some help.
Mon. Nov. 12 After dinner seeing about wood and had a walk, 3 miles or so, before tea. Got fire lit in hall. Sang 'Tidings happy tidings', and 'Whosoever will', outside before meeting.

Tue. Nov. 13 Walked out to visit old Mrs. Smith, over 10 miles. Found her reachable. Trust God will give blessing. Home for dinner. Beautiful day. Went over to hall to wait for man with wood but he didn't come. Walked out 2 miles and back. Sang on street before meeting. Read 1st Cor. 14 - Sound.

Wed. Nov. 14 Dull day but may clear up. Mrs. Smith got team and we got a load of wood and got it sawed, $4.00, and piled in barn at hall. After dinner out to visit Mrs. Watson, Mrs. Smith's daughter, also met a Mrs. Banger there. Preached Christ to them. Sang on street again. Read Prov. 26 - Ruin.

Fri. Nov. 16 Mrs. Tompkins says she got saved since we came. She may be. Love hopeth all things. Split a little kindling after dinner at hall. Then went out to visit Mrs. Nathaniel Smith. Found her concerned - more or less. Nice few out, 2nd Kings 4.

Sat. Nov. 17 Lovely day again. Leo and I took walk out a mile or so. Wrote Maude some after dinner. Called to see Mr. and Mrs. McKenzie (Scotch). Split some wood at hall. Had 4 mile walk before tea. A lot stood and listened on street. Some help.

Sun. Nov. 18 Had reading and prayer together in the home, Matt. 20. Leo and I went over to hall. Got fire going. Cold windy day. Lights not good. Read Ps. 22 and John 19 and tried to think of Him 'Who loved me.' Prayed some. About 20 out at 3 oc. Some help to preach. A few more at night, John 19 - It is finished.

Tue. Nov. 20 Took walk in am. After dinner visited Mrs. Armstrong, her brother was there, Mr. Kerr, and her daughter. Andy and his mother back from Soo. Andy must go to the war. All of the Smiths at mtg. Read Prov. 6 - How long. Mtg in Orange Hall. Sang, 'Jesus is a rock in a weary land,' and 'Take the name of Jesus with you.'

Thu. Nov. 22 Smiths all went to the Soo to see Andy off. Had nice visit with Watsons and then went over to Nathaniel Smith's. Found Mrs. S. not far from the Kingdom. 6 out to mtg.

Fri. Nov. 23 Nice bright morning but cold. Read Matt. 25 in home together. Visited Mrs. Gough, Mrs. Smith's daughter. She says she is saved. We trust she is real. Had good walk. Very cold. Nice few out to mtg. Felt encouraged. Read Isa. 57 - Rest.

Sat. Nov. 24 Nice bright morning but cold. Read Math. 26 and prayed. Mr. ——— here. <u>Didn't kneel</u>. Had walk before dinner, 2 miles. Cold clear day. Had tea out at Sterling's. Had long talk with them. No street mtg. Pretty cold. Walked 6 miles.

Sun. Nov. 25 Last mtg in theatre. God watch over His word.

The Light of His Presence

We know that at last with our loved ones 'tis well,
They do rest from their labours, such rest, who can tell?
To dwell with their Saviour in glory above,
To bask in the Light of His wonderful love.

To see Him who on Calvary suffered and died,
Despised and rejected, a King crucified.
Sharing together forever that joy,
Which never a sin nor a tear can destroy.

Their labours do follow them, happy release!
Now their's is the Glory, the rest and the peace.
We sorrow, not even as some without hope,
Nor left in the gloom and the darkness to grope.

Soon, soon shall we see them and greet them again,
Together with Jesus forever to reign.
We wait for His coming - the shout in the air,
Then what a rejoicing, to meet again there.

G. L. S.

Sure-fire diary recipes!

For Falling Hair.
To about a pint of hot water put three tablespoonfuls of pure ascetic acid. Rub into roots of hair, two or three times a week.

Recipe for Rheumatism.

Wood alcohol	1/3 pint.
Spirits of turpentine	2/3 pint.
Oil of mustard	1/2 ounce.
Unjuent	1 ounce.

Oil of hemlock and origanum 1 ounce. Apply daily.
From Mrs. Hicks, Magnetawan, Feb. 14, 1913.

Burdock Blood Bitters.

Sarsaparilla, Mandrake, Burdock	2 ounces of each.
Yellow dock	1 ounce.

Put 1 gallon rain water onto roots and boil down to 1 quart. Strain and add 1/2 pound granulated sugar. One tablespoonful before meals. Miss Eva Watson - 1915.

For Worms in Horses.
Boil potatoes in water. Then boil handful of pumpkin seeds, and handful of oats in the potato water. Feed to horse.

How to Tan a Hide.

Japonica	1 pound.
Salt	1 pound.
Water	4 gallons.

Have skins clean from fat or flesh.
Leave in solution 4 to 6 weeks till tanned.
Wash thoroughly, and oil with tanner's oil. Stretch and dry.
From Mr. Wilfred Johnston, R. R. 1, Seabright, Ont.

> God and a doctor we adore
> On the brink of danger, not before.
> The danger gone, both are requited,
> God is forgotten, the doctor slighted.

1918

The diary for this year records gospel meetings in Victoria Road and Collingwood, Ontario, and again at Pickford, Michigan. Portions of the Victoria Road and Collingwood meetings follow.

Also listed are the entries for four consecutive weeks in the fall of 1918, when public gatherings were banned due to the influenza epidemic which took many lives, both in Canada and the United States.

Sat. Mar. 02 Left Orillia at 4.40 for **Victoria Road** (Eldon). Reached McLeod's about 12.

Sun. Mar. 03 Rather good day. Nice mtg at 2 oc. Kept the feast. Mr. McClintock read about the love of Christ. Had walk after. Nice lot to mtg at 8.

Mon. Mar. 04 Visited Mrs. G. Parrington, paralyzed. Professed when Cecil Clark and I were here 2 years ago. It was a cheer. She seemed bright. Meeting, Job 3.

Tue. Mar. 05 At Bell's for dinner and Hargrave's for tea.

Wed. Mar. 06 Called at Hargrave's and came on to W. Parrington's for dinner. Mrs. R. Parrington's for tea. Meeting, 2nd Kings 4.

Thu. Mar. 07 Visited Brentnells for dinner also McNinchs and Stones in pm. Good number out and some help.

Sat. Mar. 09 Drove with Roy Forman's horse to Gilmore's for dinner. Safe journey and not very cold. At Gilmore's all day. Turned very stormy at night. Read Luke 22.

Sun. Mar. 10 Cold stormy drive to McLeod's. Got here in time for dinner. Rather nice mtg at 2 oc. Remembered the Lord's death once more. Nice few unsaved in at night, with help.

Tue. Mar. 12 Mr. McClintock was going to visit Brentnell's people with John B. I came to Truman's with Mr. McLeod. At Truman's for dinner and tea.

Thu. Mar. 14 Large meeting last night, over 40 out.

Fri. Mar. 15 Clear and cold. Ida McCaughey professed faith in Christ. Good number out. Prov. 26 - 3 R's.

Sat. Mar. 16 At Brentnell's for dinner and aft. Word about no exemption for brethren.

Sun. Mar. 17 Beautiful soft day, with high wind. Lot out to remember the Lord Jesus at 2 oc. Mr. McC. spoke - Himself. Gilmores stayed for tea. Large crowd at night, 50 or more.

Tue. Mar. 19 Another beautiful day. Heard first robins. At Truman's for dinner and tea, also visited Nicholsons in pm. Good number out at night.

Wed. Mar. 20 Mr. McLeod drove us to Brentnell's. He drove across lake to Kennedy's, safely. Dinner at K.'s and nice visit. Safe journey back. Tea at Brentnell's. Walked. A few out - How long.

Thu. Mar. 21 Wrote Maude. At Bell's for dinner. Beautiful warm day. Visited Ewers after dinner. At Hargrave's for tea. Talk with Robbie. Nice few out. God gave help. Acts 4 - Saved.

Fri. Mar. 22 Nice morning again, colder. Water on road nearly 2 feet. Nice few out - It is finished.

Sat. Mar. 23 Visited Mrs. Stone in pm. Called at Brentnell's for a little again. Walked most of way home.

Mon. Mar. 25 Mr. McLeod drove Mr. McClintock to station. Mr. Bell drove me. Home safe to Orillia about noon.

Tue. Apr. 23 John Silvester and I left at 7 oc for **Collingwood**. Called at Guest's and Beattie's. Mr. Taylor met us.

Wed. Apr. 24 Made sign. At Winny's for tea. Nice lot out.

Thu. Apr. 25 Called on Mrs. Scobie, Mrs. Jim Latimer & Mrs. McHendry. Latimer's for tea. Meeting - It is finished.

Fri. Apr. 26 Helped Mr. Taylor bring in a load of hay from stack. Too windy. Nice few out to mtg. Read - No soundness.

Sat. Apr. 27 Helped Mr. Taylor bring in 2 loads more of hay, almost all. Jim Latimer's for dinner. Drove to Creemore with Jim. McCullough's for tea. Street meeting in Collingwood.

Sun. Apr. 28 Rather good day. At Winny's for dinner. Luke 15 at S.S. Jim Latimer's for tea. Large mtg at night. Read 1 Cor. 14.

Mon. Apr. 29 Helped Mr. Taylor move furniture for Mrs. Welsh.

Tue. Apr. 30 At dock and saw boats. Left some tracts. Called to see Joe Davis. At Latimer's for tea. Throat hoarse.

Wed. May 01 Cold morning. Wrote Maude. Drove out to Willie Latimer's for dinner with Bryan's horse and buggy. Came back about 4 and had adjustment. At Bryan's for tea. Nice few out.

Thu. May 02 Helped Mr. Taylor a little. Cut strings off raspberries. Came to Mrs. Winny's for dinner. Called on Mrs. Wood. At chiropractor's, Scobie's for tea. Nice few in to mtg.

Fri. May 03 Piling wood in am. John hurt his back. Elsie T. drove us down in car to station. Called on Mrs. McHendry.

Sat. May 04 At Scobie's for dinner. Visited Hunters and Carmichaels and McHendrys.

Sun. May 05 John went to Creemore with Jas. Latimer in car. I stayed. Rather nice morning mtg.

Tue. May 07 Helped Mr. Taylor plant some trees and bushes. Called on Mrs. J. Latimer, Mrs. Jamieson. Meeting at night.

Fri. May 10 Helped Mr. Taylor for a little to get away with rhubarb etc. Rain today. Meeting, 2 Kings 5.

Mon. May 13 Came with Jim Latimer to **Creemore**. Dinner here at A. Kitt's. God grant mercy. Nice few out. Mtg - Thirst again.

Tue. May 14 At Kyle's for dinner. Had walk in pm and gave away a few tracts. At A. Kitt's for tea. Not many out.

Wed. May 15 At W. Mackay's. Some help and encouragement from God.

Thu. May 16 Beautiful morning. Visited Hiseys and for tea.

Fri. May 17 Another lovely day. God is faithful. At Kyle's for dinner. Visited Mrs. Kitch, Mrs. Bulmer and Manning's for tea.

Sat. May 18 Meeting on street, Kyle and I out with tracts.

Sun. May 19 Rather nice morning mtg, though small.

Mon. May 20 At Jim Latimer's all night. Called at Latimer Sr.'s and Taylor's for dinner. Called on Mrs. Baxter for tea.

Sun. June 09 August Heidman and I went to **Severn** on motorcycle. Rather wet day, but God managed for us. At Kitt's for dinner and at Lloyd's for tea. Home after 11 pm.

Thu. June 13 Maude and I left about 8 with J. Latimer, reached **Craighurst** about 9.30. I walked to Leslie Clark's funeral, 5 miles. Very warm. Mr. Telfer there. To conference at night.

Fri. June 14 At **Sunnidale** Conference. R. Telfer, W. P. Douglas, R. McCrory, J. C. Beattie, and J. Silvester. M&I at Johnston's.

Sat. June 15 Meetings all day in Mennonite's Hall.

Sun. June 16 Meetings all day. Spoke in gospel at night.

Sat. Oct. 12 Arr'd safely at Cheboygan, 6.30. At Bannister's.

Sun. Oct. 13 **No meetings** on account of influenza. Read and prayed together in am. At Greenlees' in pm and for tea. Down town for a walk and gave away a few tracts.

Sun. Oct. 20 Canadian Soo. **No meetings** on account of influenza.

Sun. Oct. 27 2 deaths in South River this morning. Ed Steen nursing at one place. **No feast of love divine.** August and I wheeled out to Kion's in afternoon.

Tue. Oct. 29 Phone message from N. Kion at Severn re Seymour Canning's death.

Wed. Oct. 30 Willie drove me to station at 8.45 for Severn. Charlie
Canning met me. At Canning's all night.

Thu. Oct. 31 Seymour Canning's funeral at noon. Nice few at grave
side. Read from Numbers - Death of righteous. Back to Canning's
for dinner and home in car with Beattie C.

Sun. Nov. 03 **No meetings.** The time was long. Read Luke 23 together
and prayed.

Sun. Nov. 10 Kept the feast once more.

Mon. Nov. 11 Armistice signed. Peace declared. Great celebration.

"Thy Brother Shall Rise Again."

Jesus saith unto her, Thy brother shall rise again.

John 11.23.

Thy brother shall rise again;
Thou shalt not sorrow in sad despair,
As one without hope as others do bear;
Soon thou shalt meet him again in the air,
    "Thy brother shall rise again."

Though he were dead, he shall live,
We look with grief at the dear loved face,
Absent in this, but in that glad place
Singing that song of redeeming grace,
    Yes, he shall live again.

Jesus is coming again;
Coming in glory. Believest thou this?
Bringing back with Him the dear ones we miss;
Oh what reunion, rejoicing, and bliss,
    Jesus is coming again.

G. L. S.

1919

During this year gospel meetings were held in Arnstein, Ontario, for six weeks in February and March, with brother Ed Steen. The diary indicates many familiar names.

From the middle of May to the middle of August, there were thirteen weeks of gospel meetings in Chapman Valley, Ontario, also with bro. Steen. The daily pattern of these meetings was; helping the farmers in the field in the morning, visiting in the afternoon, and preaching at night (with the occasional hair cut given in between). The Lord chose to save souls at these meetings, and twenty eight were baptized at five baptisms. These were held on Lord's Day afternoons, after a meal at the Hall. The baptisms took place in the Distress River, down the road from the Hall.

In September, Mr. Shivas and brother Ormer Sprunt held two weeks of gospel meetings at Deer Lake. Parts of the record of these meetings follow, along with a short portion regarding Orillia Conference over Labour Day of 1919, and Victoria Road Conference, Dec. 28, 1919.

Sat. Feb. 08 Left on early train for Trout Creek and at 7 oc for **Arnstein**. Arr'd safely about 7pm. *(Twelve hours is a long time to travel 60 kilometres.)* At DeBernardo's all night.

Sun. Feb. 09 A real good day. Lot out in am. Culin's for dinner. Julius' for tea. Hall full at night.

Mon. Feb. 10 At Sommacal's for dinner, also Ed and Ena. Lot out again. Help to preach.

Sun. Feb. 16 The Lord's day. Rejoice and be glad in it. Soft morning mtg. At Tuppelsea's for dinner. B. Class, Acts 17. At Julius' for tea. Good meeting - It is finished.

Mon. Feb. 17 Down to store after dinner. Ed and I visited Mrs. Cudmore and Simms. Talk with Rowbotham. Nice lot out.

Wed. Feb. 19 Walked down the lake a little way with Willie Simms, seems troubled. Mtg - Dwellings.

Thu. Feb. 20 Wrote more texts in book. Cudmore's for tea. Willie Simms professed.

Fri. Feb. 21 Read Matt. 25. John and I fixed oven door on stove. Called at Mrs. Simms' and Dellandrea Sr.'s. Mtg, Luke 10.

Sat. Feb. 22 Went with John to DeBernardo's. Painting chairs for Julius most of day. John and I drove Teno M. and Frank B. part way home. Wet snow.

Sun. Feb. 23 This is my rest forever. At Corbin's for dinner. Good number out at night - In no wise.

Mon. Feb. 24 Called at R. Brunne's and went out to Julius'. Helped him a little till tea time. Good number out to meeting.

Wed. Feb. 26 Stage didn't get in last night. Called on Gooleys, and Swanstrums.

Sat. Mar. 01 March lion. High wind all night. God is faithful. Drove with John to store. Tea with Teno Maestri.

Mon. Mar. 03 Nice morning. Had talk with Mr. Sommacal in barn.

Wed. Mar. 05 Cold night. At Tuppelsea's for dinner. Called at school, Ed and I. Saw Fred and Willie Simms. Cut Ed's hair.

Thu. Mar. 06 Went with Mr. DeB. Sr. to see traps, got beaver. Beautiful day. Mrs. Swanstrum here for tea.

Sat. Mar. 08 Frosty night. Beautiful bright day. Ed and I at R. Brunne's in am. Drove with John and met R. Culin and Bob D.

Sun. Mar. 09 Very stormy day. Snowed 8 or 9 inches.

Thu. Mar. 13 Spoke to children at school in pm from Samuel.

Mon. Mar. 17 Walked out to DeB.'s in am and got to West Road, but raining, so didn't go. Culin's for tea, and all night.

Tue. Mar. 18 A little cooler with snow. Eddy DeB. drove Ed and I to West Road. Came to Chas. Culin's for dinner. Jim Rogerson's for tea and all night. Nice lot at mtg - His own sins.

Thu. Mar. 20 Another bright day. Read John 1 in home. Sang 'Behold what love'. At Bruce's camp in pm and for tea. Mtg - Whosoever.

Fri. Mar. 21 At Archie Brook's in am and for dinner. Called on Culins, Browns and Bowers and back to Rogerson's for tea. Called at Mark R.'s. Meeting - There is.

Sat. Mar. 22 Down at Bruce's camp in am. Came as far as Mrs. Bower's for dinner. Called on Waltons.

Sun. Mar. 23 Lovely bright day. Walked with Mr. S. to hall to remember God's beloved Son.

Tue. Mar. 25 Another beautiful day. Helped John grind up meat in am. Out to see Quinn boys at bush. Visited Mrs. Brunne.

Wed. Mar. 26 Henry Hample drove us to Trout Creek with DeB.'s team. Rough road but fine day. <u>God is faithful</u>. Reached South River in due time about midnight. Slept in front room.

Usually the trip from Arnstein to Trout Creek was accomplished by stage coach and connected with the train at Trout Creek. We recall Mr. Shivas telling of one such trip in early spring. The road was beginning to break up and it was heavy going for the horses. Beside a swamp the horses floundered. The stage got out of the ruts, and tipped over into the swamp. There was just enough ice on the water to support the trunks and suitcases that fell off the top of the stage. They broke open, and skidded across the ice, scattering their contents as they went. The passengers retrieved them by carefully crawling out on their hands and knees. Then came the arduous task of getting the stage righted and back on the road.

The outcome of the day's adventure was that they were some 8 to 10 hours late for their train connection at Trout Creek, and presumed the train had gone long before.

When they reached the railway station at Trout Creek, tired, wet and cold, the station master said, "I've been wondering why the train was so very late, but now I know. God must have delayed it for you. You are just in time to catch it."

Sat. May 17 Getting ready to leave for **Chapman Valley**. Arr'd safely at Sundridge 5 oc. Tea at McCabe's. Visited Kions.

Sun. May 18 Walked as far as Castles and rest of way to Valley with Bobbie Hicks, too late for Breaking of Bread. Good Bible reading. Harrison's for dinner and tea. Large gospel mtg.

Mon. May 19 At Hicks' all night. Good rest and sleep. God is faithful. Called on Tarrants, Kings, T. Hicks'. Good crowd.

Thu. May 22 Wet day. At King's for dinner. Will Harrison there. At Tom Hicks' for tea. Early to hall to fix lamps. Lot out.

Sat. May 24 Visited Joe Millers, Miller Srs., and Stewarts.

Mon. May 26 Went as far as J. Hicks'. Talked with him in field. Also visited Alexanders, Sinclairs, and tea at Mrs. House's.

Tue. May 27 Lovely morning. Wrote R. Culin. Drove to the Mag. with Mrs H. Gave away tracts. Tea at Mrs. Mills', who professed faith in Christ. Meeting - No more.

Wed. May 28 Still beautiful weather. Good number out last night in spite of dance at Mag. 'I will work and who will hinder'. Called at H. Lennox's. Tea at Mills Sr.'s. Good number out.

Sat. May 31 At Harrison's all night. Long talk with Willie in am. Called on Sinclairs in afternoon, and had tea at Alexander's.

Mon. June 02 Visited McCabes about Cecil's pigs and spoke with Tom about eternity. Tea at Mumford's. Very warm. Nice few out.

Wed. June 04 After dinner visited Mr. Mills, Whalleys, Smiths. Mrs. Mills' for tea. Mtg - Persuade.

Sat. June 07 Down to hall after dinner and to Mrs. House's. Fixed bad steps etc. King's for tea. Home for night.

Sun. June 08 Very heavy rains. Good morning mtg, some softness and I trust, praise to God. Good large meeting at night.

Mon. June 09 Heavy rain again through the night. 3 feet over road.

Tue. June 10 Called on Mrs. Boyes and Mrs. House's for tea.

Wed. June 11 At Harrison's all night. Went up to Mrs. Miller's and was there all day reasoning out of the Scriptures.

Sat. June 14 Warm day. Miss Green, school teacher here for dinner. All over at Harrison's camp for tea and out to the bush where they were peeling bark. Miss Green professed to be saved.

Sun. June 15 Ed got back before mtg. Rather nice time in His presence. Some softness. At Wm. Hughs' for dinner and Mrs. Mills' for tea. Walked to mtg, large crowd inside and out.

Wed. June 18 Visited men in bush and at Alexander's camp.

Sat. June 21 Drove with Freddie to Sundridge. Shipped 13 pigs. Rode with Mr. Miller Sr. Visited Bobbie Hicks and Kions.

Sun. June 22 A good day. This day is salvation come to this house. Ellen Hughs got saved. Nice morning mtg, and gospel meeting.

Thu. June 26 Helped Mr. Hicks all day take out stumps near gate. All went to mtg in wagon.

Fri. June 27 At Harrison's bark bush and at camp for tea. Mtg.

Sun. June 29 The Lord's Day. Sweet feast of love divine. Nice soft mtg in am. Large mtg at night, good interest, - Come down.

Tue. July 01 At Clifford Miller's all day. Out to see men in bush.

Wed. July 02 Drove with Mrs. H. and Sarah to Mag. and to Mrs. Mills'. Birdie M. professed faith in Christ.

Thu. July 03 Warm day. Visited at Arch Alexander's camp for dinner, and the boys in the bush. Archie A. professed.

Fri. July 04 Drove to Mag. Wrote Maude. Called at Mrs. Mills'. Mrs. D. Hughs may have gotten saved. God grant it. At Harrison's for dinner, and Joe Miller's for tea. Mtg - One thing.

Sun. July 06 A good day in Thy courts. Large crowds. Dinner at Hall. Mtg at 2.30 - Arise. Baptism at river, 8 obeyed God in baptism. At Mumford's for tea. Meeting, Luke 15 - 3 L's.

Tue. July 08 At J. Boyes' in pm & for tea. Meeting, Isa. 51.

Thu. July 10 Thunder storm last night. Basil Howe may have gotten saved. God grant it. At Tarrant's in am, and Harrison's camp.

Sun. July 13 At Hall all day, a good day. Mtg outside at 2.30. Baptized 7 in the river. Mtg outside at 7.30 pm.
Tue. July 15 Quite a lot at meeting, many adversaries.
Sat. July 19 Helping with hay. Had bath in lake in evening. At Robertson's all night. Drove Ford car a few miles.
Sun. July 20 Another good day in Thy courts. Large mtg in am, precious time. Mtg at 3. Large gospel meeting.
Mon. July 21 Bob Hicks got saved in afternoon. All at Harrison's.
Thu. July 24 Called at Stewart's and Jos. Miller's and helped him draw in hay. Barton's for tea. Meeting - Found.
Fri. July 25 Helped Mr. Hicks at hay all day, with Bob Hicks.
Wed. July 30 Helped some at the hay. Nice lot out to meeting.
Thu. July 31 At Mrs. Tarrant's in pm helping at hay and for tea.
Fri. Aug. 01 At berry patch all day with young Tom Hicks. Rather good day. Manson Hicks professed. Meeting - Except.
Sat. Aug. 02 Drove with team to berry patch. Art McKee went. Picking berries all day. Ash Harrison professed faith in Christ. At Harrison's for tea. Sent 4 baskets of berries to Orillia.
Sun. Aug. 03 A feast and a good day. At Hall for dinner. Mrs. Bob Hicks professed. Mtg at 3. Ed baptized 5. Meeting - Cometh.
Mon. Aug. 04 Helped at the hay at Tarrant's. Meeting.
Tue. Aug. 05 Wrote F. G. Watson. Ed & I walked to Tom Boyes', 5 miles. Reasoned out of the Scriptures. Lot out to meeting.
Sun. Aug. 10 A good day again. Nice soft mtg, some brokenness. Mtg at 2.30. Dinner and tea in Hall. 7 baptized in the river. God gave help. Large meeting at 7.30, Gen. 3 - Where?
Mon. Aug. 11 Drove Mrs. Bob Hicks to the boat, M&I, then went home with her to Ahmic Harbor. To Robertson's in pm and for tea. Allan brought us to meeting - Depth.
Tue. Aug. 12 At King's for dinner & tea. W. Harrison there, helped at harvest. Large meeting, Num. 23 - Last.
Wed. Aug. 13 Helped J. Boyes at oats a while in am. There for dinner and tea and spoke a lot of God's word.
Thu. Aug. 14 "Eternal life" last night. At graveyard in pm, painting texts. Harrison's for tea. Had Bible Reading.
Fri. Aug. 15 Dull morning. Got some stones for graves. At Harrison's for dinner. Dear Will professed to be saved. At Joe Miller's and Wilson's. Harrison's for tea. Bible reading.
Sat. Aug. 16 Painted texts on 5 stones for the graveyard.

Sun. Aug. 17 Last Lord's Day at the Valley. Another 'Day in Thy courts.' Spoke after Breaking of Bread - Thanks be unto God. Tea and mtg at 2.30. W. Harrison baptized. Large mtg at 7.30.

Mon. Aug. 18 Manson Hicks drove us to South River. Made many calls on way up. Dinner at McCabe's, Sundridge.

Tue. Aug. 19 Good rest in sleep. God is faithful. Wrote Bob Hicks.

Wed. Aug. 27 Still wet. Down to store before breakfast. Phoned up home. Busy preparing for **Orillia conference**, etc.

Thu. Aug. 28 Still making preparations. Delivering mattresses. Herb Harris, Cecil & I. Prayer meeting.

Fri. Aug. 29 Busy all day. Handling chairs etc. Quite a few came before night. Our house about full. First mtg of Conference.

Sat. Aug. 30 Over 30 stayed at our home. What a privilege to entertain so many under our roof. Good meetings all day.

Sun. Aug. 31 The Lord's Day. Good morning mtg. Largest meetings for some years. Meals at curling rink. Helped in gospel mtg at night, Ed and I. Spoke from - Why?

Mon. Sep. 01 Good meetings all day. Orillia Conference.

Tue. Sep. 02 Good mtg at 9 oc. Telfer, Livingstone, McCartney, and Binch. Most of people went away home. God is faithful.

Sat. Sep. 06 Ormer Sprunt met me on train. We came to **Deer Lake**. Mr. Nickason met us.

Sun. Sep. 07 Rather good day at Deer Lake at Nickason's. Ormer and I had mtg at 7. Good crowd. Spoke on - Is come.

Mon. Sep. 08 Ormer and I walked to Port Sydney with mail. Made quite a few calls. Fixed hall steps. Mtg, Math. 27 - Do.

Tue. Sep. 09 Good sleep. God is faithful. Ormer and I visited Mr. Keeler, 86, across the lake. Tea at Hughs'. Good mtg.

Wed. Sep. 10 Cool and cloudy. Ormer and I walked to Oliver's, 6 miles and back. Oliver's for dinner, Forsythe's for tea.

Thu. Sep. 11 Visited old Mr. Keeler in am. Visited 3 homes. Mtg.

Fri. Sep. 12 Cold and windy. After dinner visited at Robt Orr's, Arthur Orr's, and Erwin Orr's for tea. Meeting, Acts 4 - Saved. Visited Mr. Keeler in am, also Dillaboughs & Hughs.

Sun. Sep. 14 Rather soft time at the feast, 10 of us. Some words of God at dinner table. Good number to gospel meeting.

Mon. Sep. 15 Working at the hall all day, putting on Cal. siding, Mr. Orr, Mr. M., Ormer and me.

Tue. Sep. 16 Working at hall at Deer Lake, Ormer and me. Meeting.

Wed. Sep. 17 Painting hall. Mtg at night.

Thu. Sep. 18 Ormer and I had bath in lake before breakfast. Came to Huntsville Conference. Prayer meeting.

Fri. Sep. 19 R. Telfer, R. McClintock, McCartney, F. G. Watson, Mr. & Mrs. Livingstone at Huntsville Conference.

A baptism was held at the Conference, on the Lord's Day aft. Sept. 21. From notes we learn that Mr. and Mrs. Forsythe, and another brother were baptized by Mr. F. G. Watson, at 2 pm.

There was more blessing from the gospel meetings at Chapman Valley in the summer, for at the Conference, on Lord's Day, Sept. 29th, Mr. Alex Robertson was baptized in the early afternoon. Mr. J. Silvester spoke to a large crowd at the riverside, Acts 8.

Sat. Dec. 27 **Conference at Victoria Road.** Meetings all day.

Stayed at McLeod's. Slept with W. P. Douglas.

Sun. Dec. 28 **Meetings all day in new hall.** W. P. Douglas, McClintock, McCartney, Watson, Silvester, Johnston, Bruce.

Mon. Dec. 29 Meetings all day. Helped at night, Luke 19 - Chief.

The Ants and The Conies

The ants are a people not very strong,
And so they work harder all the day long.
When the sun shines bright each warm summer day
They lay up their food in the house where they stay.

The conies are feeble and can't dig a hole,
They can't climb a tree, and they can't climb a pole.
So when lions and bears come and give them a shock
They run to their nest which is safe in the rock.

G. L. S.

Psalm 133

Behold how good and how pleasant it is for brethren to dwell together in unity! It is like the precious ointment upon the head, that ran down upon the beard, even Aaron's beard: that went down to the skirts of his garments; As the dew of Hermon, and as the dew that descended upon the mountains of Zion: for there the Lord commanded the blessing, even life for evermore.

Behold how pleasant and how good
It is for saints to dwell
In unity by grace subdued,
Such comfort who can tell.

'Tis like the ointment's fragrant breath
On Israel's priest of old;
It tells of Christ's most precious death,
By God so long foretold.

And like to morning's sparkling dew
Refreshing all the ground,
So like the Lord who lowly grew,
But now with glory crowned.

God's blessing He doth there command,
E'en life for ever more,
Until we reach that better land,
And rest on Heaven's shore.

For every foretaste here below
Our gratitude we raise,
And may our lives and lips still show
Our great Redeemer's praise.

G. L. S.

Three discoveries

There are several things about the "good old days" I have learned as I have gone over these diaries, that help keep our modern technological sophistication in proper perspective.

The first is the efficient mail service that was enjoyed. Letters and postcards were sent off with abandon, and why not, postage was 1 cent. It was taken for granted that they would be delivered within a day or two.

Even funeral arrangements were made by mail. Note the following entries.

1919 Sat. Oct. 04   Wrote R. McClintock yesterday re Jos. Smith's funeral.

Mon. Oct. 06   Up early and met Mr. McClintock at 8 train from Deer Lake. Roy Smith drove us to his father's funeral. God cleared up the weather. Good time. Read Psalm 73.

As well, note the following postcards.

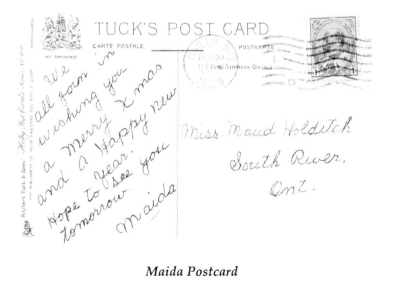

Maida Postcard

The Grass Never Grew Greener!

This postcard looks quite ordinary at first glance. Maida wished Miss Maude Holditch in South River the season's greetings, and mailed the postcard from Orillia.

When you note that it was <u>postmarked</u> midnight, Dec. 24th, in Orillia, and that Maida said "Hope to see you tomorrow," you realize that the postcard was expected to reach Miss Maude Holditch <u>in</u> South River, the following day, <u>before</u> the family arrived by train. Not only that, but the next day was Dec. 25th, Christmas Day. The Post Office must have been open!

Now if you or I mailed such a card on the 24th of December, when would we expect it might be delivered?

Would you agree, some time in the new year?

Note another postcard.

Mother Postcard

This postcard was written to G. L. Shivas in Orillia, from his mother in Bracebridge, on Friday, Sept. 15, 1905.

When Mrs. Samuel Shivas stepped off the train at Orillia the next afternoon, she fully expected George would be there with the horse and buggy to meet them. This postcard had to move very efficiently to reach G. L. Shivas in Orillia on a Saturday, so that he would meet the train.

Today, we wouldn't even think of sending such a notice as this, and anyway, there is no train on which to ride!

Nor was such postal efficiency limited to local mail.

Another postcard was postmarked Indianapolis, Indiana, 4 pm, October 20, 1904. A second postmark read Detroit, Michigan, TRANSIT, 9.30am, October 21, while a third postmark read Orillia, Ontario, PM, October 22. That is 48 hours from origin to destination.

Yet another card in the opposite direction was marked Orillia, PM, Sept 27, 1906, and Indianapolis, 4.30 am, Sept 29.

That is a total of 36 hours travelling time!

Finally, a card from Aberdeen, Scotland, postmarked 3 am, May 29, 1906, was also stamped Orillia, PM, June 8, 1906. When you consider that the card moved from Aberdeen to a seaport, crossed the ocean in a boat, and travelled by train from Montreal to Orillia, ten days time is good service.

It is no better today, via airmail!

The second feature of those times was the efficiency of the passenger train service. Mr. Shivas could get a train to almost any place, large or small, day or night.

Note the following diary notations from early years.

1907 Wed. Jan. 16 Marion R. went away on 4.40 train to Barrie.

Tue. Feb. 12 Met folks at 4.30 train, rec'd letter from Maude.

Thu. Feb. 14 Fine soft day, went down to 8.10 Midland train, saw Mr. Douglas on way from Foxmead to Toronto, pleased to see him.

Wed. Feb. 20 Rec'd letter from Maude, decided to go up to South River. Went up to Irwin's after dinner, Mrs. I. made me some lunch, went down town, wired Maude at 4.00, left on 4.40, arrived at S.R. about 9.00, Maude met me. Was glad to see her.

Sun. Feb. 24 Maude and I went to station after night mtg, train late, had tea and a little talk, left S.R. about one oc.

Mon. Feb. 25 Arr'd home about 6.00, didn't do much all day.

1912 Sat. Mar. 16 Hope to meet Maude on the 8 oc at Sundridge.

Met 8 oc train. Dear Maude brought on her way safely, went to South River together.

Mon. Mar. 18 Came down to Harrison's, Sundridge on noon train.

1915 Fri. May 21 Went to Toronto at noon.

Sat. May 22 Went to Bolton at 5.35.

Mon. May 24 Went to Toronto at 7 pm, got home to Orillia at 11.40.

Thu. June 03 Went to Craighurst Conf. at 12.44 via CPR.

Sat. Oct. 30 Ed went home to Huntsville on the midnight.

Tue. Nov. 16 Ena and Marg came on 8 oc. Jane went away on 4.20.

Mon. Dec. 20 Maude and I left S.R. on train, came as far as Huntsville safely, thank God. Maude and I met Ed at station from Deer Lake.
Tue. Dec. 21 Maude and I left Huntsville at 9.15 am for Orillia. Arr'd safely on time, at noon. Father met us at station with Harold C.'s horse.
Sat. Dec. 25 Cecil and I met Jim at 9.20 train.
Mon. Dec. 27 Bre. Telfer & Pearson came on noon train. Jim and Ethel for dinner. Jim went home on 4.30, saw him off.
Tue. Dec. 28 Ethel missed her train, went by Blackwater. Phoned Mrs. A.T. for Jim to meet other train.
1916 Thu. Jan. 13 M & I went over to Harris' on 11.45 train, came back in time for Bible Reading.
Sat. Jan. 15 Helped Mrs. Swales with her things. Cecil and I shipped them before noon. Left at 3.47 by CPR for Glenarm.
Fri. Jan. 28 Left at 4.30 for Huntsville, Ena met us.
Sat. Mar. 11 Left at 3.30 am with Ed for Soo. Arrived about 6 pm.
Wed. Apr. 12 Geo. Alton and Leo saw Ed & me off for Sudbury.
Fri. Apr. 14 Left Sudbury at 7.25 am, arr'd Sturgeon 9.25, left Sturgeon 7.54 pm, arr'd S.R. about 1 am.
Sat. June 24 Left at 7.50 for Woodville.
Tue. July 04 Maude and I left at 4.30 for Severn. Will Bailey met us. Met Lewis on train.
Thu. July 06 M&I left Severn at 11.30. Got home about 1 oc.
Wed. July 12 Left at 4.30 for Atherley.
Fri. Oct. 06 Left at noon for Collingwood Conf. Arr'd there 6.00.
Tue. Oct. 10 Left C'wood at 10.50. Home at 4.30.
Fri. Nov. 03 Soo Mich. Mr. McDonald saw us off at 5.30. Took sleeper to Duluth.
Sat. Nov. 04 Safe and prosperous journey by His will. Auntie Amy met us at station. Back for grips in pm.
1917 Sat. June 30 Mother drove Ev. & children to stn at 3.35 CPR. Went to Glenarm.
Thu. July 19 Had to run to catch 7 train for Barrie. The Lord grant mercy.
Sat. Dec. 29 Left at noon for Midland Conference. Train over an hour late.

Finally, the diaries reveal the profound impact made by the automobile upon our daily lives, as the transition is made from the horse and buggy to the horseless carriage.

The novelty of a ride in an automobile was followed by the expense and responsibility of operating one's own car. One progressed from a walking pace to a long distance drive to attend a weekend conference.

The first diary entry that mentions an automobile is;

1915 Tue. May 25 Went to Warminster at night with Mr. M. C. and Vivian C. in Mac Clark's auto.

His goodness endureth continually.

Obviously it was a risky adventure that called for special thanksgiving. However, the next evening he tried it again, and his parents as well.

Wed. May 26 Went to Warminster at night with M. Clark in auto with father and mother and Vivian.

Other sightings of automobiles soon were made.

Mon. June 14 Rankins went to town in am with A. Eagle in auto.

The whole of year 1916 makes no mention of autos.

1917 has a few notations;

Wed. July 11 Maude came home in car from Severn S.S. Treat at Sparrow Lake.

Thu. Sep. 27 Went to Chapman Valley Conference in auto with Geo. Rogerson, Ena, and Cappie Harris.

The main change from horse to car occurred in 1918. The simple word "drove," changed its meaning that year. In early spring it meant, "drove with horse and buggy." In late spring it meant, "drove with car."

1918 Sat. Mar. 02 Cut wood, cleaned stove pipes. Mother brought **horse** down, and Maude and mother **drove** me to station. Left at 4.40 for Victoria Road (Eldon). Reached McLeod's about 12.

Sat. Mar. 09 **Drove** with Roy Forman's **horse** to Gilmore's for dinner. Safe journey and not very cold. At Gilmore's all day. Turned very stormy at night. Read Luke 22.

Wed. May 01 Cold morning. Wrote Maude. **Drove** out to Willie Latimer's for dinner with Bryan's **horse and buggy.** Came back about 4. At Bryan's for tea. Nice few out to mtg.

Sat. Apr. 06 Called on Mrs. Morris after dinner. **Drove** in **auto** with Geo. Roberts out to Massey Farm.

1918 Fri. May 03 Collingwood. Piling wood in am. John hurt his back. Wrote Maude. Elsie T. **drove us down in car** to stn. Called on Mrs. McHendry. At Jim Latimer's for tea. Meeting.

The idea of moving about from place to place so conveniently had become well established.

Sun. June 09 August Heidman and I went to Severn on motorcycle. Rather wet day but God managed for us.

In the summer of 1918 Mr. Shivas was having gospel meetings with Mr. Leo Sheldrake at Pickford, Michigan. Leo decided to buy a car so that they could get to the Soo on Lord's Days.

Fri. July 19 Leo went to Soo for car with Bert Smith.

There was optional equipment, of course.

Tue. July 23 Got straps for car. Put them on before dinner.

Wed. Sep. 11 Got mica put in curtain of car.

Then the trouble started as well.

Fri. Aug. 16 Cleaning spark plugs in car.

Sun. Aug. 18 Left Soo 1 pm for Pickford. In the ditch once but got there safely in time for afternoon meeting.

Sat. Sep. 14 Left about 10.30 for Soo. Car didn't run very well.

Thu. Sep. 26 Oiling car in am.

Tue. Oct. 01 Working at car in pm.

In **1919** Mr. Shivas tried driving a car.

Sat. July 19 At Robertson's, Chapman Valley, all night. Drove Ford car a few miles.

Thu. July 24 Maude & I drove with T. Hicks' car to Harrington's for dinner. Called at Jos. Stewart's and Jos. Miller's.

Fri. July 25 Drove with Bob Hicks' car to South River.

Sun. July 27 Drove down to the Valley safely by God's grace.

The first indication of personal ownership of an automobile came in the fall of **1923**.

Mon. Oct. 08 Left Arnstein at 6.30 am. Dinner at South River. Left at 12 and got to Orillia at 7 in evening in **our Ford car.**

We have often heard him quote these lines;

"Be not the first by whom the new is tried,
Nor yet the last to lay the old aside!"

In **1924** Mr. Shivas tried his hand at automobile repairs.

Thu. Jan. 24 Jacked up car on blocks. Took tire down to Dave McC.

Thu. Apr. 24 Got paint for car.

Tue. May 27 Maude and I working cleaning car for painting.

Wed. May 28 Painting car.

Wed. July 16 Fixing car.
Tue. Aug. 12 Helped Norman Clark a little with his car in am.
Fri. Sep. 05 Got car radiator fixed, $1.
Wed. Oct. 01 Working at car.
Thu. Oct. 09 Put new piece on car, front axle.
Tue. Nov. 25 Working at car. Put in 2 new springs in rear.
Fri. Nov. 28 Started for Victoria Road, and broke wheel.
Fri. Dec. 05 Fixing tire on car.
Wed. Dec. 10 Working at tire, etc.
Thu. Dec. 11 Cleaned and oiled car.

An entry in **1926** reminds us of an incident related by Mr. Shivas, revealing how resourceful they were, when travelling.

Thu. June 03 Came up to South River last night. Washed and cleaned car. Ed and I came to Arnstein in afternoon.
Fri. June 04 At Amiel Culin's all night. Fixing Ed's car.

Mr. Shivas and Mr. Ed Steen were coming from Arnstein to South River, in Mr. Steen's car, via the "back way."

This route turned south at Commanda, followed the Old Muskoka Road, turned east a few miles west of Eagle Lake, and ended in South River. The normal route from Arnstein to South River was directly east on Highway 522 to Trout Creek, and south on Highway 11 to South River. For Mr. Shivas the highway route had no challenge, and it was a few miles longer.

They were proceeding south on this back road, which hardly deserved to be called a road, and had bounced onto a low plank bridge over a shallow creek.

At that moment, the nut came off the front of the tie rod on the passenger side, and the tie rod promptly wedged between two planks. It bent into a "U" shape, and had enough tension to lift the car, tip it over sideways, and deposit it upside down in the creek!

They scrambled out, found a wrench, and unfastened the end of the tie rod that was still connected to the car. Mr. Shivas took the bent rod, and walked down the road a few miles to the blacksmith's shop at Rye. He obligingly pounded it out straight. Mr. Shivas walked back to the car, they reconnected the rod, got the car back on its wheels, and managed to drive it onto the road. Then they continued on their way.

We recall a few trips via the back way to Arnstein with our own car, as late as the '50's, with Mr. Shivas walking ahead, moving stones, throwing brush into holes, all the while waving us on, saying, "Come on, it's fine, keep coming!"

In **1927** he acquired a Gray Dort automobile. This was not a good used car as the records clearly indicate.

Fri. May 06 Getting gas tank fixed at Ron's.

Thu. May 12 Painting car.

Mon. May 16 Working at generator of car.

Sat. May 21 Planted garden and fixed car, and drove to Midland.

Wed. May 25 Working at car at Boyce's, most of day.

Fri. May 27 Got generator fixed at Blackburn's, $4.

Sat. May 28 Put new spring in car.

Tue. May 31 Took gas tank out of car and got repaired, and mostly put in again.

Wed. June 01 Fixed gas tap in car.

Tue. June 07 Working at gas tank.

Wed. June 08 Fixed windows in car. Trouble with switch in car.

Thu. June 09 Got new switch in car and other jobs.

Mon. July 11 Tire trouble.

In the spring of **1928**, it wasn't performing much better.

Thu. Mar. 29 Got car out and down to garage.

Fri. Mar. 30 Working at car at D. McC.'s garage till 3 pm.

Tue. Apr. 03 Getting car ready, licence, etc. Left for Toronto.

Wed. Apr. 04 Took car to Frank Adams'.

Sun. Apr. 15 Welland. Out to Fonthill in aft. Got car stuck.

Mon. Apr. 23 Got new windows in car, $2.

Wed. Apr. 25 Joe W. and I called at garages trying to change Gray Dort car.

Tue. May 01 Seeing about car. Eagle's for dinner. Bought new car in evening, $63., Ford Sedan.

Thu. May 03 Got new car, 1920 Ford Sedan, $65. New fender & tire.

There was not much satisfaction with this one either.

Thu. May 10 Started for Barrie last night, father and mother, Maude, Betty & I. **Trouble with car.**

Here we shall leave the history of travel by automobile in the "good old days," well aware of the problems we all have had with these "luxuries of necessity".

On Giving

It's not what I'd do with the million
If riches should e'er be my lot,
But it's what will I do at the present
With the dollar and a quarter I've got.

For the million I'll not have to render
An account in the glory, but I've
A stewardship in Heaven to tender —
What I did with the one twenty-five.

God has filled up our garners with plenty,
And furnished our houses with store,
Made the one twenty-five into twenty,
And is able to give more and more.

The million would be too much trouble,
And sure be a burdensome lot;
The little we have He can double,
May we use for Him now what we've got.

G. L. S.

My Beloved

Yea, he is altogether lovely. This is my beloved, and this is my
friend, O daughters of Jerusalem.   Song of Solomon 5. 10-16.
The Son of God, who loved me, and gave Himself for me. Gal. 2.20.

Oh He's lovely altogether, of ten thousand He's the chief,
And there's nought from Him can sever, neither doubt
nor pain nor grief;
What marks Him out in Glory is the banner of His love,
There we'll sing the blessed story in our Father's house above.

Black and bushy are His tresses, crowns of gold His head adorn,
Where once, as olive presses, sinners pressed the crown of thorn;
But now He lives in power, Who for our sake was dead,
Pleading for us every hour, coming soon, our glorious Head.

His eyes so true and tender over sinners oft did weep,
As a sheep with no defender, to save from death's dark deep,
With one object set before Him and no other, as the dove,
But to cause us to adore Him and forever share His love.

His cheeks like sweetest spices are, compared to flowers most rare,
Yet sinners spat upon that face, and rudely plucked the hair;
But that visage scarred and riven now shines brighter
than the sun,
Looking for the bride God gave Him, waiting for His only one.

His blessed body given for us, compared to ivory strong,
Has borne that mighty load, and thus turned weeping into song,
That I might now a member be, in union so complete,
And keep His word "Remember Me," and worship at His feet.

The sweetest mouth that ever spake, and sweet the words He said,
Yet dumb He was, and for our sake, a sheep to slaughter led;
But sweeter far than sweetest wine, is from His mouth one kiss,
And oh how sweet to know He's mine, and I forever His.

Owen Sound, December, 1923. G.L.S

1920

This was a productive year for Mr. Shivas. There were three weeks of gospel meetings at Victoria Road, with brother R. McClintock in February, one week under adverse winter conditions at Rathburn in March, four weeks at Chapman Valley in June, five weeks at Cambray in July and August, one week at Chapman Valley in October, and at least seven weeks at Sault Ste. Marie in November and December, all of these places being in Ontario.

Excerpts from some of these series follow.

Sat. Jan. 24 Mr. McClintock and I left 3.35 CPR for Balsam Lake. God giveth the increase. May we see His good hand.

Sun. Jan. 25 **Victoria Road**. A feast and a good day. Very cold weather. Large mtg at 11 am. Good number out to our first mtg.

Mon. Jan. 26 Still cold. Helped Mr. McLeod cut some wood at hall, pump lamps etc. Hargrave's for tea. Nice few out for Monday.

Tue. Jan. 27 Milder today and more snow. Wrote announcement of meetings on a lot of tracts and put some in mail boxes after dinner. Roy Forman's for tea. Num. 32 - Be sure.

Wed. Jan. 28 Mr. McClintock not well. Went to bed in afternoon. Over to hall, cleaned floor, pumped lamps etc. Rubbed Mr. McC.'s back. Had mtg alone. God gave help. Luke 19 - Press.

Thu. Jan. 29 Not so cold and a little snow. Mr. McC. feeling better. Helped Mr. McLeod cut wood at hall. Nice few out at night. Some strangers. Mtg alone. Spoke on "One of them."

Fri. Jan. 30 Milder today. Roads filled in. Heavy walking. Came over to Bell's till about 4. Lit fire at hall. Some came to mtg.

Sat. Jan. 31 Nice bright day. Drove around block with tracts.

Sun. Feb. 01 Joy and gladness, a feast and a good day.

Mon. Feb. 02 Beautiful mild day. At Hargrave's for dinner.

Tue. Feb. 03 Made board for sign in am. At Brentnell's for dinner. Called on Mrs. Stone. Meeting, 1 Sam. 20 - Truly.

Wed. Feb. 04 Painted part of sign. Nice lot out to mtg. Some help.

Thu. Feb. 05 Finished painting sign. At W. Parrington's for dinner.

Fri. Feb. 06 Made frame for sign. Painted and finished it. Cut bro. McLeod's hair. Called on Mrs. McNish.

Sat. Feb. 07 At Roy Forman's for the day. Helped chop grain.

Sun. Feb. 08 A day in Thy courts. God is faithful. Good crowd and good attention at night.

Mon. Feb. 09 Fixed 3 chairs with glue, wire and nails. At Bell's for dinner. Called on McPhails in pm. Mrs. McP. professed faith in Christ. Trust she is God's workmanship. Stormy, not many out.

Thu. Feb. 12 Wrote R. A. Bruce and W. Pole. Walked to Hargrave's and drove with their horse to Webster's. Snowy, few out.

Sat. Feb. 14 John Brentnell drove us to Kennedy's across the lake.

Sun. Feb. 15 Good time at the feast. His banner over me was love.

Mon. Feb. 16 Still cold and blowing. Roads badly drifted.

Tue. Feb. 17 Balsam Lake at 9.30. Got train for home.

Sat. Feb. 28 Maude drove me with Dan (*the horse*) within 2 miles of **Rathburn**. Walked rest of way through the snow and Wilfred Johnston met me and brought me here to their place.

Sun. Feb. 29 Rather a good day. Wilfred and his wife and I remembered the Lord Jesus in breaking of bread at 2 oc. Gospel at night, 4 of an audience! God's word.

Mon. Mar. 01 Nice day. Called on Dewells, Macks, Hamils, and Bennetts in pm. Meeting, 2 Kings 5 - Would God.

Tue. Mar. 02 Called on Sandfords, Flemings, Cathcarts and Thompsons. Just Mr. and Mrs. Bennett came to mtg.

Wed. Mar. 03 Called on Deverells, McGaheys, Wilsons and Adams'. Bennetts at mtg and the teacher. Read 2 Kings 6.

Thu. Mar. 04 Called on Flemings, Watts and Burnetts.

Fri. Mar. 05 Very stormy day. Helped Wilfred at barn. Had mtg at school in pm - Samuel. At night, John 3 - So.

Sat. Mar. 06 Bright cold day. Fixed Bible bag. Over to Bennett's. Mr. and Mrs. B. may have gotten saved. God grant it may be real. Wilfred and I left at 2 oc. Home safely 5.30. Cold west wind.

Sat. July 10 To Balsam Lake. J. McLeod met me. God is faithful. "In Him is only good, in me is only ill. My ill but draws His goodness forth, and me He loveth still." Thank God for His love.

Sun. July 11 Nice lot out and some little praise to God. Mosquitoes terrible at meeting!

Mon. July 12 Dull wet day. Examined tent in hall. Smoked hall after dinner for mosquitoes. Meeting.

Tue. July 13 Working at tent all day. Got it up in evening.

Thu. July 15 Finished tent. Mtg at night, Luke 15 - Give.

Fri. July 16 Drove with John McLeod to **Cambray**. John Cory's for dinner. Got tent pitched in afternoon. Cory's all night.

Sat. July 17 Working at tent in am. Helping at hay in pm. Fixed lamps etc. God is faithful!

Sun. July 18 Drove with John Cory to Victoria Road to remember the Lord. First meeting in Cambray, Gen. 2 - Come.

Tue. July 20 Changed sign at tent. Down to P.O. and spoke to a few people. Nice few to meeting, Prov. 26 - 3 R's.

Wed. July 21 Brentnells to meeting, about 25 or more.

Sun. July 25 Sweet feast of love divine. Hymn 134 and John 21 - Lovest thou Me. Nice lot to meeting, 2 Kings 5.

Mon. July 26 Called on Mrs. Kerr & Miss Newson. Nice few to mtg.

Wed. July 28 Helped hunt horse shoes in pasture. At Mrs. Boyd's.

Thu. July 29 <u>Tent blew down</u>. Meeting at Jordan's.

Fri. July 30 Working at tent all day. Got tent up and fixed all right in time for mtg. A few came. Ps. 49 - Ransom.

Sun. Aug. 01 Drove up to Victoria Road in democrat. Good time.

Thu. Aug. 05 Helping at hay all day. Meeting at night, Acts 4.

Fri. Aug. 06 Helping at hay all day and got it all in. Meeting.

Sun. Aug. 08 Drove up to the feast. Good time.

Thu. Aug. 12 Helped John start his harvest. Cutting barley in am. Visiting in afternoon. Nice few out to meeting.

Fri. Aug. 13 Down to P.O. after dinner, several conversations with the people, Mr. Kerr and others. Very wet night.

Sat. Aug. 14 Phone message from Norman Clark re Mrs. Kyle's death.

Mon. Aug. 16 Drove with W. Parrington and J. Cory right through Orillia to Creemore, about 100 miles, to Mrs. Kyle's funeral.

Wed. Aug. 18 Helped John at wheat. Called on Mrs. Jordan & others.

Thu. Aug. 19 Cut oats behind barn with binder. Meeting at night.

Fri. Aug. 20 Cutting oats on binder in am. Gospel at night.

Sun. Aug. 22 Ed and I drove to Victoria Road for the feast. Last meeting in tent at Cambray.

Mon. Aug. 23 Taking down tent. Ed left at 11 oc, CPR. John and I stored away tent. Helped him a little fixing binder. Visiting till 7.30, Boyds, Jordans, Tomkins. To Roy Forman's place.

Tue. Aug. 24 Grinding meal at Roy's. Left by CPR at 11.20.

The Grass Never Grew Greener!

Brackendale, B. C.
February 23, 1976.

Dear brother Clark,

I presume you have to be related to the late Cecil Clark, so have relationship to dear bro. Shivas. His memory is always a tonic. He is, no doubt, one of the most often quoted among us because he had a pithy, homespun humour that hit you right between the eyes. I intend to recall many of the things that "stuck."

Was just reminded of Mr. Shivas this morning and quoted him. He gave a word at a prayer meeting somewhere locally on Israel's march around Jericho. He said, "Are you getting tired going around the walls, brother, without any sign of a crack — the rounds of meetings, prayer meeting, bible reading, worship meeting, gospel meeting? Give it another whirl, brother, the walls might come down." (Meaning we may get the blessing we've so long hoped for, the touch of God we desire to feel.)

Once he had his gas tank filled, and while waiting, a little fellow stuck his head through the open driver's window. Mr. Shivas asked, "What does your father think of you, son?" Somewhat stunned, but finally gathering his composure, the young fellow replied, "What does my father think of me? He thinks the world of me!" As they drove off, Mr. Shivas said to Frank Pearcey, "See, Frank, that's what our heavenly Father thinks of us, he thinks the world of us!"

I had spoken first on a conference gospel night. He followed and opened his remarks with, "Read so-and-so. You know, I had something else in mind, but after what my brother has said, I have changed my mind. When I buy a new writing tablet, do you know the first thing I do? I tear away the page with the lines on it, because I don't believe in going in another man's line of things!"

At another conference in the gospel I remember him telling of a little girl coming to him after a gospel meeting somewhere and telling him she was saved during the meeting. "Fine," he said. "Which one of us was preaching?" "Neither of you were," she replied. "It was when you were *singing, Just as I was I received Him." She misquoted, of course, and Mr. Shivas put that in, too. "Oh, well," he said, "thank God, I gave out the hymn!"*

When introducing him to my wife for the first time, which was several years after we were married, he said in his droll way, "I have heard of thee by the hearing of the ear, but now mine eye seeth thee." (From Job 42.5.)

Once after six weeks of gospel with a partner in a certain place, he was asked how the meetings were going. Disgustedly he replied, "Oh, I get up there every night and try to take the people to Calvary, and he gets up after and takes them to Russia!" (Meaning prophecy.)

Once at a conference during depression days, he complained of Christians enjoying 3 days of ministry, food, and hospitality, and putting a quarter in the offering Lord's Day morning. "God have mercy on your stingy soul," he said. Some took exception, but shouldn't have, knowing him. He wasn't thinking of those who couldn't, but of those who wouldn't.

I remember him once in the car commenting on 1st Cor. 7. He said he thought he could hear Paul say over the whole chapter, "I don't know." Not sure I agree with him exactly, but it was something to think about.

As you know, everyone enjoyed him getting up near the end of a heavy afternoon meeting. We'd all be about asleep, and he'd have us wide awake in about two minutes.

Once at a conference he told of burning leaves off his lawn in the fall. When scarcely anything but ashes were left, he noticed something shiny in the ashes. Come to find out, it was a piece of old electric wire with the insulation burned off. "That's what we need, brethren, to get some of the world's insulation burned off, so we can shine for Jesus!"

Again, at a conference he was speaking loudly as only he could, when he acted as if he suddenly noticed the microphone. Approaching it calmly he said, "This is a nice rig, you don't have to shout so loud." Then, as if on second thought, he added, "But I'd rather give a little shout for Jesus!" And he was off again as loud as ever.

(Sgd) Hector Alves

The Grass Never Grew Greener!

And **even to your old age** I am he; and even to hoar hairs
will I carry you: I have made and I will bear; even I will
carry, and will deliver you.   Isaiah 46.4.

To your old age I am He,
And e'en to hoar hairs will I carry;
Though enemies rage, trust in Me,
My strong arm bears thee when thou'rt weary.

Now also when I am old and greyheaded, O God, forsake me
not; until I have shewed thy strength unto this generation,
and thy power to every one that is to come.
                                        Psalm 71.18.

Although I'm gray headed and old,
Me thou wilt never forsake;
Till Thy glorious gospel I've told,
To my home then forever Thou'lt take.

For this God is our God for ever and ever: he will be our
guide even unto death.   Psalm 48.14.

For this God is ever our God,
Right on to the end will He guide;
From the path never turning He trod;
I the glory will spend by His side.

Surely goodness and mercy shall follow me all the days of
my life: and I will dwell in the house of the Lord forever.
                                        Psalm 23.6.

Surely goodness and mercy shall stay
Close behind to the last of my days;
When I see without dimness His way,
Each step of the past calls for praise.

                                        G. L. S.

1921

There was no diary for 1921, except for the first four days, which were recorded at the end of 1920, when Mr. Shivas was in Sault Ste. Marie, Ontario.

However, brother Clarence Hodgson of Lakeshore assembly supplied the Hamilton Conference notes of brother Harold Kay, for November 5, 6, and 7, 1921. Mr. Shivas spoke on the Monday night, (Thanksgiving Day), on Four Thanksgivings to God, found in Corinthians. Even the notes of his message sound like him.

2 Cor. 9.15. **Thanks** be unto God for His unspeakable gift.

Things in Corinth were in a bad condition, but the apostle rises above all difficulties, and gives thanks to God. If there is anybody under heaven who ought to be able to celebrate this day (Thanksgiving Day) it should be God's people. Before the throne of God there is the sprinkled blood, and round about that throne, a rainbow. The rainbow speaks of God's covenant mercies; but note, at the great white throne there will be no blood and no rainbow.

What a good God we have! His people have a thanksgiving day **every day** in the year. The ungodly **expect** God's people to be a happy people. When we go to Ironton, forty miles from the railway, as soon as we are in the stage coach and fairly started on the journey, the old stage-driver will say, "Can't ye sing us a song?" And we have to say, "All right, wait a while, we have to pray first." You can't **sing** yourself right with God. Paul and Silas with their feet fast in the stocks, **prayed first**; then they **sang**, and the prisoners heard them.

Dear child of God, what is your chief joy? What is there to live for in this poor world if we get away from God? Let us cleave to God and to the Word of His grace, with a **tender heart**, and a **good stiff backbone**. Note Psalm 126. 1-3. The world should be saying about us, "They're queer people, they won't smoke, or go to the show, but we have to admit, the Lord has done great things for them."

I was saved sixteen years ago, the 16th of April, standing beside a kitchen table, reading one of those oldfashioned, shiny-back Bibles, a lost, guilty, helpless sinner. I could not believe, see, feel, nor understand. I gave up all hope, and felt there was no salvation for me. But as I read John 3. 16, God saved my soul. "He spake and it was done;

He commanded and it stood fast." Psalm 33.9. "Thanks be unto God for His unspeakable gift."

2 Cor. 8.16. But **thanks** be to God, which put the same earnest care into the heart of Titus for you.

A gentleman noticed a girl carrying a boy nearly as big as herself, and he said to her, "What a burden you have got!" She answered in broad Scotch, "He's no a burden, he's my brither." Do we think of one another as a burden? Oh that God would help us to **care for one another**, even as He cares for us.

2 Cor. 2.14. Now **thanks** be unto God, which always causeth us to triumph in Christ.

1 Cor. 15. 57. But **thanks** be to God, which giveth us the victory through our Lord Jesus Christ.

The eternal glories gleam afar, to nerve my faint endeavour, so now to watch, to work, to war — our armistice is not signed yet. We have the **devil** and the **world** and the **flesh** against us, but thank God we are more than conquerors through Him that loved us.

First Cor. 15 ends, "Therefore, my beloved brethren, be ye stedfast, unmoveable, always abounding in the work of the Lord, forasmuch as ye know that your labour is not in vain in the Lord."

The Labourers Are Few

Then saith he unto his disciples, The harvest truly is plenteous, but the labourers are few. Math. 9.37.

The labourers are few.
There are many stand idle of every race,
Loitering still in the marketplace,
But few to tell of God's saving grace,
The labourers are few.

The labourers are few.
Yes, few there are with a heart to labour,
To speak for Jesus to friend and neighbour.
To be to God of Christ a savour,
The labourers are few.

The labourers are few.
Who would not serve such a Master true,
Toiling for Him with the goal in view,
To hear His "Well done," shall I, shall you?
 The labourers are few.

G. L. S.

To Dear Mother

February 20th, 1922 — "Seventy Seven."

My Ebenezer now I raise,
A tribute to Jehovah's praise,
I'm drawing nearer Heaven.
My harp's in tune in sweetest lays
To Him who led me all my ways,
Today I'm seventy seven.

The way at times was rough and long,
Yet still I sing my happy song,
My sins are all forgiven.
My home is with the blood-bought throng,
He still can keep me from all wrong,
Though now I'm seventy seven.

God's goodness all the way I trace;
He saved me by His wondrous grace
Before I was eleven.
He on the Cross died in my place,
That I might live and see His face,
And now I'm seventy seven.

I'd walk with Him another mile
If I wait yet a little while
Along the way to Heaven.
Lord, keep me from all sin and guile,
Let me still see Thy lovely smile,
Although I'm seventy seven.

With much love and best wishes and many happy returns

"Till He come."   From George and Maude.

1922

This year there were three weeks of gospel meetings at Collingwood in April, and three weeks at Victoria Road in May, both series with blessing. Then there were nine weeks of tent meetings at Udney in July and August, with bro. Herb Harris and other Orillia brethren helping. At the end of the year there were four weeks of gospel meetings in Lansing, Toronto, Ontario.

Sat. Mar. 18 Left at 4.15, **Collingwood** at 9.30 pm. At Garratt's.

Sun. Mar. 19 Nice feast in am. Good B. Class, Acts 5. Gospel at 7.

Mon. Mar. 20 Geo. G. and I went to Stayner. Called on Thompsons and Armstrongs.

Wed. Mar. 22 Visited Bryans and Jim Latimers. Meeting.

Thu. Mar. 23 At houses with tracts. Called on Gendrons. Meeting.

Fri. Mar. 24 We need more prayer. At Arthur Johnston's for tea.

Sat. Mar. 25 At Taylor's for dinner & tea. Street mtg at night.

Sun. Mar. 26 A feast and a good day. Good mtg at night, Prov. 25.6. Mrs. Varley professed. Street meeting.

Tue. Mar. 28 Geo. G. & I called on Gendrons and Mrs. Winnie, and McKendricks. Wet night. Real good mtg, Ps. 107 - Soul.

Thu. Mar. 30 Mr. Varley & Jean McNicol professed to be saved last night. Called on Winnies & Mrs. McCutcheon. Young's for tea.

Sat. Apr. 01 Visited Mrs. Bendle and Taylors. Mr. & Mrs. Gaylor called here for talk this pm.

Sun. Apr. 02 A great and a good day. John 4 - Such. At Hammil's (Clara Vanderburg) for dinner. B. Class good, and gospel mtg.

Mon. Apr. 03 Visited Mrs. Mack and Mrs. Wood. Nice few out.

Tue. Apr. 04 Called to see Chief Johnston, and Varley's shop.

Wed. Apr. 05 Called on Mrs. Vowes and Williams' and Kenwells.

Thu. Apr. 06 Cut Geo's hair. Put gilt on Bible bag. Visited bro. Bryan. Called on Owens and Varley at shop, and Mrs. Scobie.

Fri. Apr. 07 Thunderstorm. Visited Harmans in aft, and Latimers.

Sat. Apr. 08 Our wedding day 1909 (before breakfast). God's blessing on the day! "Till He come." Walked out to Taylor's.

Sun. Apr. 09 C'wood for the Lord's Day. Street meeting.

Sun. Apr. 16 16 years ago today at 2 pm God saved my precious soul. Thank God. "There was no day like that."

Sat. Apr. 29 Left at 3.38 for **Victoria Road** (Balsam Lake).

Sun. Apr. 30 Victoria Road. Nice few in at night.

Fri. May 05 Still dull & drizzling, but "God is love" no matter how weather is. Jean Hargrave told us she was saved last night.

Sat. May 06 Harold Brentnell and I motored to Orillia. Left about 8.30, arr'd 10.15. Moved things down from attic.

Sun. May 07 Harold B. & I returned to V.R. same time as yday. Rather happy feast. At McLeod's all day. Night mtg, 2 Kings 5.

Mon. May 08 Dear Norman Truman saved last night. Thank God. At Brentnell's for dinner, Rea's for tea. Mtg, Ps. 103 - As for.

Tue. May 09 Called on Hargraves & Parringtons. Tea at Stone's.

Fri. May 12 Helping Wilder Ewers paper most of day. Meeting.

Sat. May 13 Over to see Russell Forman in am, Bells & Hargraves.

Sun. May 14 "Gathered together, Math. 23." At McLeod's all day. Large crowd at night mtg. Winnie Barber professed.

Mon. May 15 At Brentnell's for dinner. Cut 5 hairs. Stone's for tea. Two girls professed after meeting, Acts 4 - Saved.

Tue. May 16 Called at Black's in aft. Mrs. Hurren professed, her sister later at Hargrave's. Good meeting, John 12 - Now.

Wed. May 17 Drove to V.R. with Bell's horse. Dinner at Crarey's. Called on Mrs. McNish & Brothersons. Mrs. Crarey Jr. professed.

Thu. May 18 Dreary wet day. Sang 304. Drove with Brentnells to Black's by car. Met Herb Harris.

Fri. May 19 Called on Ewers in am, Herb & I. At Black's in aft. and Hargrave's for tea. Meeting, Rom. 2 - No more.

Sat. May 20 At Brentnell's for dinner. Called at Chas. Bell's and at Roy Forman's for tea.

Thu. June 15 Went to Sunnidale Conf. Staying at Armstrong's.

Fri. June 16 - Sun. June 18 **Strongville Conference**. Slept with R. McCrory. Came home at night with Dave McClelland.

Mon. June 19 Phoned Jim McClintock re shipping tent in am.

Tue. June 20 Sent money for tent seats, $90. Made sign for tent.

Sat. June 24 Pitched the tent at **Udney**. John Seers, Cecil, Willie, Herb Harris and I.

Sun. June 25 At home for the feast. At Cory's for dinner. Drove out to Udney with Herb Harris. First meeting in tent.

Mon. June 26 At Harris' for tea. At Udney for tent meeting.

Sun. July 09 At Victoria Road. Sweet feast of love divine. Dinner at Stone's. Baptism at 2.30. Tea at Roy Forman's. Good crowd.

Wed. July 12 Herb and I visited in pm. At Lamb's for tea. Tent threatened by storm. Helped Harris' move some. Meeting.

Tue. July 18 Visited 7 homes and back to the tent for tea and mtg.

Fri. July 21 Visited Dobbs for dinner, at Gray's and Martin's.

Tue. July 25 Visited at Warren's, Henry Speiran's. Meeting.

Sun. July 30 <u>Sweet feast</u>! Walker's for dinner and Cecil Stephenson's for tea. Geo. S, Herb and I. Mtg, John 12 - Now.

Mon. July 31 Visited in the village in the afternoon. Meeting.

Tue. Aug. 01 Visited Mundies. Heavy rain storm. Mtg, Isa. 45.22.

Wed. Aug. 02 <u>Tent blew down</u>. Very severe storm.

Thu. Aug. 03 Got tent up again by God's mercy. Isa. 57.4.

Fri. Aug. 04 Working at tent. Meeting, Heb. 11 - Moses' choice.

Tue. Aug. 08 Visited Lambs in pm. Very cool, 9 in to meeting.

Thu. Aug. 10 Visited Speirans. Stubbs' truck load out to meeting.

Wed. Aug. 16 Making tent stakes. Visited Martins, and Givens.

Thu. Aug. 17 Visited Mundies etc. Meeting, Job - Lay thy hand.

Wed. Aug. 23 Put rings on stakes. Visited Tiffins, Barnes', and Speirans. Harris's out to meeting, Isa. 49.1.

Fri. Aug. 25 Called to see ———— who put us off the place. At P. Snodden's for dinner. Tom Warren's for tea. Car from Victoria Road with a load.

Mon. Aug. 28 At Udney. Spoke with different ones about God and eternity. Mundie's for tea. Meeting, Heb. 7 - His own.

Tue. Aug. 29 At Moore's for dinner. Called on Dobles and Warrens. Nice few in to mtg. Cool eve. Luke 10 - 4 falls.

Wed. Aug. 30 At Tiffin's for dinner and Barnes' for tea. Last meeting in tent. Mark 10 - Calls.

Sun. Nov. 12 First meeting at **Lansing**. Hall full. Spoke on - Come.

Mon. Nov. 13 At Street's all night. Visited in two homes.

Tue. Nov. 14 At Robertson's. Out with Mr. Street in car. <u>Saved</u>.

Wed. Nov. 15 Visited at homes with tracts. Carlyle's for tea. Mtg.

Thu. Nov. 16 Called at one house & Williamson's for tea.

Fri. Nov. 17 At G. Street's for tea. Mrs. Street professed.

Sat. Nov. 18 Called on Lloyd Guests in am, Mrs. Russell in eve.

Mon. Nov. 20 Called at a lot of houses. Mrs. Lucas' for tea. Mtg.

Tue. Nov. 21 Painted windows at hall. Tea at Alex Robertson's.

Wed. Nov. 22 Phil Carley here. Went to quite a few homes.

Thu. Nov. 23 Albert Eagle fixing car in aft. Had word with Mrs. Clark S. & Geo. Meeting, Isa. 38 - Great.

Fri. Nov. 24 Went up to see Jimmie Brown. Mtg, 2 Cor. 5.
Tue. Nov. 28 Visit with Mrs. C. Street. Went to see Jim Brown.
Wed. Nov. 29 Walked part of way to Walker's for dinner. Meeting.
Thu. Nov. 30 Visiting in the afternoon. At Lucas' for tea. Bro. Pearson
and I had meeting, Luke 13 - In no wise.
Fri. Dec. 01 Made some calls. G. Street's for tea. Mtg - Better.
Sat. Dec. 02 Got new shoes from Dan Sommacal at Dacks, $3.13. How
good God is. Steen's for tea. Called at O. Sprunt's & Guest's.
Sun. Dec. 03 R. McC. & I at Miss Poidevin's for dinner. At B. Class.
Jim's for tea. Meeting, Prov. 26 - 3 R's.
Mon. Dec. 04 Painting gables of hall. At Street's & Gordon's.
Tue. Dec. 05 Made some calls. At Burford's. Very cold & windy.
Wed. Dec. 06 At S. Sommacal's for dinner. At Mrs. Jas. Lynn's funeral,
hymn 353 and prayer. Eagle's for tea. Meeting.
Thu. Dec. 07 Snowy day. Called on Goods, Clark Streets, Kirbys and
Browns. Robertson's for tea. Meeting, Joshua 20.
Fri. Dec. 08 Visited Moules. Street's for tea. Meeting.
Sat. Dec. 09 Called to see Janet H. At Fred Radford's for tea.
Sun. Dec. 10 Hymn 134. Last meeting, Mark 10 - Called.

Companion to - Only a Lad Called David

Only a lad called Samuel, only a little bed,
Only a lad called Samuel lay down his sleepy head.
Only a lad called Samuel who did not know the Lord,
Only a lad called Samuel, one night he heard His Word.
Somebody called his name out loud and he answered right away,
Somebody called again and again and he knew not what to say.
But God called and He called and He called and He called
As He calls to you and me,
And Samuel came to know the Lord and a faithful boy was he.

G. L. S.

1923

In 1923 Mr. and Mrs. Shivas travelled by boat to visit his aunt Lydia, who lived in Insch, Scotland. She had asked his help in selling her home, and then returned with them to Canada for a visit. While in Great Britain, they visited many assemblies in Scotland and England, the names of which may be a pleasant reminder to believers from the Old Country.

Within a week of disembarking at Montreal, Mr. Shivas had a Gospel tent pitched there, and conducted five weeks of meetings, with the help of brother Hugh Walker of Toronto.

Near the end of the year, Mr. Shivas had five weeks of gospel meetings at Owen Sound.

Thu. Apr. 12 Left N. Falls at 5.35 am, Newburgh 4.35, McLean's for tea and all night.

Fri. Apr. 13 Over to Beacon and checked baggage in am. Called on Ellen & Mary. McLean's for tea.

Sat. Apr. 14 Left Newburgh 9 pm by boat for N.Y. Came aboard S.S.Columbia, leaving at noon for Glasgow. The Lord grant mercy. 9.35 pm all well. Good passage so far. No sickness, thank God.

Sun. Apr. 15 Thought on His Name on board ship. Maude and I read Mark 11 and Ps. 118 and sang a hymn. Gave out tracts at night.

Mon. Apr. 16 17 years ago today God saved my soul. Thank God for all His mercy. Tonight rather stormy.

Tue. Apr. 17 Rather heavy sea, yet safe by God's mercy and made good time, Sat. to Sun. noon 306 miles, Monday, 377, today, 373.

Wed. Apr. 18 Nice warm day again though quite a sea on. Did 371 miles to noon, 3011 miles from N.Y. to Glasgow. Saw large steamer in am, small French sailing boat in pm. Quite warm. Met Jas. Smith and wife from Burbank.

Sun. Apr. 22 The second Lord's Day on ship. Had meeting in 1st Cabin at 11 am. God graciously helped. 352 miles today at noon.

Mon. Apr. 23 Touched Ireland about 5 am. Disembarked at Greenock about noon. Left Glasgow at 5. Aberdeen at 9.05.

Wed. Apr. 25 Spence's for dinner. Left at 3.30, Insch at 5. Auntie Lyd met us. At "Ramesgreen". Out to Bible Reading, Rom.7.

Fri. Apr. 27 Cold wet day. 39 years old today. God is faithful.

Sat. Apr. 28 Saw internment in old graveyard. Out with tracts.

Sun. Apr. 29 **Insch.** 17 of us kept the feast. Gospel mtg at night.

Wed. May 02 Working around house packing up. Nice evening.

Sat. May 05 Did some work in house. Left at 2 pm for MacDuff. Tea at C. Milne's. B. Rdg, Esther. At Rankin's all night.

Sun. May 06 At **MacDuff, Banffshire.** Gospel meeting and street mtg.

Sun. May 13 **Dufftown** for the day.

Mon. May 21 Auntie Lyd's sale. Fine day on the whole. God's goodness to us today. Up early and worked hard getting things ready, things sold well.

Tue. May 22 Got Ford car to go to Oyne and up Benshie. The Lord grant mercy. Real nice day. Managed fine and safely.

Wed. May 23 Up to Jamieson's, Brindy Hill for tea.

Thu. May 24 Cruickshank's for tea, also Willie Taylor. Drove to Arichterless to Mr. P. Bruce's meeting.

Fri. May 25 Drove to Glass by Huntly. Called on Jas. and John McGrinnwn. Very wet, cold day.

Sat. May 26 Finished packing up and left at 2 pm for New Deer Maud Stn. At Taylor's for tea. Over night at Milne's.

Sun. May 27 At **New Deer** Assembly. Had sing in evening.

Tue. May 29 At Peterhead, Uncle Jamie's, Stephens'. Shivas' for tea. To Aberdeen in evening.

Sun. June 03 **Aberdeen. Round Room** in am, **Hebron Hall** at 2.30, Mrs. Lyon's for tea. Torry at 6.15.

Mon. June 04 Walked down by old **St.Paul Street Hall** after tea, and to Hebron Hall for missionary meeting.

Thu. June 07 At Sangster's all night. Settled on "Megantic," White Star Line, D.V., by His mercy. Meeting at **Torry.**

Wed. June 13 At Bullates, Balmoral, and Braemar.

Sat. June 16 Called on Geo. Shivas'. Up to **Haydhead** to S.S. treat. Open air meeting at night. Cold and wet.

Sun. June 17 Round Room for the day.

Wed. June 20 Left Aberdeen at 10.05. Called at Stonehaven, Glasgow. Farquhar's for tea. **Albert Hall** Prayer mtg.

Thu. June 21 Out to Paisley. Prayer mtg at **Springburn.**

Fri. June 22 Down town with Sam Lynn, at Princess Pier.

Sat. June 23 Down to Pickering, and met A. E. Hodgkinson. Saw him off on train. At Loch Lomond in afternoon.

Sun. June 24 **Glasgow Springburn** assembly. At Forbes McLeod's tent.

The Diaries of George L. Shivas

Mon. June 25 Left Glasgow at 9 for **Kilmarnock**. Saw John Ritchie. Tea at Leeds with A. E. Hodgkinsons. Sheffield all night.
Tue. June 26 Left Sheffield at 10.53, St. Paucras at 2.10, Crowborough at 5.30. Came on to Susie's, "Eastmeon." Lovely.
Sun. July 01 **Crowborough** assembly for the day. At street meeting.
Wed. July 04 Jay and Susie, M&I went up to London and spent the day in the zoological gardens. Beautiful day. Back at 8.05.
Fri. July 06 M&I came up to London in am. Saw through art gallery. Lunch in Lyon's Cafe. Tea with McLennan. All night at Adams'.
Sat. July 07 Saw through St.Paul's Cathedral, also Westminster Abbey and Houses of Parliament. Joe Adams' for tea.
Sun. July 08 At London, **E. Finchley** assembly. Visited Mr. & Mrs. Webb and family for tea. Gospel mtg, Isa. 49.1.
Mon. July 09 Met Susie at Victoria 10.20. Did shopping. Saw Natural Museum. Interview with Hy Pickering. Home at 6.06.
Thu. July 12 Jay & Susie, M&I at Brighton on the pier. Motored by Charabang to Eastbourne, via Peasehaven Newhara. Back by Lewes.
Sun. July 15 At **Sheffield**. Kept the feast with assembly in room in YWCA. With Mr. Ferguson for day. Gospel mtg in **Fitzwilliam St.**
Mon. July 16 Wrote Mr. Hodgkinson. To park and museum. Visited Stinchcombes, Darnalls. At old Uncle Leonard's in eve.
Thu. July 19 To Manchester safely. Saw Alex Jack Wallace.
Sun. July 22 **Manchester**, England. At **Warwick St. Hall**.
Wed. July 25 Up to London in am, saw London Tower in am. Met J. C. Steen at noon. Saw Tate Gallery.
Fri. July 27 Left Crowborough at 9.10. Susie accompanied us to London. Left Euston at 11.45. Adams' also saw us off. Boarded S.S. Megantic at 4 oc.
Sat. July 28 Reached Glasgow about 10 am. Auntie Lyd came aboard and left again about 5. Boat very comfortable. Fine night.
Thu. Aug. 02 Saw land (Newfoundland), icebergs and ships.
Fri. Aug. 03 Sailed through the Gulf of St. Lawrence. Pleasant.
Sat. Aug. 04 Reached Quebec about 7 am. Left again at noon and anchored in the river all night.
Sun. Aug. 05 Disembarked at **Montreal** about 8 oc. J. White and B.Sutton met us. At the feast, and for the day.
Mon. Aug. 06 Seeing about lot for tent etc. Meeting at night.
Tue. Aug. 07 Secured lot for tent. Painted poles.
Wed. Aug. 08 Pitched tent in afternoon.

Thu. Aug. 09 Got cards printed. Chairs from Rosemount. First meeting in tent, Gen. 7 - Come.

Fri. Aug. 10 Working around tent. Good meeting at night, Math. 12.

Sat. Aug. 11 Gave out cards at houses. Prayer meeting.

Sun. Aug. 12 Hugh Walker came at 7.30. Good morning. James Rea, Vancouver here. At Sutton's for tea. Tent about full.

Mon. Aug. 13 Hugh and I had a walk down to docks in afternoon. Saw over S.S. Montclare, Marburn, and Melita. Nice mtg.

Tue. Aug. 14 Hugh and I put cards in the houses in pm. Rain. Mtg.

Wed. Aug. 15 Down town in am. Saw the Cassandra and Parthenia. A.D. Line, and was through the Doric. At Coull Sr.'s. Meeting.

Fri. Aug. 17 Children's mtg at 3. Gospel at night.

Sun. Aug. 19 Montreal. A good day. Up to tent before breakfast. Good morning meeting. At Wray's for dinner. Side of tent blew in. Helping put it up. Mr. Spencer professed. Good gospel mtg.

Tue. Aug. 21 Wet day. Motored with Bert Sutton and Wilfred Coull, H. and I, about 30 miles out. Good meeting, Luke 4 - All this.

Wed. Aug. 22 Hugh Walker went home last night. Very strong wind. At tent all morning. Gospel at night.

Thu. Aug. 23 No lights last night.

Fri. Aug. 24 Herbert White came from Toronto. Children's mtg.

Sun. Aug. 26 Feast and a good day. Hugh W. came at 7.30. Good morning mtg. At Miss Brown's for dinner and tea. **Large gospel meeting, about 150.**

Mon. Aug. 27 Photo taken at the tent. Down to docks in afternoon, saw through battleship Calcutta. Meeting, Prov. 6 - How long.

Tue. Aug. 28 Visited Mrs. Irwin and Mrs. Davidson in pm. Dunsmore's for tea. Meeting, Job 40 - I am.

Wed. Aug. 29 Dougood's for tea. Gospel at night.

Fri. Aug. 31 Bob Davidson saved last night. Meeting.

Sat. Sep. 01 Good testimony mtg at night. J. Halliford baptized.

Sun. Sep. 02 Largest mtg in tent. Girl got saved.

Mon. Sep. 03 Wrote R. T. At Wilfrid Coull's for tea. Nice lot out.

Tue. Sep. 04 Bre. from Stratford in, in am. Down to docks. Saw the Kastalia, the Saturnia, the Megantic. Dunsmore's for tea.

Thu. Sep. 06 Mrs. Mason saved. At Coull Sr.'s for tea.

Sat. Sep. 08 Visited Rawlings, Spencers, and B. Suttons.

Sun. Sep. 09 Montreal. Good mtg in am. Last meeting in tent.

Tue. Sep. 11 Took down tent. All through before dinner. Lovely day. Visited Wm. Shivas. <u>God is faithful.</u>

Left,
Mr. Hugh Walker
Right,
Mr. Geo. Shivas

Tent at Montreal 1923

Sat. Nov. 17 Left at 8 am for **Owen Sound**. Met J. Silvester at Collingwood. At Owen Sound about 3 oc. At Shaw's.

Sun. Nov. 18 Owen Sound. Spoke with bre. Mtg at night, Zech. 12.

Mon. Nov. 19 God is faithful. Made sign for hall. Nice few out.

Tue. Nov. 20 At Loom's for tea. Meeting, Ps. 103 - As for.

Wed. Nov. 21 Called on Lawrences and Swords. Nice lot out.

Thu. Nov. 22 Called on Reiths in pm. Wood's for tea. Meeting.

Fri. Nov. 23 Tea at Brigg's. Wet snow. Nice lot out.

Sat. Nov. 24 Loom's for dinner, Shaw's for tea. Had walk.

Sun. Nov. 25 Owen Sound. Read Gen. 22 in am. Had walk, John and I, and gave out tracts. Good mtg, Isa. 49.1.

Mon. Nov. 26 Fixed door for Mrs. Shaw. Made few calls. Meeting.

Tue. Nov. 27 At Reith's for dinner. Called on Mrs. Crook. Meeting.

Wed. Nov. 28 Miss Spence's for dinner. Brigg's for tea. Meeting.

Mon. Dec. 03 Wrote Maude. Sent poem. Lovely day. Called on several and at Sword's for tea. Meeting, Prov. 30 - 4 things.

Wed. Dec. 05 Made calls and at Brigg's for tea. Wet night. Mtg.

Thu. Dec. 06 Called on Crooks and Mr. Kelso. Wood's for tea. Mtg.

Sat. Dec. 08 Loom's for dinner. Put tracts in mail boxes.

Tue. Dec. 11 Wrote verses on Song of Solomon 5. Meeting.

Wed. Dec. 12 Called on Peutons and at Brigg's for tea. Meeting.

Thu. Dec. 13 Called on Mrs. Brealey and at Loom's for tea. Mtg.

Fri. Dec. 14 Called on Davenports, at Reith's for tea. Meeting.

Sat. Dec. 15 Loom's for dinner. Called to see Mr. Wood. Sword's for tea and had walk.

Sun. Dec. 16 Owen Sound. Sweet feast of love divine. Good mtg. Spoke to children at 4 - Lam. 4.4. Gospel mtg good, 2 Kings 6.

Wed. Dec. 19 Visited Reiths, Hicks' and to cemetery. Loom's for tea and helped at hall.

Thu. Dec. 20 Snow all gone. Very mild. S.S. Treat.

Fri. Dec. 21 Left Owen Sound at 1 oc with W. Hicks. Called at Beattie's. Home at 9. Thank God.

1924

At the first of the year Mr. Shivas worked at his printing press at home in Orillia. In March, Mr. John Silvester joined him there for three weeks in the Gospel.

In May they were together at Midland, Ontario, for four weeks. During the first week he lettered and painted the text, John 3.16, either for the Hall, or for the meetings. Some mornings they were out before breakfast with invitations and tracts.

One notation states, "Evelyn S.F. got saved. God grant it may be real." In August, seven were baptized by A. Morrison at the Midland Sunday School Picnic.

On Tuesday, July 1st, a tent was pitched on Gill Street in Orillia, and the gospel proclaimed for almost eight weeks. There were 3 funerals during that time, those of Mrs. Irene Vanderburg, Mrs. Rankin, and of Mr. Arthur Heels, who had drowned.

After Orillia Conference over Labour Day weekend, Mr. Shivas went to Strongville for most of September and October.

Sun. Sep. 07 **Strongville.** Motored over in time for mtg at 10.30, M&I. At Robert Armstrong's for dinner and tea and all night.

Mon. Sep. 08 Lincoln Johnston's for dinner. H. Black's for tea. Cold and wet. Nice number to meeting, - Go thy way.

Tue. Sep. 09 Still cold and wet. Geo. Johnston's for dinner and at David Smith's for tea. Meeting, John 3.16 - God's love.

Wed. Sep. 10 Still cold and cloudy. D. Partridge's for dinner. Called on John Armstrongs and at McKinnon's for tea.

Thu. Sep. 11 At Peter Fleming's for dinner. Long talk with Mr. F. Called on Mrs. Howie and McLeish's for tea. Large meeting.

Fri. Sep. 12 Nice day. At Geo. Johnston's for dinner and John Armstrong's for tea. Hugh McMillan was saved by God's grace.

Sat. Sep. 13 Called at L. & G. Johnston's and Cole's for dinner. Home about 2.30. Willie Pole with us, also Hope Cole.

Sun. Sep. 14 Strongville. Mr. Livingstone here. Mtg at 2.30. At R. Armstrong's for dinner and tea. Geo. Johnston's all night.

Mon. Sep. 14 Fixing car in am. At Geo. Johnston's for dinner and Smith's for tea. Meeting, Mark 11 - Never man.

Tue. Sep. 16 At Hugh Black's for dinner and tea. Helping draw in barley. Meeting, Heb. 11 - Rahab.

Wed. Sep. 16 Lovely day. Going to Stayner, D.V. At Armstrong's for dinner and tea and with them to mtg. Acts 4 - Saved.

Mrs. Sandford Fleming (Maudie Black) recalls her Sunday School class in the corner of the old Strongville Hall. One day she overheard remarks made in the adult Bible Class concerning unscriptural statements. Mr. Shivas was there that day, and when he closed the Sunday School he said, "We'll sing, 'Jesus loves me this I know, for the Bible tells me so', — because it's scriptural!"

She also remembers an Orillia Conference when Mr. Silvester gave out a hymn just as Mr. Shivas was going to the platform. He said, "Brother Silvester, we will sing that hymn after we read Hebrews 13, 13 and 13 (words)." The Lord used the message to give the conference a lift. She adds, "One thing we all will say is that our fellowship and help from Mr. Shivas will not be forgotten."

Sun. Oct. 19 Strongville. At Armstrong's for dinner. Mtg at 2.30. L. Johnston's for tea. Hall full at night.

Thu. Oct. 23 Voting day on O.T.A. God grant mercy for the Gospel's sake. (*Would that be the Ontario Temperance Act?*)

Sat. Oct. 25 To New Lowell for street meeting.

Sun. Nov. 02 Good day. Baptism at Creemore. Donald Partridge baptized H. McMillan and Denim Black. Read Luke 12 at baptism.

Mon. Nov. 03 Armstrong's for dinner. Black's for tea. Down at bush to see men cutting wood. Meeting, Math. 12 - Uttermost.

Tue. Nov. 04 At L. Johnston's for dinner. Smith's for tea. Called on Blacks and Partridges in pm. God helped at mtg.

Fri. Nov. 28 Started for **Victoria Road** and broke wheel. Mrs. Ross' for tea. At father's in evening.

Sat. Nov. 29 Left early for Victoria Road. Safe journey by 10.15. Mrs. McDonald's funeral at 12. Read Ps. 73. 22-24.

Sun. Nov. 30 Victoria Road. Hargrave's for dinner. McLeod's for tea. Lorne Ball, Herb H. and I had meeting.

1925

1925 began with six weeks of gospel meetings in South River, Ont. with Mr. Ben Widdifield, with some blessing along with the snow storms.

Wed. Jan. 21 Maude and I visited Mrs. H. Wilkinson in afternoon, who professed to be saved. "A Damaris," thank God. Nice crowd.

Thu. Jan. 22 Very cold and stormy. Brought wood from big house.

Wed. Jan. 28 38 below last night. Mrs. Shaver saved.

Fri. Jan. 30 Large meeting. Simon S. professed.

Sat. Jan. 31 Ben and I out all day. Walked about 10 miles.

Sat. Feb. 07 Roads very heavy. Ben and I at Allan's, and at Loney's for dinner. Mrs. Loney may have gotten saved. God grant it.

In July the gospel tent was pitched in Montreal, Que. and Mr. Alexander Livingstone joined Mr. Shivas for seven weeks. They made texts for the tent. Haircuts had reached the price of 25 cents. It was noted that a Mr. Burt had been saved, and on August 30, 2 were baptized.

On September 9th, Mr. Shivas read Psalm 73 at the funeral of his wife's mother, Mrs. Elizabeth Holditch, who was laid to rest in South River cemetery.

In November there were a few cottage meetings in a place called Donald, in the Haliburtons.

Sun. Nov. 15 Victoria Road. Read Prov. 12 in am. Bible Rdg, 2 Tim. 2. Left at 2.30 and got to **Donald** about 10. <u>Terrible</u> <u>roads</u>. God is faithful.

Mon. Nov. 16 Staying at Bolton's. The Lord grant mercy. Snowing. Had walk. Meeting at night, Isa. 38 - House.

Wed. Nov. 18 Working at car. Also called on Exons and Brooms before tea. Meeting at Exon's. Nice few came.

Fri. Nov. 20 Snowing a little. Put gas in car, etc. Down to bush in afternoon. Meeting at Bolton's, 2 Kings 5 - Went away.

Sat. Nov. 21 Lovely day. Left Bolton's about 9 oclock and got to McLeod's about 5.30. <u>God is faithful.</u>

An interesting item near the end of December states, "Took Betty to meeting in am. She was good. Thank God."

The Grass Never Grew Greener!

Midland, Ontario.
March 3, 1976.

Dear brother Ross,

Here are a few recollections of Mr. Shivas.

He got up at a Toronto Conference Prayer meeting for the first time, after there had been a long pause, saying in his deep voice, "There is a lad here that hath five barley loaves, but what are they among so many." He was the lad (a younger man then) and had five texts that he referred to in his message.

I have heard him speak of David taking 5 smooth stones and using only one for Goliath. Then in a booming voice he would say, "Goliath had 4 brothers, you know." The others were not slain by David personally, but this did not worry brother Shivas.

I was told by one present at a conference how a preacher droned on for an hour and fifteen minutes, and left 15 minutes for another speaker, in a morning session. Mr. Shivas got up and opened with, "Even the sun in the heaven knows when to set, but some of the sons of God do not know when to sit."

At another conference I heard him say, "Don't try to go down the middle of the road, brother. They will hit you on both sides." I recall him saying when a brother had left him a little extra time to speak (which is rare), "I like to pull into a parking place and find someone has left me a few minutes on the meter."

Speaking about those in the prayer meeting before the gospel meeting who bend only one knee, he said, "They look to me like a man in a track event waiting for the starting shot. They don't intend to stay long where they are."

He often said, "I don't find time for God, I have to take it."

And again, "Where wrongs are preached against, they are not practiced, and where they are practiced, they are not preached about."

Print only what is worthy of the man.

Yours through grace,
(Sgd) Edward Doherty

1926

In February Mr. Shivas returned to Cheboygan, Mich., for four weeks of gospel meetings. Not many of us would try singing hymns on the street corner in the middle of February to advertise gospel meetings, but he evidently enjoyed it.

Thu. Feb. 18 **Cheboygan.** Sang on street for first time.
Sat. Feb. 20 Had meeting on street. Sang 'Peace, sweet Peace.'
Mon. Feb. 22 Made calls in afternoon. Sang on street.
Fri. Feb. 26 Went from door to door and called on Keys. Good meeting on the street.
Sat. Feb. 27 Had meeting on street. Sang 'Christ is the Saviour' and 'I know He's mine.'
Tue. Mar. 09 Jeanette G. saved last night.

In July the tent was pitched at Eldon, Ont. and the glad message sent forth for seven weeks, with Mr. John Gilchrist.
Fri. July 09 Pitched tent in **Eldon** in afternoon.
Sun. July 11 First meeting in tent. Herb Harris helped.
Wed. July 14 Drove with Roy to Victoria Road. Mr. Gilchrist came.
Wed. July 28 Visiting around the farms. Tramped over 6 miles.

In November Mr. Shivas joined Mr. Ben Widdifield in five weeks of gospel meetings in **Collingwood**, Ont., with a brief record of blessing.
Mon. Dec. 06 Heard of a soul being saved.
Thu. Dec. 09 Alex Sammonds told us he was saved Tuesday night.
   Thanks be unto God for His unspeakable gift.

The Grass Never Grew Greener!

Sault Ste. Marie, Ontario.
November 15, 1991.

Dear brother Murray,

Well, I got your pile of sheets from the diary of Mr. Shivas and have read them all over.

I didn't realize he had been to the Sault that long ago. The first I remember was when he and Mrs. Shivas and Betty came to our place when we were still living in the shack. Betty was about two years of age at the time, and she said John 3.16, not the words, just "John 3.16."

He had a Ford car, a model T, with what they called an Ames body. I don't know what year that was, but you can judge by Betty's age now.

I noticed that Mr. Shivas and Ed Steen were at the Sault on March 11, 1916. Well, my brother Ed was born on March 10, 1916, so he was named Edmund George after the names of the two preachers.

My brother Will was saved as a result of Mr. Shivas taking an interest in him and speaking to him.

We took his car once and filled it with gas. He thanked us for it, but wanted to know how much we had put in it, as he was trying to keep track of the mileage.

Sincerely in the Lord.
(Sgd) Jim Clark

1927

The year was just three weeks old when Mr. Shivas and Mr. John Silvester commenced eight weeks of gospel meetings in Midland, Ontario. After five weeks, Mr. Earl Cummings professed, and at seven weeks, Mr. Tripp was saved, and on Sunday, March 13th, the diary records, "Good gospel meeting, four professed. Spoke on - Everlasting."

Mr. Shivas was back to Midland again in April and May for a baptism each time.

On Sunday, May 29, he baptized five in the lake at **Victoria Road**, Mrs. Parrington Sr., W. Fleming, E. Moynes, M. Fleming, and A. Stone. "God is faithful."

Entry for Wednesday, July 13 reads, Went to Eldon for tent with Peacock's truck. Got tent pitched at **Gravenhurst**. Baptism, Joshua 3.

There are no further diary entries until October.

October 9th, he commenced meetings at **Earlton**, Ont. for five weeks, helping with the grain in the fields, as well as sowing the good seed of the word of God.

Tue. Oct. 11 Out at field threshing grass seed.
Thu. Oct. 20 Helped in the field, pitching oats, 15 loads.
Wed. Oct. 26 Pitched load of seed hay in am.

On Sundays were listed a Sunday School at Tomstown, and at the "other school house," as well as the regular meetings.

On November 4 the first snow fell, and on November 15th, he attempted to drive to Orillia, but had to turn back because of the stormy weather. However, on Sunday, the 13th, David F. was saved, which made it all worthwhile. Thank God.

"Forgetting"

Forgetting those things which are behind, and reaching forth unto those things that are before, I press toward the mark for the prize of the high calling of God in Christ Jesus.   Phil. 3.13.

My God would have me to forget the things that are behind,
The things o'er which I chafe and fret, which often come to mind,
The idols which I used to know, the sins that I have done;
And in His knowledge seek to grow, He who my heart has won.

Ask of the woman from the well, who to the city fled,
With one desire, and that to tell of One her heart had read.
Say "Woman, where is now thy pot, which oft the waters bore?"
Smiling she answers, "I forgot, I'll thirst again no more."

Enquire of the beloved Paul, who once esteemed it gain
To be a Pharisee called Saul, and cause God's people pain,
"Where now is all thy sin and pride, which often long did blind thee?"
His answer reaches far and wide, "Forgetting things behind me."

The dear disciples left their nets, to seek for souls of men,
To work for Him who ne'er forgets, or brings them up again.
"What shall we have," said Peter bold, "who all for Thee have given?"
The answer was, "An hundred fold, with endless life in heaven."

God in His blessed Word doth tell, He freely will forget
Our many sins deserving hell, to which our path was set;
Then surely all our griefs and cares, which cause us pain and fretting,
We'll cast on Him who all will bear, and journey on "Forgetting."

G. L. S.

1928

In January, Mr. Shivas had five weeks of gospel meetings with brother Ed Steen, in Grimsby, Ontario. Then during July and August he had seven weeks of tent meetings in Bracebridge, Ontario with brother Robert Bruce. Tent meetings in Barrie, Ontario followed in September for two weeks, and in October there were two weeks of meetings in Chicago, Ill. He made his way home via Cleveland, Ohio, Niagara Falls, and Welland, Ontario.

Selections of diary records follow.

Sun. Jan. 08 **At Grimsby.** Drove from Toronto with F. G. Watson. Good gospel meeting by God's mercy, Ps. 112 - Tidings.

Mon. Jan. 09 Ed Steen and brethren from St. Catharines came over last night. Called at houses with tracts. Nice lot out.

Sun. Jan. 29 Grimsby. At the table with Him. Open S.S. Jos. Warburton came. 3 of us preached. God is faithful.

Fri. Feb. 03 Lovely day. Had conversation together in home. Mrs. Snider professed. Good meeting, Math. 21 - Leaves only.

Mon. Feb. 06 With Julius to Hamilton and called at sanatorium. Nice few out to night meeting, Prov. 8 - Finding.

Sun. Feb. 12 Grimsby, 5th Lord's Day. Real good day.

Mr. Eli Davis, a native Indian, and his family were reached with the gospel at these meetings. More details given in the year 1944.

Sat. Mar. 03 Orillia. Down to market and got eggs and butter, 38 and 40 cents. John Silvester up for dinner.

Fri. Mar. 30 Working at car at Dave McClelland's garage till 3 pm.

Sun. Apr. 15 Welland. Out to Fonthill, Klager's in afternoon. Got car stuck. Dalton's for tea. Good gospel meeting.

Mon. Apr. 16 Lovely bright day. 'Oh happy day that fixed my choice, on Thee my Saviour and my God.' Saved 22 years today.

Tue. Apr. 17 Niagara Falls. Visited James', Mrs. McKay, Marshs, Mattices, Baileys, Krahlings, Jacksons, Mrs. Pinches, Adams', saw Mr. Cleland at hospital.

Fri. June 01 At Lang and Belleville on way to Deseronto Conf.

Sat. June 02 Staying at Root's with R. Bruce.

Fri. June 08 Victoria Road Conference.

Mon. June 18 22 preachers at Stayner Conference.

The Grass Never Grew Greener!

Sun. July 01 Craighurst. Baptism at Orr Lake. Jas. Gunn and I.
Wed. July 04 Wrote R. Bruce re Bracebridge. Getting tent and tent
stakes ready. Making text for platform.
Fri. July 06 Got site for tent at **Bracebridge.**
Sat. July 07 Met R. Bruce at Scotia at 12.30, Bracebridge at 3.45. Boys
brought up tent about 6.30. Got tent pitched amidst the storm and
rain. All night in hay loft.
Sun. July 08 Bracebridge, 1st Lord's Day. Sought to be in the Spirit.
Read and prayed together. At houses in pm. Prayer mtg.
Tue. July 10 Put signs out at corner. Called at houses. 8 out.
Sat. July 14 Wet day. Fixing seats, etc. Had meeting on street, and
gave out tracts.
Sun. July 15 **Huntsville.** Robt. Bruce and I drove up in am. Back to
Bracebridge at 6. Over 20 in. Spoke from Deut. 26 - Ready.
Fri. July 20 Called at houses with some joy. 20 to meeting.
Sat. July 21 Left at 7.30 for Parry Sound. Called at Pearson's. Saw Mr.
& Mrs. H. Fletcher, Mr. & Mrs. McLean from Chicago, and Mrs.
Faulkner. Dinner at Hayes', Twitle Lake. P. Sound at 6.
Sun. July 22 **Parry Sound.** 13 broke bread. Left at 2.30. Called at
Twitle Lake. Bracebridge before 6.20 for tent meeting.
Sat. Aug. 04 Street meeting at night with some help. Thank God.
Sun. Aug. 05 Bracebridge. More rain. Read Isa. 53 together and sang a
few hymns, and thought of Him. Called to see W. Johnston,
dying. About 30 to meeting, Luke 18 - Trusted.
Sun. Aug. 12 **Severn Bridge.** Kept the feast with the saints. Mr. Bruce
and I went with S. Moore. Dinner at Bayley's. Banks' for tea. Back
for gospel meeting in the tent.
Mon. Aug. 13 **Orillia** Sunday School treat. Called on several in pm. N.
Hunt professed. Nice meeting, Luke 4 - All this.
Tue. Aug. 14 Bright warm days. Wrote Dr. Martin in am. Made calls in
pm. J. Smith and A. Pile from Cleveland, for tea at tent.
Wed. Aug. 15 Wrote Jim in am. MB&I at Willson's Falls for dinner.
Robt. and I called on some houses. Meeting, Isa. 57 - Dwellings.
Sat. Aug. 18 Street meeting, 2 of us.
Tue. Aug. 21 Mrs. McGreggor professed. Ralph Baxter and wife out.
Wed. Aug. 22 Maude and Betty went with others on boat trip.
Lovely day. At Deer Lake all day, Robert and I.
Sun. Aug. 26 Bracebridge. "Thought on His Name" together in the
tent. Last meeting, Rom. 6 - End.

Mon. Aug. 27 Lovely day. Taking down tent. R. Bruce went to Parry Sound at 12. We got home with tent about 7.30.
After Orillia Conference, Mr. Shivas had two weeks of tent meetings at **Allandale**, near Barrie, Ont.

Sun. Sep. 30 **Chicago**, Ill. Mr A. Livingstone and I had meeting at 3.30, at **Normal & 66th**. Mr. Gilchrist and I at 7.30.
Wed. Oct. 03 At Gould's for dinner with Steve Mick. At D. Barns' in afternoon and Shearer's. Meeting at Avondale, Proverbs 8.
Sat. Oct. 06 Lovely day. Letter from Maude. At Gould's for lunch. Mr. Buick Sr.'s funeral in pm. Drove 25 miles to cemetery. Lovely day. Cooper's from Valparaiso for tea.
Sun. Oct. 07 **Chicago, Avondale**. Real good morning meeting. Buick's for dinner and tea. Large meeting, John 3.16 - Everlasting.
Sun. Oct. 14 **Valparaiso**. At Cooper's. Jacob Cotton's for tea. Good meeting, Math. 7 - Nothing under. (*Note following letter.*)
Mon. Oct. 15 Left at 8.45 for **Kendallville**. Arr'd 2 pm. Mtg.
Wed. Oct. 17 Left Kendallville at 5.50 am. Arrived Cleveland by God's mercy, 225 miles, about 3 pm. Came to Crawford's.
Fri. Oct. 19 Got cuff links 10c, pants fixed 50c. Had walk. At W. P. Douglas' for tea. Large meeting, Luke 18 - Bartimeaus.
Sun. Oct. 21 **Cleveland**. Good time at the feast. At J. Oliver's. Large gospel meeting, Luke 4 - All this.
Thu. Oct. 25 Left Cleveland at 6.10 am. **Niagara Falls** at 3.15 pm. Adams' for tea and night meeting, Gen. 45 - Enough.

Sat. Dec. 15 **Toronto**. At **Gledhill** Sunday School Treat.
Sun. Dec. 16 At **Swanwick** in am. Gledhill at 3 and 7 pm.
Mon. Dec. 24 Got Sunday School books at Sprunt's.
Tue. Dec. 25 Home by God's mercy by 4 pm. At Prayer meeting.

The Grass Never Grew Greener!

Valparaiso, Indiana
May 14, 1975.

Dear brother,

Just a note from an old friend of George Shivas.

He was indeed a unique character and one of the Lord's jewels.

One year at the Soo Conference, brother Shivas got up to speak. Leonard Sheldrake said "Speak up, George, so the people can hear you." You would have to know Mr. Shivas to appreciate this.

He was at our prayer meeting in Valparaiso one night and was greeting people at the door as they went out. He asked a young lady, "And are you saved?" Upon a negative reply he said, "What a pity, likely you never will be." Strange thing to say, but it was the work of the Holy Spirit. Shortly after we got home from the meeting, the young couple rapped at our door, and she was surely shook up. It didn't take George long to point her to Christ, and she was ready to accept Him. This happened years ago, and the girl, now a middle-aged woman, is still in the assembly.

Many memories flood my mind of dear George Shivas.

Yours by grace,
(Sgd) Wilbur D. Cooper

It Wasn't An Accident

And we know that all things work together for good to them that
love God, to them who are the called according to his purpose.

Romans 8.28.

We often call it an accident,
And say it just happened that way.
And some, that a little bad luck was sent.
While others explain it away.

But we believe that in love it was meant,
To cause us to praise and to pray.
Above from God in Heaven 'twas sent,
Who giveth us strength as our day.

And when we are done with this frail earthly tent,
Or hear the glad shout - "Come away!"
Each sore accident, causing many a rent,
We shall read in the light of that day.

The trial at times to worship gives vent,
As we bow to His will and obey.
And remember His love who to Calvary went,
Knowing all, yet had nothing to say.

G. L. S.

January 1st, 1929

Here's a brief little line
Dear wifie of mine
A faint echo of God's love divine;
May each day as you dine,
Bring bread, honey, and wine,
All through ninteen twenty and nine.

Abide still in 'The Vine'
May your affections entwine,
Nor from Him let your way e'er decline;
May the gold still be 'fine,'
Never dim, but still shine,
This year nineteen twenty and nine.

If in sorrow, don't pine,
On God's love still recline,
In His will, joy and sorrow combine;
To His pleasure resign,
May His blessings be thine
Each day <u>nineteen twenty and nine</u>.

G. L. S.

1929

In the summer of this year, Mr. Shivas reached Manitoulin Island by way of Earlton Conference and the Soo. He was on the island for six weeks of gospel meetings.

In October he started out with his family by auto for the west coast of the United States — no mean feat, considering the automobiles and the roads of that era.

Wed. July 03 J. Silvester and Crocker came on 8 train. Silvester, Crocker, & I left at 1.10 for South River. Arrived safely by God's mercy about 7 o'clock.

Thu. July 04 Left about 8 for Earlton in Ed's car. Silvester, Crocker, C. Devries. Tea at Haileybury. Earlton about 7.30. Good prayer meeting.

Fri. July 05 Conference at **Earlton**. Silvester, Crocker, Steen, Widdifield, Fletcher. Staying at Carr's, Crocker and I.

Fri. July 12 Left Sudbury at 8. Broke down at Espanola at 10. Ernie *(Mrs. Shivas' brother)* came for us. Sudbury all night.

Sat. July 13 A. Crocker and I left at noon for the **Soo**. Arrived safely at 5. Staying at Wright's. Street meeting at Echo Bay.

Mon. July 15 Seeing about car. Looked at many. Mr. Keller's meeting. Called on Mrs. Parr, Hunters, McIntyres, Hills.

Wed. July 17 Got Ford car in am. Left at 2.

Thu. July 18 Came on to Spragge in am. **Gore Bay** at 6. Staying at Kinney's.

Sat. July 20 Lovely morning. At **Providence Bay** all day. Over to dock etc. Back to Gore Bay after tea - Street meeting. Large crowd, 300.

Sun. July 21 Not feeling well. Kept the feast at 1.30. Meeting in school at 3. Wilson's for tea.

Mon. July 22 Had walk to lighthouse with tracts. Mtg in school.

Tue. July 23 At Wilson's. Helped pitch 4 loads of hay. At Kagawong in afternoon. Meeting full, Math. 12 - Uttermost.

Thu. July 25 Helped pitch 5 loads of hay after dinner. Very warm day. Meeting, good crowd - Ps. 73.22-24.

Fri. July 26 Called on 11 or 12 homes. Meeting at Neeley's.

Sat. July 27 Kinney's, Gore Bay all night. Out to Thorburn's for dinner and drove Mr. Mitchell to Providence Bay after. Street meeting, Isa. 45.22.

Sun. July 28 Heavy rain. **Ice Lake.** Kept the feast at 2, with the few. McArthur's for dinner. Mtg at school at 3.15.

Tue. July 30 At Kagawong in afternoon. Had walk, gave out papers.

Thu. Aug. 01 Helped Mr. Kinney draw in hay. McArthur's for tea.

Sat. Aug. 03 Drove in to Gore Bay to boat with mail in am. Got 7 gals gas, 1 pint oil - $2.75. Helped with 2 loads of hay. Called on Grangers and Neeleys. Street meeting at night.

Sun. Aug. 04 Ice Lake. Read Eccl. 9 in am. Mrs. Nolan's for tea. Had walk. Large gospel meeting, Luke 12.

Wed. Aug. 07 Came in from Ice Lake. Drove Mr. Crocker to Little Current. Gas & oil 1.55.

Thu. Aug. 08 Meeting last night at S.S. - Not alone. Out to lighthouse in aft. and gave away some tracts. Put tracts in cars in evening (100). At Kinney's all night.

Sat. Aug. 10 Called on Crofts and McArthurs.

Wed. Aug. 14 Meeting in **No.1 school,** John 3.16 - Everlasting.

Sun. Aug. 18 Ice Lake. Drove to Providence Bay with Mac McA. Met Mr. Crocker. Back for the feast at 2. Mtg in school at 3.30, and at **Brittainville** at 8, Luke 13 - Trusted.

Mon. Aug. 19 Meeting in **Orange Hall, Mills.** Ford's all night.

Tue. Aug. 20 Meeting at Mills. Luke 19 - Trees.

Thu. Aug. 22 McArthur's all night. Gore Bay for mail, gas etc. Little Current. Morphet's for dinner. Walked to town. Made calls. Meeting in **W. I. Hall,** Ps. 142 - Cared.

Fri. Aug. 23 Came to White's, Green Bay for dinner. Meeting in church, John 4 - Altogether.

Sat. Aug. 24 Good street meeting.

Sun. Aug. 25 Ice Lake. Feast at 2. Baptism at 3.30. Left at 6 for Providence Bay. Meeting in Hall at 8. At McGillivary's.

Tue. Aug. 27 Cleaned wheels of car. Changed oil. At McDermid's, Mindenoya, for dinner. Learmont's for tea. Meeting at night.

Thu. Aug. 29 Left Gore Bay by boat 10 am. Lovely day. Got safely to Sudbury, 5.45 pm. Thank God.

Sun. Sep. 01 **Soo, Mich.** Conference. Good meetings and large. Sheldrake, Silvester, Crocker, Joyce, Ferguson, Warke, Kay, Dobbin, Govan, Steen and self.

Mon. Sep. 02 Soo Conference. Read 2 Chron. 18 at 2.30. Baptism at night, 7 obeyed the Lord.

Sun. Sep. 15 **Bay City,** Mich. for the day. At Mowatt's and Southgate's.

Fri. Sep. 20 Flint, Mich. At Allen's blacksmith shop. Got bumper.

Sat. Sep. 21 At Anderson's for tea with Govans, Stewarts, etc. Nice time, singing, reading, and praying.
Sat. Sep. 28 **Detroit Conference**. Large meetings. 44 preachers.
Thu. Oct. 03 Mr. Waugh helped me with car side curtains in am. Left for Cass City, arrived about 6.
Sun. Oct. 06 **Ubly**. Read Ecc. 9 in am. With Dr. Morris for dinner and tea. MB&I had walk. Meeting, **Deckerville**, Crocker & I.
Mon. Oct. 07 Bright day. 11 am, Betty had tonsils out. Thank God.
Fri. Oct. 11 Got to Grand Rapids, 4.30. At Johnson's all night.
Sat. Oct. 12 Down town with W. Pell in am, took car to garage. With Johnsons shopping in pm. Thank God for all.
Sun. Oct. 13 **Grand Rapids** for the day.
Mon. Oct. 14 F. Schwartz helped at meeting.
Wed. Oct. 16 Put new window in rear of car. Washing. Called on Peter Pell. Mr. Barr at meeting.
Fri. Oct. 18 Left at 9 am. Mr. & Mrs. Barr and us. At Sturgis all night. Mr. Waugh's meetings.
Sat. Oct. 19 Left Sturgis about 9.30, dinner at Elkhart, got to Chicago about 4. At Stevensons.
Sun. Oct. 20 **Chicago. New hall**, 10 am and 2.30. McEwen brothers. **Rosedale Hall**, Barr and I. George Conover professed.

From here the trip westward began in earnest via the following route, with stops for meetings with the saints at many assemblies, **Indianapolis**, Ind., **St.Louis**, Mo., **Kansas City**, Mo., **Tulsa**, Okla., **Sherman**, Okla, and a call at "God's Mercy store", in Waller, Texas. They were at **Houston**, Texas, for their Conference in early November, and for two weeks of meetings. Next stop was **San Antonio**, Texas, for one week. Monday, December 2 notes, "Young Fried boy professed", then on to **El Paso**, Texas, and **Phoenix**, Arizona, via Deming, Willcox, and Florence Jct., over very dusty roads.

Thu. Dec. 12 Left Phoenix, Ariz. about 8.10. Lovely warm day. Very dusty. Not very good roads. All night in Yuma, Arizona, auto camp, $1. <u>God is faithful</u>.
Fri. Dec. 13 Left Yuma at 6.30. Dinner on the road. Came over the Rockies, about 200 miles. San Diego, California all night.
Sat. Dec. 14 Left S. Diego about 9.30, and got to Long Beach, Cal., at 1.30 or 2. Soon found Lycurgas *(Mrs. Shivas' brother)* and Mary. At Sunday School Teacher's Prayer meeting in Mrs. Blair's house.

The family found an apartment to rent at 1207 Atlantic, for $25., and Mr. Shivas started gospel meetings with Mr. Robert A. Barr, immediately.

Some readers will recall that Mr. and Mrs. Robert Barr were killed in an automobile accident four years later.

1933 Tue. Dec. 11 Julius Bernardo brought word of Mr. and Mrs. Barr's homecall. Considered going to Bay City to funeral. Left at 3.30 for London. E. Plewes' at night.

Wed. Dec. 12 E. Plewes and I left at 6 am. Bay City at noon. Robert and Amy Barr's funeral at 2.30. Helped carry Robert's body and prayed at cemetery.

The Shivas family enroute to California 1930

1930

January of this year found the Shivas family in Long Beach, California. Mr. Shivas and Mr. Robert A. Barr were continuing gospel meetings there. Meetings in Los Angeles and Monrovia, Cal. followed in February and March.

Wed. Jan. 01 **Los Angeles Conference**. Last day. Read chapter 19, verse 30, in Lev., 2 Sam., 2 Kings. Home for our meeting.

Tue. Jan. 07 Out with tracts with Robert Barr. At Lyc. for tea.

Thu. Jan. 09 Out with tracts in pm. Children's treat at 7. Good time. Marjory Colborne saved last night.

Mon. Jan. 13 Out in aft with tracts to houses. Anna Dean saved last night.

Tue. Jan. 14 Wet day again. R. A. Barr drove me to San Pedro to see U.S. Customs re car. 30 out. Good for wet night.

Fri. Jan. 17 Drove up to Los A. in the morning in our car. MB&I, Lyc, Mary and Robert. Got settled with U. S. Customs. 25% on $50. Appraisment $12.50. Got back about 4.30. Home for tea.

Sun. Jan. 19 Large meeting & street mtg, John 9.

Sat. Jan. 25 Prayer mtg in hall and on street, 5th & Pine.

Mon. Jan. 27 Seeing about car. Got connecting rods tightened up in am. Had walk and drove over to Lindsay's for tea, down 3rd to Winnipeg, 3000 block.

Tue. Jan. 28 We all drove out to see Mrs. Witham. Philip Vasileau, 1035 Orange, Apt D. for tea. Meeting.

Thu. Jan. 30 Getting ready to move. At Mrs. Lindsay's. Made calls. At Harrison's (McConnell's) for dinner. Prudie's for tea. Back in time for meeting. Good crowd, last meeting, Mark 5 - Often.

Fri. Jan. 31 Packing up and left about 11 oc, Barr's and us. Came up to L.A. and secured room. Ash Harrison drove me to **Pomona** Sunday School Treat. At Martin's all night.

Sat. Feb. 01 Saw through orange packing house, and picked box of oranges in am. Up to mountains in pm. Got oranges and grapefruit sent off, $8. Harrison's for tea, and back to L. A., MB&I.

Sun. Feb. 02 Los Angeles. Large and good gospel meeting.

Mon. Feb. 03 Had walk in pm and gave away some tracts. Meeting.

Wed. Feb. 12 M&I seeing about new Ford coach and bought it for $75. difference on our Touring. S. Greer met us. At Garris for mtg at 2.30 on baptism, and, Gathering to His Name.

Thu. Feb. 13 Mr. Caldwell drove us and the Barr's to 104th St. for mtg at 2.30. Caldwell's for tea, MB&I. Meeting, Mark 5.

Sat. Feb. 15 At Long Beach. Drove down in our new car, MB&I. Called at Harrison's (McConnell's) on the way. Lyc. for dinner. Called to see Mrs. Henley and Philip Vasileau. Also at ocean. Smith's, L. A. for tea. Street meeting and prayer meeting.

Sun. Feb. 16 Los Angeles. At Dr. Wells' (Ida Harrison's) for dinner. Mtg at 3 at Gehring's. Prayer mtg and gospel mtg and baptism, Rev. 2 - Depths.

Mon. Feb. 17 Lovely day. Like July. Got car licence transferred. Put top dressing on. Meeting, Prov. 8 - Finding.

Tue. Feb. 18 Lovely day, like summer. Down town with Dr. Wells and Ida. Out to mtg at 103rd St.

Wed. Feb. 19 To go to John Worter's, 3517 10th Ave, end of J car, for tea, D.V.

Sat. Feb. 22 Got packed up last night. Up at 7. Got away from L. A. about 9.45 am, and got to Monrovia in good time for dinner at Thompson's. Secured apt.

Sun. Feb. 23 **Monrovia**, 1st Lord's Day. Spoke to children at 9.45 from Wordless Book. Feast at 11. Had walk up mountain in pm.

Mon. Feb. 24 Bought cooker at store. Gave out tracts. Meeting.

Tue. Feb. 25 Over to hall in am and made sign on blackboard for meetings. Lovely day. Got oranges. Meeting.

Wed. Feb. 26 Got word of Marion Davis being saved. Mr. Thompson brought 64 oranges. Meeting, Ps. 112 - Tidings.

Fri. Feb. 28 MB&I out in am. Up canyon with car and had walk up the mountain path. At bro. Ross, 628 W. Palm for supper. Mtg.

Sun. Mar. 02 Monrovia, 2nd Lord's Day. Quite large mtg & help.

Mon. Mar. 03 MB&I up the canyon in am. Had our lunch there.

Mon. Mar. 10 Resting most of day. Out in pm up mountain. Nice lot out to mtg. God is faithful.

Sat. Mar. 15 Decided to stay 1 more week. God grant mercy. Got hair cut .35c. More rain.

Sun. Mar. 16 Monrovia. Gathering sticks, at 9.45. Feast at 11. Mtg at 3 - Required. Gospel meeting. Rain.

Tue. Mar. 18 T. D. W. Muir & wife for dinner, had nice visit. Mtg.

Wed. Mar. 19 Called to see Mrs. Letourneau. *(See 1907).*

Fri. Mar. 21 Did some packing and getting ready to move.

Sat. Mar. 22 MB&I called on Adair's. Mr. Bruce Adair professed to receive Christ.

Sun. Mar. 23 Monrovia, 5th Lord's Day. Very warm.

Wed. Mar. 26 Ready to move. Last mtg, Math. 23 - Would not.

Thu. Mar. 27 Leaving Monrovia. Got to Visalia for the night.

Tue. Apr. 01 Got to **Fresno** about 6. Meeting in Hall.

Fri. Mar. 04 Over to see bro. Wright at store, had talk with Tom Woods from Ireland about his soul in am. Meeting.

Sat. Mar. 05 Left Fresno at 6.30, MB&I. Got to Oakland at 11.30 safely by God's mercy, 170 miles. Got car fixed, center main bearing, $2.65. Hill's all night. Thank God.

Sun. Mar. 06 **Oakland**, Cal. S.S. at 9.30 - Two sons in Old & New Testament. At W. J. McClure's mtg at 3.30 on Tabernacle. At Berkeley Hall at 7.45. Linfoots and Ness boys there. Good mtg.

Mon. Apr. 07 Met S. Greer and W. J. McClure. To Sacramento by 4. Marysville (across river) all night. Thank God for His mercy.

Tue. Apr. 08 Left about 8. Dinner at Redding. All night at Yreka. Had walk and tightened brake bands in auto camp.

Wed. Apr. 09 Left about 8. Got new fan belt. Dinner at Grants Pass. Had some work done on car at noon. Roseburg all night.

Thu. Apr. 10 Left Roseburg about 6.30. Dinner at Eugene. Bad knock in car. Got to Salem at noon. Dinner and tea at Jim Linfoot's. Got car fixed. At Aunt Grace's for evening.

Fri. Apr. 11 Left Salem at 9 am. Dinner at Bullivant's, Portland, Oregon. Lovely day. "God is faithful". Bullivant's came with us to **Forest Grove**. Eddie Goff's all night. Meeting in Hall.

Sat. Apr. 12 Called at houses in Dilley with tracts in am. Haylett's for tea. Street meeting.

The following tract was written by Mr. Shivas as the result of meeting a gentleman in Forest Grove, Oregon, on that Saturday morning, April 12, 1930.

"Did He Really Believe It?"

The winter of 1929-30 we spent in the Western States and Canada. During a visit at Forest Grove, Oregon, on a Saturday afternoon we were calling from house to house giving away gospel tracts and inviting the people to an evangelistic service on the Sunday evening. We found an old man sitting by the south side of his barn getting a sunbath on his rheumatic limbs. We told him our story and gave him a tract and this was his response.

"Do you know what I believe?" "No," I said. "I believe," said he, "that a man dies like a dog and that's the end of him!"

"**You do?**" said I. My first impulse was to say goodbye and leave him, but something seemed to say — does he **really** believe that?

The Lord gave me two traps to set for him and I nearly caught him in the first one, but the second caught him solid.

"Is your father still alive, Mister?" I said. I knew he wasn't, for he was a gray-headed man himself. "No, Mister," he said, "My father died 25 years ago."

"Did your father die like a dog?" I said gently. The poor man was nearly caught but said he supposed and allowed that maybe he did.

So I set the next trap. "Is your mother still alive, Mister?" "Oh no," said he, "My mother died many years ago." I started to repeat the same question regarding his mother, but the dear man was shocked and wouldn't let me finish. "No, mister, I don't believe she did," he said. I said to him: "No, she certainly did not. She died and went to heaven, or, died and went to hell."

Then I spoke plainly to him and told him that he might live like a dog but he certainly would not die like a dog. I told him of the Saviour who loved him and died that shameful death on the cross of Calvary that he might be saved from the power of sin, and death, and hell; and be sure of a home in heaven.

The title of this tract is in the form of a question. He certainly did not really believe it and it took but the mention of the memory of his dear departed mother to make him refute such a God-dishonouring lie of Satan.

No — the poor dog is a faithful, noble creature and fulfils the purpose for which he was created, returning to his original state, having no further responsibility; but God made man in His own likeness — Gen. 1. 26,27. God breathed into Adam's nostrils the breath of life and man became a **living soul**, Gen. 2.7. A living soul is a **creature of Eternity.**

Job said in the book that bears his name, Chapter 14, verse 10: "But man dieth and wasteth away, yea, man giveth up the ghost; and where is he?" Does he die like a dog and that's the end of him, as the dear man at Forest Grove said long ago? (I'm sure he is dead and gone before this, but where?)

In Luke 16 the Lord Jesus tells us of two men who lived and died, and then draws aside the curtain between time and eternity to let us see just where they are; the one in perfect peace and comfort, — the other in endless pain and torment. It would be a mercy for those who wilfully reject the loving Saviour whom God has provided, **if they could** die like a dog, and that would be the end of them — but God has said in Heb. 9.27, "It is appointed unto men once to die, but after this the judgment."

"Be sure your sin will find you out," Numbers 32.23. The only sin that will send men to hell and the lake of fire forever is the crowning sin of the **rejection of Christ!** "If ye die in your sins," He has said, "where I am ye cannot come." "For if ye believe not that I am He, ye shall die in your sins." John 8.21.

The Scriptures declare, "Christ died for the ungodly." "Christ Jesus came into the world to save sinners." "The Son of God who loved me, and gave Himself for me." "Believe on the Lord Jesus Christ, and thou shalt be saved."

I was a guilty sinner, but Jesus died for me!

For a Christian to die, means to be absent from the body, and present (at home) with the Lord. To die in one's sins — "better never to have been born," Mark 4.14 - 21.

"For God so loved the world, that he gave his only begotten Son, that whosoever believeth in him should not perish, but have everlasting life." John 3.16.

G. L. S.

The Grass Never Grew Greener!

Tue. Apr. 15 Left Forest Grove at 8 am and got to **Tacoma** city limits
3.10. Went to Chas. Summer's for tea and night. Put new brake lin-
ing on rear wheel. Chas. Summers helped me.
Wed. Apr. 16 24 years in Christ today. Thank God for all His mercy.
Left Tacoma about 7 am. Passed the Customs at Blain about 3.30.
Paid duty on car at New Westminster, B.C. $55. F.W. Goff's,
Vancouver, for tea. All night at Matheson's.
Thu. Apr. 17 Phoned Jas. Rae. Met J. J. Rouse. Visited Richilieu Binch
and at Stanley Budd's. First meeting of Vancouver Conf.
Fri. Apr. 18 **Vancouver Conference,** Seymour St. W. J. McClure, Greer,
Cameron, Rouse, Barr.
Sun. Apr. 20 Meetings good. Helped in gospel Sunday eve, Acts 12.
Wed. Apr. 23 Mrs. Boyle (Mary B.) drove us around Stanley Park in
pm. Had walk. Fairly good mtg for first. Thank God.
    Six weeks of gospel meetings in Vancouver, B. C.
Sun. Apr. 27 Vancouver B.C. Read Deut. 23.9 in am. F. W. Goff's for
dinner. S.S. at 2 - Wordless Book. Believer's meeting at 3.
Matheson's for tea. Mtg at night, Luke 2 - Saviour. Rainy.
Mon. Apr. 28 Funeral at 3 at 11th & Kingsway, 1 Thess. 4 at grave. At
R. Marshall's, ll747 13 Ave. E. Broadway E. off at Scott.
Tue. Apr. 29 Got car in am, 27 Chev. coach at Begg Bros.
Thu. May 01 Called for S. Greer. Budd's for dinner. Stan Budd's for
tea. Meeting, Rom. 3.
Fri. May 02 Down town with car in am, got cards ordered. Called at
Leeson's Garage. Cloggie's for tea, 3436 W 12th. Meeting.
Sat. May 03 Working at cement sidewalk at rear of Matheson's in am.
At Mercer's (Alice Taylor) for dinner. At walk in pm. Mr.
Cloggie and Jack More helping. Jack and I at street meeting.
Sun. May 04 Vancouver B.C. At the feast at 11. Meeting at 3. Large
gospel meeting - Everlasting.
Mon. May 05 Got wind shields put on 27 Chev. coach after dinner
$2.65. At Mervin Clark's for supper. Had walk. Meeting.
Tue. May 06 Saw John Rea. Mrs. Belyca for tea, 2823 Waterloo.
Wed. May 07 Mrs. Key's for dinner and tea. Back for prayer mtg.
Thu. May 08 Drove Mrs. Matheson downtown. At Seed's most of day.
Fri. May 09 Morrison's for tea, 1210 Melson Ave, Jubilee. Meeting.
Sat. May 10 Working at wood, Maude and I. Threw 2 loads over
fence. Mr. Greer and us at Mercer's for dinner. Did some digging
in garden at Mercer's. At C. G. McLean's in pm and for tea. Called
on Mr. & Mrs. Hern. Street meeting - A sinner.

Sun. May 11 Vancouver B.C. At the feast at 11, good. F. W. Goff's for dinner and tea. Had walk. Mtg at 3, John 3 - Whosoever. Large meeting at 7.30 and prayer mtg, Luke 14 - Gospel supper.

Mon. May 12 Calls this week at D. Wallace's, Topping's, Trench's, Matheson's, Mrs. Anderson's (nee Annie Coulter), Mrs. Toole's.

Sun. May 18 Vancouver B.C. Large gospel meeting and good.

Mon. May 19 Had talk with Frank Boyle in evening. There for tea. Funeral at 1.30, Jones boy. Hymn 84. No meeting.

Wed. May 21 Got Speedo gas, 6.5 gals, $1.92.

Thu. May 22 Called on Hector Alves. Meeting, John 5 - Place.

Sat. May 24 At **Fairview Conference** in am. Dinner at Hall. Albert Ragan's funeral at 2 at Cloverdale. Spoke at grave, He is risen. Fairview at night, Dan and I. Heard C. Summers at both meetings.

Tue. May 27 Called on Hector Alves and Hill at factory. Called on Mrs. Harris and Calder. At Willox's for supper. Mtg.

Thu. May 29 At Seed's for dinner and tea. At Capilano River and bridges in aft. Meeting, Job 40 - I am.

Fri. May 30 Over to N. Van. for dinner. Called at Dennis's and had visit. Key's for dinner and tea. Back for mtg, Luke 12 - Barns.

Sat. May 31 Cleaned car. Called at Belyca's and John Taylor's. Rich Binch's for lunch. Had walk, and at McLean's for supper and evening. J. Taylor there.

Sun. June 01 Vancouver B.C. Large gospel meeting.

Thu. June 05 Packing up in am, getting ready to leave.

Sun. June 08 **Langley Prairie**. Called on Ragans after S.S.

Mon. June 09 Called on homes with B. W. Brown in pm. At Ried's.

Tue. June 10 Out with Mr. Brown calling after dinner. Large gospel meeting, Luke 15. Raymond Ragan professed.

Wed. June 11 Made calls with tracts in pm, Mr. Brown and I. At **Abbotsford** meeting, read Acts 16 and Luke 16.

Fri. June 13 Got car partly loaded up. Out with Mr. Brown in pm making calls. Had good time. Home for supper. Dan and Lydie out for meeting. Good lot out. Read Isa. 38 - Dwellings.

Sat. June 14 Raymond Ragan called in am before we left. Thank God for all His mercy. Took our leave from the dear Browns with some mutual sorrow. Journeying mercies all the way to Seattle.

Sun. June 15 **Seattle**, Wash. Feast at 10.30. S.S. and B. Class at 12.15. Home for dinner at Matthew's. Gospel at 7.30, Bartimaeus.

Mon. June 16 At Roache's and Geo. Morrison's. Meeting, 7.45 pm.

Tue. June 17 Got front wheels of car lined up, washers on hind wheels in am. At McNicoll's and Martin's. Children's meeting, 6.45 pm, Wordless Book. Meeting at 7.45, Luke 14 - Extra.

Wed. June 18 Left Seattle at 6 am, and got to Wenatchee at 11.40, 172 miles, over mountains. Malott at 3.40, 256 miles. At Lester Hinde's all night in camp. Had walk, supper, and read in eve.

Thu. June 19 Visited with Mr. Arnold and Ralph Goff. Walked with Ralph up to place where boys were working. Meeting at night in **Okanagan**. Read John 3.16 - Whosoever.

Fri. June 20 Got to **Penticton** about 3. Got car fixed some. Felt washers in front wheels, etc. Meeting in Penticton.

Sat. June 21 Stayed all night at Mrs. Clifton's, Penticton, and came on to Glenrosa in am. Rain. Got to Gates' at noon, staying there. Over to Kelowna in evening, saw Ribelin's.

Sun. June 22 **Glenrosa**, B.C. Feast at 11. Meeting at 2.30. Hussey's for supper. Gospel meeting at 8.

Tue. June 24 Cleaned and greased car in am. Out with Gilbert and Daisy in pm. Made several calls. At Webber's for tea. Good mtg.

Wed. June 25 Left Glenrosa at 5.30. Met Alex McDonald near Osoyoos. Passed customs etc, via Tonasket, Republic, and Wilbur. Got safely to Spokane about 7 oc. Got to John Whitfield's for tea & all night.

Thu. June 26 Left Spokane 6.30 am. Got in the ditch, bent axle etc, but by God's mercy were able to proceed on our journey. Passed the border and got to Wasa, 23 miles past Cranbrook at 5.30. Auto camp all night. Lots of mosquitos, ? but God?

Fri. June 27 Left Wasa 4.45 am. Had good sleep and rest. Crossed the Rockies and got to Banff at noon, **Calgary** at 4. Came to Mrs. Ross' for supper and night. Prayer meeting, Acts 16, Luke 16.

From here the Shivas family began the trek eastward across the Canadian Prairie, visiting the Lord's people and seeking to encourage them in the things of God, as well as enduring the early summer rains and roads, and a pesky bent front car axle.

Sat. June 28 Took car to garage in am. Got it back in pm. Raining 8 to 5. Ross' for supper. Called on Wallis', Russels, Rieds.

Sun. June 29 Calgary, Alta. Good meeting, and a good day.

Mon. June 30 Left Calgary about 9 and got to **Edmonton** about 5.30, 215 miles by God's mercy. Good roads. Dinner at Red Deer. Staying at Twittey's, 93 St. Meeting in Hall at 8 - Whosoever.

The Diaries of George L. Shivas

Tue. July 01 Out at Mark's farm for dinner and supper with Twittey's and others, 40 in all. Had mtg in pm. Came through heavy rains.
Thu. July 03 At Winter's, Edmonton. Meeting at night.
Fri. July 04 Left Edmonton at 6 am. Found bad roads, <u>mud</u>, part of way, but got safely by God's mercy to Lloydminster for night.
Sat. July 05 Came on to **Waseca Conference** in am. R. Telfer, R. J. Dickson, and C. H. Willoughby there. Read Gen. 18 - Abraham.
Sun. July 06 Waseca Conf. Took part in pm, and also in gospel.
Tue. July 08 Left Waseca at 9 am, and came to Sinclair's for dinner. Getting axle straightened. Meeting in school.
Wed. July 09 Called on blacksmith and had walk. Trouble with Sinclair's car on way to mtg, Haviland and I, Ps. 103.
Thu. July 10 At A. Grant's for dinner. Called on Herb Ray, Carltons, and at Baynton's for supper. School house full.
Fri. July 11 Got car ready to leave Sinclair's after dinner. Left Baldwinton about 1 oc, and got safely to Cox Sr.'s for supper. Came on to **Mervin** for meeting at 8, John 4 - Again.
Sat. July 12 Took car to garage at Turtleford in am. Had to get rear end in. Street meeting.
Sun. July 13 Mervin, Sask. Mtg at Louisville school at 3, and in Parkdale school at 8.
Mon. July 14 Got car from Turtleford, $15. in am, and left Mervin at 12. Got to Saskatoon about 7, 6 hours driving, 186 miles. *Not too brisk a speed, to average 30 miles per hour!* Thank God for His mercy. Stayed all night with Norton and Annie Greer.
Tue. July 15 Called on Mrs. Bush in Saskatoon and Maymie Stubbs (Holley), and left Saskatoon about 10. Got to Aberdeen for dinner. Called on Armstrongs and at Will Stewart's for dinner. **Taylorside** about 8 oclock for meeting. Read Prov. 8 - Finding.
Wed. July 16 At Herbert Taylor's all night. At Halverson's for dinner and supper. Very warm day. Meeting at night, John 3.
Thu. July 17 Dinner at Ernest Taylor's. Called on Evans. Mtg.
Fri. July 18 Children's treat day, Taylorside Sask. Spoke to children and all <u>200</u> at 5 oclock before tea, from Gen. 3.8 - Trees. Lovely day. God is faithful.
Sat. July 19 Tightened bolts in rear wheel in am. At Fred Clark's in pm and for supper. Rained a little. Drove with them to Beatty for street meeting. Back to H. Taylor's all night.
Sun. July 20 Taylorside, Sask. Meeting at 2.30 for children and all. Good weather. Gospel at 7.30, Teno Maestri helped.

Mon. July 21 Had conversation with Fred Clark in am. Got ready and left about 9.30. Called to see Wm. Paul at Melfort. Left about 12, and to Esk. Howard Clark's about 4. Mtg in school.

Wed. July 23 Adjusted front wheels of car. At Mrs. Barber's (Waters) for dinner. Tom King's for night. Lot out to mtg.

Thu. July 24 Rain. At Henry King's. Larger meeting.

Sat. July 26 Street meeting at Lanigan at night.

Sun. July 27 **Esk (Hiawatha)**. Good meetings. Johnston's for dinner. Mtg at 3, Eph. 2 - Children. Mehaffy's for supper. Prayer mtg at 7. Gospel, 7.30. Reg White helped.

Mon. July 28 Dinner at Sheho, 100 miles at 12. Got to R. McNicol's about 4.30, Saltcoats, 189 miles. Some muddy roads but on the whole, good. God is faithful. McNicol's all night. Good sleep.

Wed. July 30 Got to W. J. Stewart's, **Minnetonas**, Man. 3.30. Mtg.

Thu. July 31 Lovely day. Jack Stewart and I working at car, straightening front axle and tire. At R. Cleaveley's for dinner. Called on Mrs. Abbott and had a rest there. Very warm. At Geo. Cleaveley's for supper. Mr. & Mrs. Peterson there.

Fri. Aug. 01 Getting ready to leave at noon. Had dinner with Stewart's, chicken, ice cream, etc. Had read and prayer with Dorothy. Left Stewart's at 12.45. Roads fairly good. Got to Frank Martin's, **Saltcoats** at 7.00. Very warm, and mosquitoes. Meeting out doors. Nicol's all night.

Sat Aug. 02 Martin's for dinner and supper. In hay field at noon. Over to Saltcoats in pm and got front axle straightened. Called on Chamberlains and others in pm. Baptized 2 men in lake, read Acts 10.8. Meeting at Martin's. Street meeting in Saltcoats.

Sun. Aug. 03 Saltcoats, Sask. Kept the Feast at 2 pm at Frank Martin's house. Gospel mtg at 3.45. To Yorkton for street mtg.

Mon. Aug. 04 Up at 5.30 and left R. McNicol's at 7.10 for **Portage La Prairie**. Stopped at Shoal Lake at noon for a few mins. Maude drove 100 miles from Shoal Lake to Gladstone. Arr'd Portage, 4.30. At Ronald's, Main St. S. for supper and all night. "God is faithful". 268 miles. Meeting, Gen. 18 - Sat.

Tue. Aug. 05 Called on Geo. Fuller, baker. Got some work done on car. At their place for dinner. Called on Mr. Rey, tailor, in afternoon. Got hat cleaned. Good mtg, John 3 - Whosoever.

Wed. Aug. 06 Called on Mr. Fuller, and then at flour mill. Saw Mr. Tonkin and others there and saw through the mill. Called on Mr. Rey, and at Ronald's for dinner. Left P.L.P. at 2. Winnipeg at 5.30. Geo Keeling's for supper and at W. D. Stewart's all night.

Thu. Aug. 07 Did some work at car, fixed tire, etc. Mr. Haviland and I down town in am. Unloaded car after dinner. Went for Mrs. Morrow Sr. and called on Adam Morning. At Keeling's for tea, prayer mtg.

Fri. Aug. 08 Down to the city in am with Mr. & Mrs. Stewart. Helped Mr. Haviland with car. Keeling's for supper. Tent with Fred Watson.

Sat. Aug. 09 At Stewart's with F. G. Watson and R. Ronald.

Sun. Aug. 10 **Winnipeg (West End).** S.S. at 3 - Wordless Book. Mtg at 3.30. Robertson's for supper. Gospel and street meeting.

Mon. Aug. 11 Lovely morning. "God is good." Got front axle heated and straightened. Got carbon cleaned and valves ground after dinner, and at Hobday's for supper.

Wed. Aug. 13 Got gas, oil in car. Called on Mrs. Rose, Milton Ball, and McManns after dinner. Got car loaded up and at Lindsay Stewart's for supper. Geo. Keeling and wife in.

Thu. Aug. 14 Left Winnipeg at 7 oc and got as far as Iowane Camp for night, 325 miles, with no trouble. Thank God for His mercy. Slept in car all night.

Fri. Aug. 15 Left about 9, and got to Duluth about 3, 150 miles. In auto camp all night, Indian Head. Comfortable night in tent.

Sun. Aug. 17 **Duluth.** Spoke to children at 9.15 am. Feast at 10.30, good. Bennett's for dinner. Mtg at 3, and gospel meeting.

Wed. Aug. 20 Took car to Luhm's to get wheels painted. Came back on street car. At the zoo in pm and saw animals fed. At J. Brown's for supper. Nice few out to meeting.

Mon. Aug. 25 Packing up camp. Lovely day. Thank God. At Bennett's for dinner. Came to **Hinckley** to Moffat's for supper and all night. Meeting in home, John 11 - Come forth.

Thu. Aug. 28 Left at 9. Got safely to **Minneapolis**, 3.30. At Upton's for night. Nice visit. At Jas. F. Spink's meeting.

Fri. Aug. 29 Left Mpls. 8.30 and got to La Crosse, 150 miles at 4. At Sam Hamilton's all night. Prayer mtg of conference, Heb. 9.

Sat. Aug. 30 Stewart of Detroit, Warke of Chicago, Smith of Waterloo, Hamilton of La Crosse, J. Rea of London. Good mtgs.

Mon. Sep. 01 **La Crosse Conf.** Street mtg and gospel mtg at night.

Wed. Sep. 03 Mrs. Helen Turmo got saved. Left La Crosse at 2.30, got to **Beetown** at 8 for mtg, thank God. Tire trouble. At Jamieson's.

Thu. Sep. 04 Good mtg last night. Five souls professed to be saved. Neil & Cecelia Christianson, Davis & Grace Schlat, and Gerald. Left Beetown at 1.30, Waterloo 5.30. Tent at **Cloutier**, Acts 4 - Saved.

Fri. Sep. 05 On to Hitesville, Kesley for meeting.

Sun. Sep. 07 **Hitesville** for the day.

Mon. Sep. 08 At garage all day. Walter Eltze's for dinner. Drove with Geo. Uhlenhopp's to Applington for supper. At Paul Elliott's meeting at **Stout**.

Tue. Sep. 09 Got car from garage, Kesley, and left about 10. Dinner at O. Smith's, Waterloo, with J. Ferguson, W. Warke. Got to Manchester at 5.30, staying with G. Roberts. Meeting.

Wed. Sep. 10 Meeting in **Garnavillo**.

Thu. Sep. 11 Visited some in am with L. Brandt. Left at 3 and got to Beetown at 5. Stayed all night at Dickson's. Meeting.

Sat. Sep. 13 Left at 8 for Lake Geneva. Dinner at Monroe. Lake Geneva, 4.30. Staying at McCohn's. Thank God for all His mercy.

Sun. Sep. 14 **Lake Geneva** for the day.

Mon. Sep. 15 Left at 9 after calling on Miss Roberts. Dinner at Elgin Gables. Through watch works. **Chicago**, 6 pm to J. H. Stevenson's.

Tue. Sep. 16 Cleaned car and pressed clothes. To Boyd's and Gould's, got front seats covered. Had visit with W. Gould. Missionary mtg.

Thu. Sep. 18 Left Chicago about 8, and got to Detroit by God's mercy at 4.30. Called at Sturgis'. Supper at Walker's and stayed there. Good conference prayer meeting.

Fri. Sep. 19 **Detroit Conference**. Lovely weather and good crowds. Helpful ministry, all day. Behold how good!

Sat. Sep. 20 Lovely day. Ross, Muir, Clark, Marshall, Dickson, Rouse, Ferguson etc, about 25 preachers.

Sun. Sep. 21 Spoke to children at 1 oc. Large mtgs and good. Some friends in at Walker's to sing after meeting.

Mon. Sep. 22 Another lovely day. "God is faithful." Called on Woods for dinner, Craws not home, Floods, McGeachys. Gavin and Ruth's for supper, Rive's in evening, Walker's all night.

Tue. Sep. 23 Left about 3. Over to **Windsor**. J. J. Rouse had mtg.

Wed. Sep. 24 Left about 9 am and on to London. Saw R. Hills, Ed, J. Cossey and Mary, and got to Grimsby by God's mercy. Called on Grandma Bernardo. Saw new Hall.

Thu. Sep. 25 **Grimsby.** Got wheel tightened up, spokes and fender fixed, changed oil, gas. At prayer mtg.

Fri. Sep. 26 Called on Mrs. Bonham, Mrs. Snider, W. Gunns in am. Got some fruit. Lovely day. Called on Jas. Gunn after dinner and got peaches. Left about 3. At Pape Ave. prayer meeting.

Sat. Sep. 27 Street meeting on Danforth - Whose side I am on.

Sun. Sep. 28 **Pape Avenue** for the day.

Wed. Oct. 01 Got packed up and left 204 about 9.30. Dinner at C. Harvie's. Called to see Jim at hospital and got home to Orillia about 5.30. Mother's for tea. <u>God is faithful</u>.

Later in October the way opened for the Shivas family to move to Grimsby, and by the 28th of the month they were residing at 15 Kidd Avenue, Grimsby, Ontario. Mr. Shivas had an interest there ever since the gospel meetings held in 1928.

I Was Saved In A Kitchen.

I was saved in a kitchen as I stood by the table,
With the window nearby where the sunshine shone in.
But my Saviour was born in a low cattle stable
Because there was found no room in the inn.

I was saved in a kitchen as I stood by the table,
Where often the victuals and bounties were spread.
But a Bible lying there told of One who is able
To save by His power, tho' once He was dead.

I was saved in a kitchen as I stood by the table,
Reading that Bible — John three and sixteen.
The anchor is sure and so is the cable.
Whosoever means me, who else could it mean?

I was saved in a kitchen as I stood by the table,
Lost and condemned on the near brink of hell.
When the Saviour drew near — it's true, and no fable.
Sought me and saved me. He loved me so well.

I was saved in a kitchen as I stood by the table,
Wearied and worried and seeking release.
Where all was confusion and darkness and babel,
Christ spoke the pardon, and filled me with peace.

G. L. S.

1931

This year commenced with the usual trip to Tillsonburg Conference over the New Year. It was uncommon to get through the Conference without an ice storm! Evidently 1931 was a good year.

Fri. Jan. 02 Leo Sheldrake and I drove to Tillsonburg in am, there for dinner. Staying at Mr. Touzeau's.

Sat. Jan. 03 **Tillsonburg Conference.** McCrory, Rouse, Sheldrake, Smith, Stewart, Wilkie, Schwartz, Gilchrist, Touzeau, Dobbin, Palin, and Cathers.

Sun. Jan. 04 I spoke on Gen. 18 Saturday, and in gospel, Sunday.

Mon. Jan. 05 Leo and I drove safely by God's mercy to Hamilton.

Sat. Jan. 17 Grimsby. Gracie Grimes saved last night.

Most of February and March were spent in gospel meetings on both sides of the border at **Sault Ste. Marie**, with Mr. Shivas and Mr. Leo Sheldrake. The names of faithful families keep recurring in the diaries. The Lord blessed their efforts.

Sun. Feb. 15 Large gospel meeting and good.

Sat. Feb. 21 Not feeling well, cold. H. Smith's for tea - saved.

Fri. Feb. 27 Wrote Maude in am. Lovely day. Leo and I called on Bert Hurley's. He got saved. Also called on Mr. Graham.

Sun. Mar. 15 American Soo. Large gospel mtg - Everlasting.

Sat. Mar. 21 Had walk and gave out tracts. Street Meeting.

(Street meeting on the 21st of March?)

Wed. Mar. 25 Mrs H. Gordon saved in afternoon. Mtg over river.

Sat. Apr. 04 **Toronto Conference.** Clean heart and a right spirit.

Thu. Apr. 16 25 years in Christ. "From my heart the burden rolled away, happy day."

Fri. May 08 **Grimsby**. Mrs. Russel Davis saved.

Sat. May 23 **Midland Conference.** Good weather and meetings. Staying at Lewis Boyce's. Telfer, McCartney, Duncan, Livingstone, Dickson, Silvester, Gould, Widdifield, Steen, Baillie, Watson, Gillespie, Goodfellow, Gunn, Crocker.

Mon. June 15 Came to **Grand Bend** with T. Wilkie. Mtg at night.

Tue. June 16 Had walk by the beach. Made some calls. Meeting.

During July and August, Mr. Shivas and Mr. Wilkie had tent meetings at Dunnville, Ontario.

Sat. June 27 Drove with Julius Bernardo to Dunnville. Seeing about lot, and hydro for site.

Wed. July 01 T. Wilkie and I home from Straffordville at noon.

Thu. July 02 Drove to **Dunnville** after dinner. Hunting for auger. Brethren came from St.C. in evening and we got the tent pitched after a rain storm.

Fri. July 03 Tom and I slept in tent all night. Getting things in readiness. Pitched one small tent.

Sat. July 04 Men wiring the tent. Got sounding board together. Brethren came from St. C. in evening and we had street meeting. Home at 12.30.

Sun. July 05 Grimsby. All at Dunnville, first mtg - Come.

Mon. July 06 Heavy rain storm in the night. God is faithful. Gave out some bills at houses.

Fri. July 10 Out with tracts. Eleven in to meeting.

Thu. July 23 Out in afternoon. At tent for supper. About 40 out.

Sat. July 25 Street meeting at Dunnville.

Mon. July 27 Had walk. Spoke to some. Large children's meeting.

Thu. July 30 At Foster's and others in pm. Kurven Foster professed to be saved. Meeting.

Sat. Aug. 08 Good street meeting, Dunnville. Tent all night.

Sun. Aug. 23 Largest crowd yet to tent.

Sun. Aug. 30 Did some sewing on tent after storm. Last meeting.

During October there were two weeks of children's meetings held in **Grimsby**, with Mr. Tom Wilkie. They were very successful meetings, but were terminated when Mr. Shivas received word of his father's homecall.

Tue. Oct. 13 Put ad in paper and ordered cards for meetings.

Fri. Oct. 16 Down town and got ads and tickets. Gave away tickets to children at 4 at school. At St.Catharines children's mtg.

Sat. Oct. 17 Put notices in all the stores. Made calls.

Mon. Oct. 19 Out to Beach school, with Tom Wilkie. Leo for tea. First children's meeting, 145 out. Spoke on Clock. *Those were depression days. We recall that every child who came received a loaf of bread.*

Tue. Oct. 20 Leo with us all night. We drove him to St.C. in pm. 47 at meeting, Luke 18. *Meetings continued till Thu. Oct. 29.*

Fri. Oct. 30 Got word at 5 am of dear father's sudden homecall.

Mon. Nov. 02 Getting ready for funeral at 2. R. Telfer and J. Silvester took it. Burial at Atherley. God sustained us all.

Mr. Shivas and Mr. Wilkie continued in gospel meetings at Grimsby for the rest of November.

Wed. Nov. 18 Sinclair called to see us and tell us he got saved.

"I and the Lad"

"I and the lad will go yonder and worship." Gen.22.5.

Yonder to worship the God I adore,
Yonder to sing His glad praise o'er and o'er,
Yonder to see His own blessed Son,
Yonder to ponder the work He has done;
   "I and the lad will go yonder."

Leaving behind the young men with the ass,
The cares of this world that fain would harass,
Things of this life in their place that are right,
Leaving them there far behind, out of sight;
   "I and the lad will go yonder."

Yonder to worship and then to return,
Yonder our offerings of incense to burn,
Yonder the place of His own blessed choosing,
Yonder the applause of the world gladly losing;
   "I and the lad will go yonder."

G. L. S.

Two Mites

And there came a certain poor widow, and she threw in two mites, which make a farthing. She of her want did cast in all that she had, even all her living.   Mark 12. 42-44.

Two mites which make up a farthing,
    The poor widow cast in her all,
And never a thought of starving —
    God hears the raven's call.

Our God is a God of knowledge,
    And by Him actions are weighed;
The widow had been in God's college,
    So her all in the balances laid.

He whose eyes are keen like a flame,
    Trying the children of men,
From His throne in the glory He came,
    Down to this sin-blighted scene.

Though rich, for our sakes became poor,
    Though high, yet He stooped down so low;
Shed His blood to forgiveness assure,
    That poor sinners to glory might go.

His great heart still yearns o'er His own,
    His ear is attent to their call,
How sweet is His voice from the throne,
    "This widow cast in more than they all."

                                        G. L. S.

1932

Following the death of his father on October 30, 1931, Mr. Shivas also lost his only brother, Jim, on March 12th, 1932, and his mother passed away six weeks later, on April 24th.

Moving to Grimsby made a considerable change in Mr. Shivas' labours for the Lord, due to the increasing ill health of Mrs. Shivas. It meant fewer long trips away from home, and a more concentrated effort in Southwestern Ontario. His field of endeavour included the Toronto, Hamilton, St.Catharines, and Niagara Falls area, as well as other assemblies such as Welland, Port Dover (Five Points), Straffordville, Tillsonburg, South Middleton, Embro, Chatham, and Merlin.

Many fond memories are stirred by the mention of places and people, and of series of meetings conducted in this part of Ontario.

Fri. Jan. 08 Maude not very good night. My soul, wait thou only upon God.

Sat. Feb. 06 Got dear Maude into hospital, Toronto, at 3 pm.

Sun. Feb. 14 **Toronto, Junction.** Mr. Jones came for me, and for dinner. Fred Radford's for tea. Gospel, McCartney and I.

Mon. Mar. 07 Over to house in Grimsby. Met Mr. Littleproud. J. Gunn's for dinner. Very stormy day. Called on Booths.

Sat. Mar. 12 With Jim for last time. God took him at 12.20 am. "Far better."

Tue. Mar. 15 Jim's service at 2 pm, W. P. Douglas, A. Livingstone, R. McCrory, and R. Telfer. Mother here.

Sun. Mar. 20 **Toronto, Pape Avenue.** At the feast. Gave thanks for the cup. Good meeting. Mr. Douglas ministered. Douglas and Telfer at 3. J. Sommacal and I at **Bracondale** for gospel.

Sun. Mar. 27 **Toronto Conference in Massey Hall.** Spoke to children at **Swanwick** at 3 with Jas. Farquharson.

Sun. Apr. 10 **Severn Bridge.** Read Gen. 43 in am. Canning's for dinner. Johnston's in aft. Walked 4 miles. Kett's for supper.

Sun. Apr. 24 **Orillia.** At the feast but had to leave early. Dear mother home with Christ at 1.20 pm. "Far better."

Tue. Apr. 26 Dear mother's body laid away at Atherley, at 2 pm. Service at house. Bre. J. Silvester, F. W. Watson, E. B. Steen spoke. Thank God for all His mercy.

The beginning of May saw the commencement of five weeks of gospel meetings with Mr. Ed Steen, in **Sundridge**, Ontario.

Mon. May 02 Walked to Bacon Lake up track in aft. Met Bob and Ed. Sundridge meeting, Ed and I.

Wed. May 04 Out to Eagle Lake after dinner. Had walk home. Meeting, Sundridge, Luke 18.

Sun. May 08 South River. Had walk across Chemical bridge. Ed at Sundridge, me at South River.

Mon. May 09 Down to Sundridge with J. Onlock. Calling at houses. Mrs. Hicks' for supper. Ed and I had mtg, John 5.

Thu. May 12 Visited McCabe's, Van Mere's and others, Ed and I in pm. Meeting in Sundridge.

Thu. May 26 Sundridge all night. Not feeling very well. Lovely day. McCabe's for dinner and called on quite a few in pm. Tom Erwin and I had meeting, Ps. 51 - Behold.

Mon. May 30 Sundridge in pm. First meeting in Orange Hall.

Wed. June 01 Lovely day. John Onlock and I at Sundridge visiting. Had walk. Hicks' for tea. Meeting, no lights, Joshua 20.1.

Fri. July 01 Drove Mr. & Mrs. McCrory to **Straffordville Conference**. Good meetings and a lovely day. McCrory, Wilkie, Lyon, McMullin, Touzeau, and Dobbin. All night at L. Garnham's.

Sat. July 02 At W. Jeffrey's, Port Dover. Helping with hay in pm.

Sun. July 03 **Port Dover**. Fergie's for dinner. S.S. at Jeffrey's at 3. Mtg at Port Dover at 7.45, 2 Kings 6 - Places.

Mon. July 04 Dinner at Mr. Jeffrey Sr.'s with Mr. & Mrs. A. Kitcher & Mr. & Mrs. P. Hynd. Home to Grimsby in pm.

Sat. July 23 Soo. Staying at Wright's. Thank God for all His mercy. At J. Clark's and F. West's. Street meeting at Buckley.

Sun. July 24 **Soo Ontario**. Chiarello's for dinner. Heart with door, at 3 with children. Gospel, Luke 13 - Barren fig tree.

Mon. July 25 Left Soo about 11 oc after calling on H. Smiths and others. Got to Bellaire at 5.45. Meeting, Gen. 3 - Trees.

Tue. July 26 Meeting last night in auto camp at Mancelona. Visited Hayne's at Bellaire, meeting at **Mancelona**.

Wed. July 27 Lovely day. Taking papers to homes in Mancelona. Mtg.

Thu. July 28 To Bellaire in am. Visited Siglers. Had walk to Lake of the Woods in pm. Large meeting, Math. 7.

Sun. July 31 **Bellaire**, Mich. Kept the feast at 10 oc in Benedict's home. Meeting in Antrim at 3. Meeting in home at 8, good.

Fri. Aug. 05 Cleaned car. Got 2 gallons oil down town $1.08. Leo & I left for Duluth. Got to Carlshend at 5.30. At Fogerberg's.

Sat. Aug. 06 Had walk and good sleep. Left about 7. Ate our lunch west of Iron River and got to Duluth by God's mercy at 4.30, 300 miles and no trouble all the way. J. G. Brown's all night.

Sun. Aug. 07 **Duluth**, Minn. Spoke to children at 9.30. Feast at 10.30. Gave out tracts at zoo. Gospel at 7.30.

The diary for August records a visit to Port Arthur, Ontario.

Thu. Aug. 18 Left Duluth at 8 am. Dinner at Williamson's, half way. Port Arthur at 6.30. Staying at Coldridge's. Thank God for journeying mercies.

Fri. Aug. 19 Fixing and changing tire. Leo & I got boot in tire. Visiting in pm, Richmonds and others. Mtg at night, Math. 6.6.

Sat. Aug. 20 Lovely morning. Visiting and giving out papers to houses with Mr. Coldridge in pm. Street meeting at night.

Sun. Aug. 21 **Port Arthur**, Ontario. The feast at 11.15, Leo spoke. S.S. at 12.30 - B B chart. Mtg in park at 4.20 - Peanut. Meeting in Hall at 7.45 pm.

Mon. Aug. 22 Calling at houses inviting people to meeting.

Tue. Aug. 23 Out to Cloud Bay and Stanley in pm. Meeting.

Wed. Aug. 24 Visited bro. Chis. in am at Fort William, and at McDowell's for dinner. Had walk and got lost in bush. McDowell's for supper. Good meeting, John 9 - Altogether.

Fri. Aug. 26 Left Port Arthur about 10 am and got to **Lutyen** about 3. Called on a lot of houses and had meeting in school - ABC.

Wed. Aug. 31 Left Carlshend about 10 oc. Trouble with the car, timing chain and rear end. Got to Mich. Soo about 3, and over river to Wright's all night. Prayer meeting.

There were three weeks of gospel meetings at Straffordville, Ontario, near the end of the year.

Sun. Nov. 27 Grimsby to **Straffordville** for 10 am by God's mercy. Thurston's for dinner, and L. Garnham's for all night. Meeting.

Mon. Nov. 28 Cold night. Went to schoolhouse to invite children. Children's meeting, Rom. 6.23 - Wages and Gift.

Wed. Nov. 30 Calling at houses in village. Walked to McAllister's for tea, and called on houses enroute. Walked about 6 miles.

Sat. Dec. 03 Went home after mtg. Trouble at Cayuga with car. Julius B. came and met me, and towed me home, about 1.30 am. Thank God for all His mercy.

Mon. Dec. 05 Nice day. At funeral in pm. Heard sermon in church. Awful. Meeting, Rev. 3.20 - Door in heart.

Sun. Dec. 11 Straffordville. To children, Time and Clock at 3.

Mon. Dec. 12 Talking with Lew Garnham in am. Had walk in pm, and at Croft Garnham's for tea. Opened children's meeting.

Many of us remember Mr. Shivas saying that he felt like taking off his hat every time he went by a cow in the field because the cow was serving it's Creator without rebelling, and knew enough to get on it's knees when it lay down, and when it rose up, which was more than most men did.

Mr. Don Garnham, son of Lew Garnham, tells of Mr. Shivas' keen interest in one of their cows that was sick, when he was staying at their place. On a later visit, while speaking, he was rehearsing the story about taking off his hat to a cow, when he suddenly stopped, and said, "Say, brother Garnham, that cow of yours that was sick, did it get better?"

Wed. Dec. 14 Helping fix texts for S.S. Visited McQuiggans, Everitts and Guntsons. Flewiston's for supper. Meeting.

Fri. Dec. 16 Clear and cold. Helping with S.S. prizes. Visited Claus Ludens and Scribbens and Frank McQuiggan's for tea. Mtg.

Sat. Dec. 17 Helping with S.S. prizes in am. Walked to Geo. Adlington's and Garnham's for tea.

Mon. Dec. 19 Drove Tom Wilkie to Tillsonburg. Saw J. C. McCormack. Left at 9.30. Home safely by God's mercy at noon. Got car fixed.

Fri. Dec. 23 **St. Catharines Treat**, Julius Bernardo and I went.

Thu. Dec. 29 To Toronto in am. Hugh Walker's for dinner. Steen's for tea. **Brock Ave Children's meeting**, Rom. 6.23.

Sat. Dec. 31 **Tillsonburg Conference**. J. Rouse, Innis, McCrory, Gilchrist, Lyon, Wilkie, Bruce, Miller, Hatherly.

The Outside Place

Outside of heaven, that glorious place,
Outside, descending in wonderful grace,
Outside the city, born in a town,
Outside the inn, in a manger laid down.
    God's only One - Outside!

Outside the land of God's wonderful choice,
Outside, to Egypt, obeying His voice,
Outside, He was driven to die from His youth,
Outside, fulfilling each letter of truth.
    God's obedient One - Outside!

Outside Jerusalem, still He must stay,
Outside Judea, the enemy's prey,
Outside, preserved in so wicked a scene,
Outside, in Galilee, called Nazarene.
    God's hated One - Outside.

Outside He wandered, no house and no home,
Outside, as a stranger and pilgrim to roam;
Outside with no place to lay His blest head,
Outside, healing sick and raising the dead.
    God's suffering One - Outside!

Outside they left him, each homeward went,
Outside on the mountain the whole night He spent,
Outside to wrestle with God and to pray,
Outside, wet with dew and with frost, there He lay,
    God's lowly One - Outside!

Outside, He prayed in the garden alone,
Outside, to agonize, labour and moan;
Outside, while disciples sorrow and sleep,
Outside, they leave Him alone there to weep,
    God's lonely One - Outside!

Outside He was led as a Lamb there to die,
Outside He stood there with not a friend nigh,
Outside they led Him, outside the gate,
Outside — the object of suffering and hate.
God's gentle One - Outside!

Outside, on the cross with the thorns on His brow,
Outside of heaven and earth, see Him now;
Outside, forsaken by God and by man,
Outside, survey such a scene if you can.
God's patient One - Outside!

Outside He cried with a loud voice and died,
Outside, behold Him, a King crucified,
Outside He paid the debt, setting us free,
Outside I see Him there dying for me.
God's redeeming One - Outside!

Outside they buried Him in a clean place,
Outside He rose again, of sin not a trace,
Outside He led those disciples so few,
Outside He ascended far up out of view.
God's risen One - Outside!

Outside of this world despised by mankind,
Outside sinners leave Him, and wander on blind,
Outside is my place, outside the camp,
Outside, He calls in grace, trim every lamp.
God's rejected One - Outside!

Inside He'll take us soon, inside to Glory,
Inside there still is room. Oh tell the story;
Outside He came for me, praise His blest Name,
Inside with Him to be forever the same.
Forever together - Inside!

G. L. S.

1933

Five weeks of gospel meetings were held in Grimsby, Ontario, with Mr. George Gould Jr. early in 1933.

Sat. Jan. 07 J. Bernardo called. G. Gould coming for meetings. Made calls in aft. inviting people. MB&I had walk. Cold & windy.

Sun. Jan. 08 **Grimsby**. Geo. Gould and I had first meeting.

Mon. Jan. 09 Nice lot out to mtg last night. Made calls at houses in afternoon. Meeting.

Thu. Jan. 26 Rested some. Put soles on overshoes. Geo. Gould and I called on Booths, Gunns, Duffields, Herns. Meeting.

Wed. Feb. 08 Cold day. Met G. G. at Post Office at 3. Called on Miss Teeft and Stewarts. Meeting.

Sun. Feb. 19 Grimsby. Large mtg in am. G. Gould and W. Agnew spoke. Rushton's for dinner. Large gospel meeting.

It was during these meetings that brother Robert Booth and his two brothers and three sisters were saved.

Their father, William Booth, had gone to school with Mr. Shivas when they were boys in Orillia. In 1929 the Booth family moved near Grimsby, and through a local Christian, Mr. James Gunn, the parents renewed the schoolday friendship. They started attending the Gospel Hall, and were saved in 1932.

Stan Booth recalls going by the Gospel Hall with a load of hay, and asking his father what kind of a place that was. Stan said he knew lots of Halls, but not a Gospel Hall.

When the above meetings began, the Booth children came to listen to the Gospel, and all six were saved, in the following order, Art, Evelyn, Robert (on Jan. 26), Stan (on Jan. 28), Violet, and Hilda.

Art's high school teacher, Miss Aiton, asked him where he was going every night. He told her, she came, and was saved at that time. Also Mrs. Jim Pirie, and the Hern family, among others.

The Grass Never Grew Greener!

In the spring Mr. Shivas made visits to London, Chatham, Merlin, Windsor, and Detroit.

Tue. Apr. 04 At **London** for night mtg, Ps. 73. 22-24.

Fri. Apr. 07 Called to see Ed Cossey. Meeting at night.

Sat. Apr. 08 Mr. Keller and I at A. Gratton's, Forrester's and Cook's for visit. To **Munsey Reserve** for meeting. Good time.

Sun. Apr. 09 London. At C. Plewes'. Meeting.

Mon. Apr. 10 Met R. McCrory and T. Wilkie at **Chatham**. Meeting.

Wed. Apr. 12 Staying at Watson's. Called on Phillips and McDowells. Spoke at Old People's Home at 6.30, Gen 7 - Come, and in Hall at 7 pm.

Thu. Apr. 13 Came to **Merlin**. Staying at Will Brown's. Called on Shivas'. *(Relatives who lived near Fletcher, Ont.)* Meeting.

Sat. Apr. 15 Down to lake in am. Left Brown's at 2 oc. Called at Jack Miner's place, Kingsville, and saw birds. Got to Detroit in time for tea at Popplestone's. At Fluter's in evening.

Sun. Apr. 16 **Detroit, Central**. At H. Gillow's. Mtg at Pontiac.

Mon. Apr. 17 Out with F. Mehl in am and for dinner. Called on Ruth & Walkers. Bobser's for tea. Dr. Cameron's in evening.

Wed. Apr. 19 At **Windsor**. At Russel's and saw Bro. McCloy. Meeting.

Fri. Apr. 21 Lovely day. Saw D. Young and Mr. Bendle and called on Mrs. Skelding and Allens. Met Mr. Lancaster and Mr. Ried.

Sun. Apr. 23 Windsor. Lever's for dinner. Mtg at 3 for children. Gospel at night, Luke 14 - Supper.

Mon. Apr. 24 Had funeral at 2 pm, Mrs. Ried, read Ex. 2 - Groans. Drove to Merlin for night meeting.

Tue. Apr. 25 Met C. McCracken. Left Merlin at 9.30. Dinner at McCormack's, Tillsonburg. Home at 5.45. Thank God.

Sun. May 28 MB&I drove to **Guelph** in am. Read Gen. 12 - Going on still. At Walsh's for dinner. Bible Class, John 7. Guthrie's for tea. Gospel. Home at 9.15. God is good.

Thu. June 01 Working at car at Albert Eagle's, gaskets and timing.

Fri. June 02 Steen's for dinner. Called for Mr. & Mrs. Gilchrist, met N. Truman at Whitby. All at **Victoria Road Conf.** At Bell's.

Fri. June 09 I left for Sarnia at 11.25, Julius Bernardo came with me. Met Ormer Sprunt at Clappison's Corners at 12.30. Sarnia at 5.30. Prayer meeting.

Sat. June 10 **Sarnia Conf.** Staying at Taylor's. Also Mr. Cox and Clifford from Mervin, Sask. R. Telfer spoke in am, 2 Kings 8.1. Douglas, Barr, Watson, Baillie, Duncan, W. B. Johnson, Stewart, Winemiller, Foster, Touzeau. Very warm weather.

Mon. June 12 Ormer Sprunt and I made call at Hall. Dinner at S. Steele's and came to **Watford** after dinner. Made calls and mtg.

Tue. June 13 At Telford Thompson's all night. We went with him to Petrolia with strawberries. At Mrs. Tanner's for supper, mtg.

Wed. June 14 Came to **Forest** for dinner at Burnham's. Called on Colin Johnston. Henry Hodgson's for supper. Had walk by lake. Mtg.

Thu. June 15 Called on J. Johnston, Rawlings and came to Grand Bend. Wilkie's for dinner. Home to Grimsby before 6. Meeting.

During the summer, six weeks of gospel meetings were held in a tent at **Dunnville**, Ontario, with brother Robert McCrory.

Wed. July 12 Made text for tent, Luke 19.10.

Fri. July 14 Getting ready to leave for Dunnville. Left about 1 oc. Got our tent pitched in tourist camp. Boys came from St. C. at 8.30 and we got large tent pitched.

Sat. July 15 Maude & I over at tent in am, fixing it up. Heavy rain in pm. Men got lights connected. Street mtg at night.

Sun. July 16 **Welland** in morning. Dunnville street meeting.

Mon. July 17 Did some work at tent. Mr. McCrory & I. At tent for dinner. Made some calls in pm. Meeting for children.

Wed. July 19 Lovely morning. Fixed bed. **Looking for car keys.** Called on Stewarts and Smiths and other houses. Meeting.

This reminds us of a day some years later when Mr. and Mrs. Shivas missed the car keys while at the cottage. They began to search for them after lunch in view of going to Chapman Valley prayer meeting that evening. The whole afternoon was spent turning the place upside down but without success.

Finally, in desperation, Mr. Shivas went into the bedroom and dropped to his knees by the bed to seek the Lord's help. Just as his hands rested on the covers, he felt a lump in the bed, and lo and behold, there were the keys.

Mr. Shivas said, "Humph, if only I had prayed about it in the first place, I could have saved all that trouble!"

Sat. July 22 Changed and fixed tire. Got shavings, new fan belt 50c. Working at tent in aft. Levelling ground and putting down shavings. R. McCrory here for supper. He and I at street mtg.

Thu. Aug. 03 Raining through night and till noon. Over to big tent, loosened poles and saw Mr. McCrory. At houses. Good mtg.

Sun. Aug. 20 St.Catharines in am. Dunnville to mtg. Nice few in.

Sat. Aug. 26 Lovely day. Working all am at big tent. Truck came at 2.45. We got small tent loaded and Mr. McCrory came with us to Grimsby about 6.15. Thank God for all His mercy.

Sat. Sep. 30 Left at 2.30 pm for Embro, Dan Steele and I. Embro at 6.30. Marsh's all night. Had walk.

Sun. Oct. 01 **Embro**. Chester Marsh's for dinner and supper. Had walk. Meeting in school, Rom 3. - ABC.

Mon. Oct. 02 Around mill in am. Drove with Marshs to Stratford. Called on Mrs. Eyce, Millers, Petersons, Larters.

Tue. Oct. 03 Around mill in am. Chester's for dinner. Left at 3.30 for home. D. Steele & family & I. Lots of tire trouble. Home 11.

A Pleading Saviour

There's a Saviour who's pleading in Glory
Pleading still for lost sinners to come;
While we tell out the blessed old story
Of His love that refuses not one.

Once He lay down His life on Calvary's mountain
Shed His blood to set guilty sinners free
While He pleads come and wash at the Fountain
Come and wash while He's pleading for thee.

To the tune,
There's an old spinning wheel in the parlor.

G. L. S.

1934

The year 1934 commenced with four weeks of gospel meetings in Straffordville with Mr. John Govan, followed by three weeks in Grimsby.

Wed. Jan. 10 Cleaned car and changed markers. Left at 2.30. Called at Jarvis, F. Lampkin's. **Straffordville** at 5. Had walk. Meeting, J. Govan and I.

Thu. Jan. 11 Staying with J. Govan at J. McQuiggan's. Made many calls. At school - 2 sons. At hall, 1 Cor. 14 - Sounds.

Fri. Jan. 12 Will Beckett called. Called on M. Nelles and Croft Garnhams. Thurston's for tea. Large crowd, 100. Mtg, Jer. 18.

Sat. Jan. 13 Snowy day. To T'burg in pm. Supper at McCormack's. Ordered suit $20. Called on Irelands, who lost their brother.

Sun. Jan. 14 Straffordville. At Willard McAllister's for dinner and tea. S.S. at 3. Large gospel mtg.

Tue. Jan. 16 Walked down to W. Humphrey's before dinner. With them to Murray Wilson's for dinner. Walked part way back. Supper at Humphrey's with Steve and Beatrice. Meeting.

Thu. Jan. 18 Anderson's for dinner. Walked 5 miles. Called on quite a few houses, and at Underhill's for supper. Mtg, Rom. 3.

Fri. Jan. 26 Got hair cut in am. Pete McQ.'s for dinner. Called on Esseltines, Tribes, Guntsons, Devries. Thurston's for supper. Good meeting, Luke 18 - Trusted.

Sun. Feb. 04 **Grimsby.** J. Govan spoke. Us all at Bernardo's for dinner and supper. Prayer mtg 6.30. Fairly good first meeting.

Tue. Feb. 06 Nice bright day, but cold. Putting signs of mtgs in stores. Lit fire in Hall. Cold night. Meeting, Eph. 2 - Without.

Tue. Feb. 13 Splitting and piling wood in basement. Repairing sweeper. Out in pm with tracts to houses in hollow and Ontario St. J. Gunn's for supper. Cold night. Mtg, Matt. 12 - Uttermost.

Wed. Feb. 14 Called at houses on Oak St, Depot St, and visited Mrs. Felker and Mrs. LePage. Not large mtg, Isa. 1 - People.

Thu. Feb. 15 Lovely bright day. Called on Johnstons, Heddons, Sniders, Stadelmyers, and houses with tracts.

Mon. Feb. 26 J. Bernardo called for John Govan about 8 am and we saw him off on train for home at 9.25. God is faithful.

Sun. Mar. 11 **Port Dover**. F. Lampkin's for dinner. He & I called on 14 homes inviting people to meeting. Home safely, thank God.
Sun. Apr. 08 Our 25th wedding anniversary. I drove to **Straffordville** alone in am. Late for mtg (car not right.) J. McQuiggan's for dinner and tea. S. S. at 3. Walked to meeting.
Tue. Apr. 10 John & I at Pete's for dinner. Up to Caulton. Visited Andersons, E. Underhills, Bernice McAllister & Mrs. McA. Sr., and at Jim Thomas' for supper. Walked. Nice lot out to meeting.
Wed. Apr. 11 Very wet night and rainy still. Showers of blessing. Called on Touzeaus in aft, R. Coopers, Oatmans, Bert Brooks'.

Tue. May 01 Drove to **Midland** by 7.15. Meeting, John 3.
Wed. May 02 All night at Swales' with G. Johnston. Over at Jas. Gunn's. Gordon & I walked out to Crull's. Swales' for tea. Mtg.
Thu. May 03 Fred Boyce did little work on car. Got 5 collars, $1. Swales' for dinner. Called on Stewarts and Elmer Blackmeres, Gunns. Swales' for tea. David Scott at meeting.
Sat. May 05 McCaw's for dinner. Gordon and I called on Borlands, Mrs. Prentice, and at Fenton's for supper. Called on Mrs. Mackie and Eunice Fenton in evening.
Tue. May 29 Staying at Manning's, **Creemore**. At Hisey's for dinner. Called on Groves, Bulmers. Mackie's for supper. McCaws came from Midland, also Armstrongs from Sunnidale. Hall full.
Fri. June 01 **Victoria Road Conference**. D. R. Scott, Watson, Silvester, Gilchrist, Blackwood, Nugent, Miller, Widdifield, Bruce, G. Johnston, Baillie, Gould. Good weather and meetings.
Sat. June 02 Fred Nugent, R. Bruce, and I went to see Russell Forman's family, whose baby had died.
Sun. June 03 F. Nugent and G. Johnston spoke to children at 1 oc. D. Scott, G. Johnston and J. Blackwood spoke at 2.30. F. Nugent, Ben Widdifield, and F. G. Watson in gospel. To Orillia after.

Fri. June 08 Cooler. J. Govan and I at Pete McQuiggan's for dinner. Called on Andersons, Essletines. Meeting.
Sat. June 09 Looked up Elvie McQ. J. Thomas' for dinner. At Geo. Adlington's, L. Garnham's seeing about baptism. Neville's in pm.
Sun. June 10 **Straffordville**. Large mtg. W. McAllister's for dinner. At 3, baptized 9 in the name of the Lord Jesus.
Mon. June 11 Left at 10 am. C. Millard as far as Delhi.
Tue. June 19 Heavy rains. Thank God. Voting day. God is over all.

There were six weeks of gospel meetings in the summer at Port Dover, Ontario, with Mr. Fred Nugent.

Sun. June 24 Drove to **Port Dover**. F. Nugent spoke in am. Calling at homes in pm. First gospel meeting, F. Nugent and I.

Tue. June 26 Out with Will Jeffrey at hay in am. Mtg at school at 2.45, 15 children. Made many calls. Porter's for supper.

Fri. July 06 Called on Collins, Belbecks, Porter's for supper. Called on Ryersies. Children's mtg, Fred spoke, I opened.

Sun. July 08 Corbett's for the day. Mtg with children at Kiwanis camp at 4.30. Good meeting in Hall.

Wed. July 18 Beryl Jeffrey professed to be saved. May it be of God.

Thu. July 19 Mtg at Children's Shelter at 3. Five Points at night.

Mon. July 23 Long talk with Mrs. Lampkin and Morley professed to be saved. Children's meeting.

Thu. July 26 Children's mtg at 3. Mr. T. Dobbin at night meeting.

Fri. July 27 Large children's meeting. Hall full, some strangers.

Sun. Aug. 12 Last Sunday. Baptism at 3.30. Fred preached. I opened and did baptizing, W. Swenson & wife, Mrs. Young, & Paul Jeffrey. Gospel at night. Mrs. Parks professed.

In the fall there were three weeks of gospel meetings at Sault Ste. Marie, Ontario, with Mr. Lorne McBain.

Sat. Sep. 01 At Clark's in am. Called to see Mrs. Collins. Conf. Prayer mtg. McGeachy, Silvester, Govan, Stewart, McBain, Dobbin.

Wed. Sep. 05 Took T. Dobbin to ferry. Called at Davis' and saw J. Silvester, and L. McBain. First mtg, Luke 20 - What shall I do?

Thu. Sep. 06 Mr. & Mrs. Simm of Chicago here all night. Dinner at Pete Chiarello's. Tea at Delubo's. Meeting.

Mon. Sep. 10 Visited Hurley Srs. and at Mrs. McIntyre's for supper. Had broken axle after mtg. Good meeting, 2 professed.

Tue. Sep. 11 Worked at car till 3 am. Jimmie Clark and I till noon today. Hasting's for supper. Meeting, Mark 5.

Wed. Sep. 12 Dinardo's for dinner. Working at car, Jimmie and I. Called on Mrs. B. Hurley, Mrs. R. Hurley, and Mrs. Collins.

Thu. Sep. 13 Lorne and I at Bert Hurley's for dinner. At Earl Hill's barber shop. F. West's for supper. Meeting.

Sun. Sep. 16 Soo. At Davis'. Children at 3. Large gospel mtg.

Tue. Sep. 18 <u>God is faithful</u>. Mrs. Parr's for dinner. Made calls. Had
walk up to locks and saw boat go through. At A. West's.
Wed. Sep. 19 At Mrs. Smith's funeral. Spoke at Hall, Lorne McBain at
grave. Clark's for tea. Meeting.
Thu. Sep. 20 Wet day. Called on Mrs. Patterson. Large meeting.

Wed. Dec. 26 Grimsby. Serious Railroad accident at Dundas last
night, 15 killed, 40 injured. (*Some readers will remember this.*)

Give and Take

And from thence, when the brethren heard of us, they came
to meet us as far as Appii forum, and The three taverns:
whom when Paul saw, he thanked God, and took courage.

Acts 28.15

Give thanks to God for all His grace,
For all He bids our souls embrace,
Salvation to our sinful race,
Give to Him the glory.
Thanks to God is due His Name,
Thanks for Christ His Son who came
Down from Heaven to bear our shame,
Thanks for all the story.

Take the courage that He gives,
Take from Him who all forgives,
Take from Him who died and lives
Courage! hearts that break.
Courage as we prove His love,
Courage coming from above,
Courage that will never move
GIVE thanks and courage TAKE.

G. L. S.

1935

In January of 1935, Mr. Shivas had nine weeks of gospel meetings at Beamsville, Ont., in the home of Russel Davis, a fine native Indian man. He and his father, Eli, were first reached when Mr. Shivas had gospel meetings in the Orange Hall, Grimsby, in 1928. Mr. Eli Davis' outstanding testimony in the town is illustrated by an article in the Grimsby Independent newspaper, given later in the book.

Sun. Jan. 20 Trumans & W. Gunn here for dinner. Eli, Russel & I to **Oswegan Indian Reserve** for gospel with Brantford brethren.

Mon. Jan. 21 Changed tire. First meeting in **Beamsville**.

Thu. Jan. 24 Very cold. Calling on houses in Beamsville. Mtg.

Fri. Jan. 25 With Russel D. to see Mr. Fletcher & Bomberrys.

Wed. Feb. 13 Beamsville. Over 40 out tonight. Good meeting.

Thu. Feb. 21 Beamsville. Mr A. Osman may have gotten saved.

Mon. Apr. 22 **Toronto**. At Eagle's in am. Got horn fixed. Albert Eagle and I called on neighbour. Saved!

Sat. June 01 **Victoria Road Conference**. Spoke Sunday night.

Tue. June 04 Mr. Gilchrist and I left 10 am. At **Bobcaygeon**.

Wed. June 05 Left B., came to Joe Parrington's via Lindsay. Saw Harry Stone. On to **Peterborough**. Meeting.

Thu. June 06 At Wager's all night. Called on Turners, Kennedys, and Blackwoods. Came on to **Lang**. At Edward's. Meeting.

Fri. June 07 Came to **Campbellford** for dinner at W. Gibson's with Mr. Bryant. Called on Bays, 93, and others. Meeting.

Sat. June 08 To Perth. Dinner at Regis' and came on to Ottawa.

Sun. June 09 **Ottawa**. Mtg in Orange Hall. S.S. at 3, & gospel.

Mon. June 10 Met Mr. Hume at 12.30 for dinner. Saw through Parliament Buildings. Heard Bennett and McKenzie King.

Wed. June 12 Came on to **Oshawa**. Barlow's for dinner. Meeting.

Late in the year four weeks of gospel meetings were held in Burlington, Ontario, with Mr. John Gilchrist.

Mon. Nov. 11 First meeting at **Burlington**, at A. Bush's.

Mon. Nov. 25 Seeing Mr. Gates at school re Legion Hall and other places we looked at with no success.

Wed. Nov. 27 Meetings continue at Burlington. 40 out tonight.

The following editorial appeared in the Grimsby Independent newspaper, sometime in 1950.

We All Need Converting

I am not very strong on the different kinds of religion which flourish in this town and in other places, because I am a busy man. But all the same I am a religious man. I even started a competition once for a place among the most religious men of the town, and if the angels would only take away a few more of my competitors, I might even reach the top.

But in the meantime there is one man I am afraid of, and some of you may even guess who he is. He is a minister of the Gospel, and has been here longer than any other reverend gentleman of the town, now that the chief of all my competitors is gone. This minister is Mr. George L. Shivas, of the Gospel Hall on Adelaide Street, and of many other places to which he goes to spread the Gospel. I must admit that I have not often heard him preaching, but I meet him on the street, and other people meet him who know a good man when they see one, and I know the kind of life he leads. When I have a talk with him he says some of the things that other people don't say, but which perhaps they ought to say, if they were not so keen on keeping their light under a bushel basket.

Now my chief business is that of printing a newspaper every Thursday morning, and to do this I read other papers of all kinds, and just lately I came across a piece in a really religious paper published in Toronto, that good city, and if this piece is not about my friend, Mr. Shivas, I lose my guess.

It tells about a godly minister who wrote a poem called "How, When, Where.", and in this poem, my friend, if my guess is right, tells about his conversion, how it happened, the day of the month, and the year, and the very place, with street and number. And it explains the difference from what he was before this happened to what he was afterwards, and is.

And the Toronto writer goes on to place our humble townsman along with Bunyan and other high saints of long ago. And I second the motion. For I know that most of us need all the converting we can get.

1936

Tue. Jan. 28 McKenzie King's funeral. Public holiday.

Sat. Feb. 01 Drove down to dear Fred Dunkley's funeral in St.C. in aft. Took N. Truman and Davis'. Supper at Tempest's. Home by 7.

Wed. Mar. 18 Orillia. Left for **Waubaushene** at 3.30. Heel's for supper. Bible Rdg, Eph. 5 - Walk, Love, Light.

Thu. Mar. 19 At Wm. Heel's all night. Called on Weavers. Went on to Victoria Harbour. Called on L. Ball, R. Heels & Brothersons. Children's meeting at **Port McNicoll** - HOME. At Jim Heel's.

Fri. Mar. 20 To Midland in am. Silvester's for dinner. J. Pearson there. **Waverley** for children's mtg with M. Paul - SHEEP.

Fri. Apr. 10 Nice day. Left at 12.30 for **Toronto**. Had blowout near Oakville. At **Brock Ave.** Conference.

Sun. May 10 Drove alone to **Woodstock**, 11 am E.S.T. At R. E. Tree's for dinner and supper. S.S. at 3 - ABC. Gospel, 7.15 pm - John 11. Home at 11.30 pm D.S.T.

Fri. Dec. 11 Doctoring sore throat. Heard ex king speak.
This would be the abdication speech of the Prince of Wales, clearing the way for George 6th, our present Queen's father, to take the throne.

Sat. Dec. 12 Eli Davis and I left at 5.30, and got to **Oswegan** for S.S. Treat at 7. At James LaDrew's all night.

Sun. Dec. 13 Eli Davis and I at **Embro** for morning meeting. At Marsh's for dinner. Meeting at the Reserve. Home at 11.

Sat. Dec. 19 Left at 2.30 for Clyde. Snow. With E. St.Clair to Galt for all night.

Sun. Dec. 20 **Clyde.** More snow. Reeve's for dinner and supper. S. S. Isa. 30 - Arithmetic. Gospel mtg alone, Luke 2 - Saviour. Home safely by God's mercy about 10.30. Roads heavy part of way.

April 16, 1937

I hail once more the happy morn
When first my heart did sing and pray,
My precious soul anew was born,
Thirty one years ago today.

He Who on Calvary died to save
A sinner, lost, undone, astray,
Himself and every good He gave
And safely led us in the way.

He changes not through all the years,
More precious now He is by far.
He cheers my heart and dries my tears,
And guides me where green pastures are.

I praise the Lord as I look back,
Remembering all the happy way.
No 'good thing' now my soul doth lack,
Though it's thirty one years ago today.

Soon He will come to call us home,
We'll hear the shout and fly away.
Our longing hearts cry 'Saviour, come,'
We then shall hail the happiest day.

G. L. S.

1937

Sun. Jan. 24 Hamilton, McNabb St. S. Gilmour and I had gospel meeting. Roads icy, but got home safely. <u>Thank God</u>.

Sun. Jan. 31 Straffordville, 10.30 am. Mr. J. McQuiggan and I had Norris baby's funeral at King's Lake. Read John 19 - It is finished. Bad roads. F. Sheldrake and I had gospel meeting.

Tue. Feb. 09 J. J. Rouse here in Grimsby, also G. G. Johnston. Out visiting at homes with tracts. Mr. Rouse for supper and night.

Thu. Feb. 11 Working at Hall most of day, lining back room. Gordon Johnston with me in gospel meetings.

Tue. Feb. 16 Did homes on Oak, Elm, Mountain, Robinson Streets and in the hollow, and John St.

Sun. Mar. 07 Grimsby. Last gospel meeting with Gordon Johnston.

Wed. Mar. 24 Russel Davis and I to St.Catharines for glass for Hall window. <u>Stormy</u>.

Wed. May 12 Coronation of King George 6th and Queen Elizabeth.

Sun. Aug. 08 Came to Arnstein. S.S. at Pt. Loring. At Bernardo's. Street meeting - NEWS.

Mon. Aug. 09 At Jas. Rogerson's all night. Mtg at E. Foreshew's.

Tue. Aug. 10 Out with Jim R. on lake in boat in am. Mtg at night.

Wed. Aug. 11 Rogerson's away huckleberrying. Archie's for dinner. Bottrell's for tea. Meeting, 2 Kings 6 - Axehead.

Thu. Aug. 12 Wet day. Made crowbar. Made calls down road & at E. Foreshew's for supper. Large meeting, John 5 - Helpless man.

Fri. Aug. 13 With Jim down to his shelter. Supper at C. Culin's.

Sun. Aug. 15 Arnstein. Dan Sommacal & I had gospel meeting.

Mon. Aug. 16 Street meeting last night. Came on up to Jas. Rogerson's, West Road. Meeting.

Tue. Aug. 17 Helping draw in hay and oats all day. Very warm. Mtg.

Wed. Aug. 18 Sommacal's for dinner, Cudmore's for tea. Meeting.

Sun. Aug. 22 Arnstein. Baptism in aft. Maestri's for dinner. Head's for supper. Mtg, Jer. 52.

Tue. Aug. 24 Down to Pt. Loring with Mr. Birch and made calls. Thompson's for dinner. At the mill. Foreshew's for supper. Mtg.

Wed. Aug. 25 At Ben Brown's for dinner. Visited B. Foreshew, Jake Brown. Had walk down near lake, and at C. Culin's. Meeting.
Thu. Aug. 26 Up East Road all day with Stanley Foreshew. R. Bain's for dinner. At Curry's and Brooks'. S. Foreshew's for supper.
Fri. Aug. 27 Very warm days. Helped Jim cut some oats. Mtg. Home.
Fri. Sep. 10 Arnstein Conference. Silvester, Watson, Widdifield, Livingstone, Bruce, Draper, Joyce, Johnston, Paul, Miller, Baillie.
Sat. Sep. 11 Staying at R. Culin's. Wet and cold. Real good spirit and wisdom in the meetings.
Sun. Sep. 12 Cool but lovely day. Opened S.S. for M. Paul. Gospel at night at South River, Watson and I.
Tue. Sep. 14 At Orillia. Saw new Hall.

Mon. Oct. 11 Thanksgiving Day! Hamilton Conference. Regis' and Watsons, Chatham, J. McQuiggan, and C. Soper with us all night. All of us at the Conference.
I recall the abundance of fresh fruit that was being passed around in the Shivas' home for the visitors to enjoy. Mr. Shivas said several times very casually, "Oh yes, my father grows all this and gives it to me." It took me a while to realize he meant his Heavenly Father.

At the end of the year there were three weeks of gospel meetings at Grassie, a small community south of Grimsby, Ontario, with Mr. Tom Wilkie.
Fri. Nov. 26 Made calls up mtn. Arranged for Hall at Grassie, D.V. Norman Truman and I at meeting.
Sat. Nov. 27 Saw Earls, Rumbles, Hills. M&I up to Grassie in aft and made some calls. Phoned Tom W. at Hamilton.
Sun. Nov. 28 Grimsby. Tom W. came. First meeting at Grassie.
Mon. Nov. 29 Up mtn in aft and made calls. Mtg, John 11.
Tue. Nov. 30 Made sign in am for mtgs. Clear and cold wind. Up to Grassie in aft and made calls. Nice few out to meeting.
Thu. Dec. 02 Clear and cold. Tom and I up to Grassie. Called at 2 schools and other places. Nice few out to meeting.
Fri. Dec. 03 Children's meeting, 50 all told.
Sat. Dec. 04 Tom and I left at 6 am for Sarnia. Snow. Got in ditch near Sarnia but God had mercy on us. Funeral - Ps. 116.
Sun. Dec. 05 Forest. Left at 1 pm. Safe journey. Home at 6. Prayer meeting and at Grassie for gospel meeting.

Fri. Dec. 10 Russel Davis called. Called on Blacks, Merritts. Davis' for supper. Children's meeting - Heart with door.
Thu. Dec. 16 Still rainy and icy, but soft. Tom & I at Cowan's, Blanchard's, Black's. Meeting, Luke 2 - Saviour.
Mon. Dec. 20 Good meeting last night. Thank God. <u>Others saved</u>.
Sat. Dec. 25 Christmas Day. All at home. Heard the King speak at 10. Nice happy day together. Thank God. M&I had walk to lake.

Life's Mortgage

God holds the mortgage on our life,
Advancing more, as time rolls on,
To cover strain and stress and strife
And every care, till days are gone.

He has the right, the cause is plain,
The upkeep to investigate,
Though some the privilege disdain
To let Him enter soon or late.

The interest should be kept intact,
The principal reduced should be,
But oh, how slow we are to act,
Or pay the Heavenly Mortgagee.

The place is all let go to rack,
The house soon shows the sore abuse,
In sad distress God gets it back,
Although it is but little use.

The Grass Never Grew Greener!

But He has found a way of grace
Through Christ to pardon all our sin,
And renovate the sin-stained place,
And put a newborn tenant in.

For Jesus precious cleansing blood
Can wash and make us white as snow;
Such is the virtue of that blood,
That not a sin nor stain can show.

The mortgage will be cancelled sure,
Paid up in full beyond all loss
By Him who did our sins endure,
And settled all on Calvary's cross.

How sad it is in many a case
That those who all His claims reject,
Despising all God's love and grace,
So great salvation still neglect.

Remember all His tender love,
He died for sin and then arose;
In judgment coming from above,
That mortgage He may soon foreclose.

Grimsby, 1954.   G.L.S.

144

1938

The year 1938 began with Mr. Shivas and Mr. Wilkie back at Grassie for another five weeks of gospel meetings, accompanied by blessing.

Mon. Jan. 03 Tom Wilkie and I at **Grassie**. Smiths saved.

Wed. Jan. 12 Lot of snow. Testimony mtg, 20 brethren from Hamilton and St.Catharines.

Mon. Jan. 17 Very stormy, snow & cold. Roads very heavy. No mtg.

Fri. Jan. 21 Out visiting. Children's meeting. I opened.

Wed. Jan. 26 Stormy day. Brethren from Simcoe came, testimony mtg.

Sat. Jan. 29 Tom & I drove to St.C, and N. Falls. Saw collapsed bridge, sang, 'On Christ the solid rock I stand.'

Fri. Feb. 04 Lovely morning. Not cold. Mtg at #20 school, and at Grassie school. Tom had children's meeting.

Sun. Feb. 06 Grimsby. Me at Mountain school. Tom at Grassie. Night meeting in our Hall, Acts 12.

Thu. Feb. 10 M&I at M. Blanchard's for dinner. Murray professed to be saved. God grant it's real! Good meeting.

Seven weeks of gospel meetings followed at St.Catharines, Ontario, with Mr. Tom Wilkie.

Sun. Feb. 20 First meeting at **St.Catharines**, Tom and I.

Tue. Mar. 01 Milder. C. Keller left for Toronto with C. Winters. Tom and I at 100 houses. Beckett's for supper. Mtg, Acts 4.

Tue. Mar. 08 At Bremmer's, Georing's, Campbell's, Vansickle's.

Mon. Mar. 14 Visiting. Pearson's for supper. Nice lot out to mtg.

Tue. Mar. 15 Mrs. Lambley's for dinner. Many calls. Mtg, Luke 18.

Thu. Mar. 17 Many calls. Warden's, Port Dalhousie for supper.

Fri. Mar. 18 Called on Notleys, James'. J. Pirie's for supper.

Mon. Mar. 21 Lovely day. First of spring. "Oh to see God's good hand in salvation." Low's for supper. Meeting - Persuade.

Tue. Mar. 22 McLaren's for supper. Meeting, Prov. 26 - Ruin.

Fri. Mar. 25 Tom & I at G. McIntee's, Bremner's, Murray's. Tempest Sr's. for supper. Children's mtg at 7, Tom. Meeting at 8, Amos 8 - Anxious souls. Good prayer meetings.

Thu. Mar. 31 Dull and raining. Visited Notleys, McIntees, Lows, and supper at Patterson's, Port Weller. Large mtg with help.

Fri. Apr. 01 Tom and I at Deluco's, Thomas', McGarvie's, Townson's for supper. Nice lot out to mtg, Lev. 19.20 - Seek.

Tue. Apr. 05 Still cool. God is faithful. Hope thou in Him. Visited Geo. McIntee. Notley saved? A. Piper's for supper. J. McGarvie saved.

Thu. Apr. 07 Jim Booth's for dinner, Tom & I. Called on McKays, V. McIntees, Bairds, and others on Hill. Low's for supper. Mtg.

Sun. Apr. 10 MB&I to St.C in am. Grassie at 3. Last mtg at St. C.

Sat. May 21 **Midland Conference**. Spoke word at night, Ps. 96 - Beauty and Strength.

Sun. May 22 Large meetings and a lovely day. Helped M. Paul at children's meeting. Gave out hymn 214. John Smythe saved.

Mon. May 23 Took Mr. Blackwood to Peterboro and came on to Edward's, Lang, all night.

Tue. May 24 Clear but cold. **Lang Conference**. Spoke from Ex. 17 - Rock, in am. At 2.30, Math. 18, Ecc. 4 - Fellowship, and - Mighty to save, Isa. 63. Edward's all night.

Wed. May 25 Came to **Campbellford** in pm. At Hall's for supper and all night. Mtg in Hall, Isa. 42 - 4 things that never fail.

Thu. May 26 Hall's all night. Gibson's for dinner. Back to Lang in aft. Fitchett's for supper. Edward's all night. Meeting.

Sun. July 17 **South River**. Baptism at 2.30. Baptized 3. R. Fenton and I shared the gospel meeting.

The year ended with four weeks of gospel meetings at **Niagara Falls**, Ontario.

Mon. Nov. 21 To Simcoe and Embro for Mrs. J. Marsh's funeral. Spoke at grave. On to N. Falls for gospel meeting.

Tue. Nov. 22 T. Warden's all night. Over to Fisher's in am, got defroster put on, also sunvisor. A. Smith & I at houses. Mtg.

Wed. Nov. 23 Snow. To N. Falls at 2. J. Bacon & I at houses. Mtg.

Thu. Nov. 24 C. Pinches and I at houses. Wurster's for tea. Mtg.

Fri. Nov. 25 Cold and damp. D. Hodgin for Prestone in car. Got sign at Hall. Albert Smith and I at houses. Pinches' for supper.

Sat. Nov. 26 Home safely last night. Thank God.

Tue. Nov. 29 Out with Arthur King. At Bacon's and many houses with tracts. King's for supper. Good number out. Mtg - In no wise.

Wed. Nov. 30 Dull & mild. Mrs. Shepherd's for dinner. At houses with tracts. Wurster's for supper. Mtg, Mark 5 - Woman.

Thu. Dec. 01 At Fisher's for dinner. At houses with tracts. Sprained ankle. Rolph's for supper. Mtg, Jer. 18 - Hands.
Sat. Dec. 03 John Smith, Cleveland, helped at mtg last night. MB&I, Mrs. Smith Sr., Arthur King & Jim Millers over to Toronto to Mr. Telfer's funeral. Back for supper.
Wed. Dec. 07 Krahling's for dinner. At Smythe's, Dobson's, Freur's, and J. Sherriffs'. Rather good meeting, Luke 18.
Thu. Dec. 08 Warden's for dinner. At Miller's, Mulholland's in aft. Marsh's for supper. Mtg, Gen. 32, John 8 - Alone.
Sun. Dec. 11 MB&I to N. Falls in am. Adams' for dinner. Mattice's for supper. Gospel mtg, John 3.16 - Everlasting.
Tue. Dec. 20 Called on Mitchesons, and at N. Bailey's for dinner. At Newburn's, and Jerow's for supper. Meeting at Miller's.
Sat. Dec. 31 MB&I and Tom Wilkie to Tillsonburg Conference. Snow and icy roads.

David the Shepherd

To the tune: Sweet hour of prayer

When David was a little boy
He kept his father's lambs and sheep.
To watch by day it gave him joy
To guard them as they lay in sleep.
Wild animals he drove away,
He kept them safe by night and day.

One day a lion came along
And stole a tender little lamb.
The lion he was fierce and strong
But David was so brave and calm
He smote the lion, rent his jaws,
And took the lamb from between his paws.

And then there came along a bear
And took a helpless little sheep.
He thought he'd take it to his lair
And have some food to eat and keep.
But David smote it on the head —
The sheep was saved, the bear fell dead.

Another day a great big man,
Goliath he was called by name,
And when they saw him, Israel ran,
They all were put to grief and shame.
There was not found a man of might
Who would with big Goliath fight.

But David said, Here! — I will dare
To fight this giant strong and great,
I killed the lion and the bear,
He soon shall meet their dreadful fate.
The God who helped me all alone
Will use to kill this man, a stone.

So from the brook five stones he took,
And put one in his little sling,
And to his God he then did look
Before that chosen stone took wing.
It struck the giant, down he fell,
God helped dear David do it well.

But David had a Shepherd true
Who died to save us one and all,
He gave His life that we anew
Might live and hear His loving call.
I call this precious Saviour mine,
And so may you by Grace Divine.

G. L. S.

1939

There were four major series of gospel meetings held by Mr. Shivas in 1939. In January, Mr. Tom Wilkie joined him for four weeks in Niagara Falls. From the middle of February to the end of March he had six weeks of meetings in Pape Avenue Gospel Hall, Toronto. Mr. Fred Nugent laboured with him in Merlin, Ontario, for six weeks in May and June, when 17 professed faith in our Lord Jesus Christ, the editor of this book among them. During October and November, six weeks of meetings were held in Bracondale assembly, Toronto, with Mr. W. Foster (who took ill). He then was helped by Mr. Tom Erwin, and Mr. J. Bernard.

A sketch of the year follows, gleaned from the diaries, along with my personal testimony, which is representative of that of many souls who were reached with the gospel through the preaching of Mr. Shivas, during his 54 years of service.

In fact, the diary for 1939 begins with the record of the salvation of his daughter Elizabeth, who in the goodness of God, became my wife some years later.

Sun. Jan. 01 Tillsonburg Conference. BETTY SAVED at 12.30 am. Praise God. Large meetings in town hall at 2.30. T. Wilkie, W. Smith and F. W. Nugent had children's mtg. T.Wilkie, W. Smith and J. Ferguson at 7.

Four weeks of gospel meetings at Niagara Falls, Ontario, with Mr. Tom Wilkie.

Sun. Jan. 08 Maude, Betty, Tom & I at Niagara Falls. First meeting in Dorchester St.

Mon. Jan. 09 Got load hardwood. H. McKay's for supper. Meeting at Miller's.

Thu. Jan. 19 Snow. I. Doan's for dinner. R. James' for tea. Mtg.

Thu. Jan. 26 Called on Baileys, Bacons, Newburns, Badgers, and at McLean's for supper. Mtg, 2 Sam. 14.14.

Wed. Feb. 01 Lovely day. Clear and cold. Sheppard's for dinner. Made a few calls. Burley's for supper. Mtg - What have I done.

Sun. Feb. 12 Drove alone to Port Dover. Stuck in snow on shortcut. F. Lampkin's for dinner. Jeffrey's for tea. Robert McCrory & I had gospel meeting.

Six weeks of gospel meetings in Pape Ave. Gospel Hall, Toronto, Ontario.

Sun. Feb. 19 To Pape Ave. At Arnold Adams'. T. Erwin & I, mtg.

Tue. Feb. 21 Cold & frosty. Over at Freeman's. Phoning Lucas', Ethel, Welsteads, Smiths, Nicols. A. Russell's for supper.

Wed. Feb. 22 With W. G. Smith at S. Moore's. Meeting.

Mon. Feb. 27 Adams' for dinner. Wallace's for tea. Meeting, W. G. Smith & I.

Tue. Feb. 28 W. G. Smith, H. McKay and I at R. Hamilton's for tea.

Wed. Mar. 01 Stormy. At Eagle's and Adams'. Meeting.

Sat. Mar. 04 Some grippe. Doctoring myself for cold. At home.

Fri. Mar. 10 Lovely bright morning. At Welstead's and Alex Adams'.

Sun. Mar. 19 To Pape Ave. At Arnold Adams'. Large gospel meeting.

Tue. Mar. 21 God is faithful. At Mulholland's for supper. Meeting.

Wed. Mar. 22 More snow. E. Joyce's for dinner. Visited Benthams, G. McDonald at boat, and at West's for supper. Mtg, Prov. 25.

Sun. Apr. 02 Drove alone to Pape Ave. Trouble with car ground wire. Simmon's for dinner. B. C. Saunder's for supper. Mtg.

Six weeks of gospel meetings in Merlin, Ontario, with Mr. Fred Nugent.

Sat. Apr. 29 Getting ready to go to Merlin and left about 1. At Nugent's for supper. Fred and I to Will Brown's, Merlin.

Sun. Apr. 30 Merlin. Read Deut. 23.9 in am. Fred, Will Brown and I out calling. At Isaac Brown's for supper. Our first meeting.

Mon. May 01 Lovely bright day. God is faithful. Fred and I made many calls. Isaac Brown's for supper. Mtg, Gen. 6 - Windows.

Wed. May 03 Lovely bright day. Warmer. Fred and I calling on many homes, Armstrong's, etc. Meeting.

Sun. May 07 Merlin. F. Nugent ministered. S.S., John 12.24 -Wheat. Coltman's, Chatham, for dinner. Watson's for supper. Meeting at Old People's Home at 3, Ecc. 12. Meeting at Merlin, Luke 14.

Mon. May 08 Cloudy like rain. Fred and I out in aft. Calling on Middle Road. Meeting.

I remember Mr. Nugent saying that at the few places where the opposition was exceptionally severe, he would have to go to the car, while Mr. Shivas tried to speak kindly to the people.

Tue. May 09 Cooler and rain through night and this am. To go to Regis' for dinner. Made calls in aft. Meeting.

Wed. May 10 Cloudy and cool. Taking young cattle to pasture in trailer. Up to Merlin. Ed Jones' for dinner. G. Baker's for tea. Meeting.

Wed. May 17 Lovely day. Folks painting house. Barlows here. At H. Brown's for dinner. F. & I made calls and at school. McCloy's for supper. Meeting, 2 Kings 6.1.

Thu. May 18 Clear and cool. F. & I visiting 3 schools and others. Baker's for supper. Meeting.

Fri. May 19 Lovely day. Clear and cool. F. & I out visiting in aft. At Lorraine Jones'. Children's mtg - Heart & Door.

Sat. May 20 Cloudy like rain. Street meeting in Merlin in evening.

Sun. May 21 Merlin. Feast and a good day. Visitors from Detroit and Straffordville. Mtg at 3. Ed Jones' for supper. Testimony meeting at 7.30, 8 took part.

From the notes of Mrs. Frieda C. Regis we learn that those who gave their testimonies that Sunday evening were: Mr. Shivas, Mr. John McQuiggan, Mr. Walter Regis, Mr. Lorne Cochrane, Mr. Clyde Soper, Mr. Geo Barlow, and Mr. Fred Nugent, all of whom have gone home to be with the Lord.

Mon. May 22 Dull day and warm. Murray Regis saved last night. Fred & I visiting. Meeting.

Thu. May 25 Lovely morning. Fred & I at houses, and at Lorne Armstrong's for supper. Meeting.

Tue. May 30 Lovely day, cool and bright. Tomato planting in am. Fred and I called at Harold (Slim) Johnson's. Meeting.

Thu. June 01 Cool and cloudy. Fred and I at Johnson's, Phelps', and E. Jones'. Good mtg, Luke 15 - Prodigal.

Fri. June 02 Mrs. Jones Sr's. for supper. Children's meeting - B B chart.

This was a lesson based on Blind Bartimaeus met the Burden Bearer, etc. Mr. Shivas improvised at this meeting by adding the Bad Brown's to the chart!

Tue. June 06 Helping Will some in am. Went with Mr. & Mrs. Brown to Chatham in afternoon to see the King and Queen at 6.40. Back in time for meeting, Luke 2 - Saviour.

Wed. June 07 Clear and dry, but more like rain. God send it, (rain). Helped Will Brown with screens in am. Visited Mr. Phelps, at Baker's for supper. Meeting, Prov. 8 - Finding.

Thu. June 08 Plentiful rain last night. Thank God. I went with Will to Leamington. Saw Bob Robertson. At Lorraine Jones'.

Sun. June 11 Merlin. At Cliff Brown's. Mtg at 3. Last gospel mtg.

The Grass Never Grew Greener!

Sun. Oct. 15 Drove alone to Bracondale. Eagle's for dinner. Our first meeting. W. Foster and I, Luke 2 - Dayspring.
Mon. Oct. 16 At C. Harvie's all night. Up to Hall before supper. Met S. Moore. Smaller mtg, 65 out.
Tue. Oct. 17 Over to J. Nickle's & J. Winter's for dinner with T. Halliday. At O. Sprunt's with Bible. More out.
Thu. Oct. 19 Cold better. At Sprunt's, Miller's, Yeat's. Mtg.
Fri. Oct. 20 Got Bible and tracts. At school. Children's mtg, 8pm.
Wed. Oct. 25 Mr. Foster in bed with cold. T. Erwin helped in mtg.
Thu. Oct. 26 Steen's for supper. T. Erwin helped in mtg, Heb. 11.
Fri. Oct. 27 Children's meeting with W. McCullough.
Sun. Oct. 29 MB&I at Bracondale. Weaver's for dinner. Mtg at 3.15. Gospel at 7, J. Bernard and I, 1 Kings 6.1.
Wed. Nov. 01 Out to Peat's, Welstead's, Steen's for dinner. Young's for supper. J. Bernard & I at meeting.
Fri. Nov. 03 At Lawrence's, Radford's, Shakespeare's, Jones', Harvie's. Young's for supper. Children's meeting, then gospel.
Wed. Nov. 08 With A. Eagle to Blair's, Gilchrist's, Bunting's.
Thu. Nov. 09 Made calls by Hall and walked to Eglinton. Harvie's for dinner. McKinley's for supper. Mtg, Math. 22 - Ready.
Mon. Nov. 13 At Alf Buckner's funeral, Pape Ave Hall, G. Gould.
Thu. Nov. 16 Called on Mrs. Buckner, Mrs. Telfer. At Mrs. Cairns for supper. Meeting, Luke 19 - Zacchaeus.
Fri. Nov. 17 At McKinley's and Fettes'. Children's meeting.
Tue. Nov. 21 Wilkie, Nugent and I at Mrs. Gordon's, and houses.
Fri. Nov. 24 Harvie's for dinner. Made calls. Got gas at Sam McIntosh's. Children's mtg - Postage stamp.
Mon. Nov. 27 To Toronto at 3. Made calls. Dean's for tea. 50 out.
Wed. Nov. 29 Eagle's for dinner. At A. Walker's, Lyman W.'s, R. Bunting's, Craik's, and Sam McIntosh's. Last meeting.

Paid In Full.

For years it has been on my heart to record the details of how God reached me in my sins, and gave me the assurance that those sins were forgiven, and that I was a child of His. This seems the ideal circumstance in which to accomplish this desire.

My father, Walter D. Regis, and my mother Frieda, were saved soon after they were married, so that all my life I was under the influence of the gospel in a home where reading of the Bible, and prayer (on our knees) was the daily convention.

My father was employed all his working days by the Canadian Pacific Railway as a telegraph operator and later as a station agent. At the time I was born he held the second hour (4pm to 12m) operator's position at Chatham, Ontario.

My early recollections were of preacher's visits. Mr. Touzeau wore a beard, and I asked my mother if I would have feathers like that when I grew up! Mr. Black was a quiet man, and very deaf. I undertook to tell a story at the dinner table once, and he asked if the person I was telling about was "a saved mon." Needless to say, that ended the story. Mr. Thomas Dobbin was a kindly man. My mother was reached for the Lord through his ministry. Mr. Steve Mick spent some time in our home, but I didn't like him because every time we went out the door he would ask me if I had gone to the bathroom. "We don't want any wet pants in meeting," he'd say. I liked him better later on!

During the depression my father was "bumped" from his position, and worked all over Southern Ontario as a spare operator. About 1934 he secured a steady night operator's position at Glentay, (near Perth), Ontario, and we moved there.

The nearest assembly was in Ottawa, 62 miles away. Needless to say, we didn't get there every Lord's Day. The saints met to remember the Lord in a cavernous room on the second or third floor of the Masonic Temple.

I well remember the imposing array of plush velvet chairs set around that room. I recall Mr. Herbert Hume, a godly gentleman, who held a high position as a civil servant in the government of the day, taking me through the Parliament Buildings on several occasions. I was soberly impressed one day as we drove along a boulevard in Ottawa which was lined with the homes of diplomats of every nation. Mr. Hume said, "Murray, there isn't a home along all this street that doesn't hold a heavy heart." Mr. Shivas mentions his visits to Ottawa, and to our place in Perth, in June of 1935, with Mr. Gilchrist. I remember how gently and sincerely Mr. Gilchrist spoke to me of my need to know the Lord Jesus Christ as my personal Saviour.

In 1938 my father "bid" on a position as station agent at Haycroft, thirty miles west of Chatham, Ontario. This was a day job with Sundays off, a real advancement after 20 years on the night shift. We went to the assembly at Merlin, Ontario, and the folk there were very good to us. Very few Lord's Days did we go the 22 miles back to the station where we lived, until after the evening gospel meeting, because we had been invited to stay for the day by some of the Christians.

My father, being a railroader, soon built up a reputation for being the first to arrive at meeting. The gospel meetings held by Mr. Shivas and Mr. Nugent in the spring of 1939 were no exception. High school studies and piano lessons could fit in where they pleased. My father saw to it that we were there every night without fail.

It seemed the wrong time of the year to hold a series of meetings. This was a farming community. The farmers had to get their seeding done, and had little time to attend meetings. But they began, and from the commencement I knew that it was an opportunity for me to settle the question of my soul's destiny.

I note from the diary that 3 weeks of meetings preceded the 21st of May. My impression of those meetings was that the speakers were in earnest. They faithfully presented the sinner's loss and eternal condemnation if he failed to come to Christ, as well as the eternal blessing of trusting the Lord Jesus as personal Saviour. I believed the Lord was speaking to me, and I was weighing the issues well. When a chum of mine, Glen Baker, trusted the Saviour, my concern deepened.

The Diaries of George L. Shivas

On Sunday, the 21st of May, we were invited to stay with Mr. and Mrs. Isaac Brown for the day. Mrs. Brown, called Aunt Liza by her friends, had an intriguing habit. After dinner was over and the dishes washed, she would drop into the rocking chair in the kitchen, throw her apron over her head, and have a wee nap. I spent the afternoon out in the fields with one of her sons, Charlie, tracing out a short in the electric fence.

The gospel meeting that evening, as already detailed, was a testimony meeting. Something about the genuine honesty and simplicity of those men reached my heart, and I felt I had to do something about getting right with God. For a young teenager to stay behind after such a meeting, and let the preachers know that he would like to be saved, was the ultimate in disclosure.

However, I did it, and when the people had left the Hall, Mr. Shivas and Mr. Nugent sat down on the front row of chairs, and brought verse after verse of Scripture before me, each of which made the way of salvation plain, but not to me.

The more they read, and the more I tried to believe, the darker the matter became. Finally, Mr. Shivas said (wisely), "Come on, Fred. I think we had better go home. I don't believe Murray wants to be saved tonight." Those words sounded as a deathknell to my soul. To think that I had confided that I wanted to be saved, and the preachers had talked with me, and I was going to go home not saved, meant to me that all was lost!

There was a square brown enamelled natural gas stove about two thirds of the way back in the Hall, and I stopped by the stove, while they shrugged on their coats, and Mr. Shivas pulled on his overshoes.

Then Mr. Shivas said to me, "Murray, it's just as if I had bought groceries on credit at the store, and because I had no money to pay, the bill became so great that it was impossible for me to pay the debt. Mr. Nugent, a friend of mine, knew my plight, asked the grocer for the total amount of my bill, and paid it himself. The grocer wrote across the bill, 'Paid in full,' signed it, and handed it to Mr. Nugent. Mr. Nugent offered me the receipt and said that because he was a good friend of mine, he had paid my bill. All I had to do was accept the receipt and that would be the end of the debt."

His illustration was perfectly clear to me. The debt which had become impossible to pay was my sin before a holy God.

As I listened intently to the story, I read the text at the front of the Hall,
> "But he was wounded for our transgressions,
> he was bruised for our iniquities:
> the chastisement of our peace was upon him;
> and with his stripes we are healed." Isaiah 53.5

I was convinced that this verse was the receipt for my debt, and that written across that bill, to guarantee its payment, were the words, "With His stripes, Murray is healed."

I rested then and there on what God said Christ had done for me on the Cross of Calvary, and I hold that receipt to this day, and will carry it into eternity.

I believe there were 17 who professed faith in our Lord Jesus Christ at that time. In August, many of them were baptized in Lake Erie, below the clay cliffs, on a sunny Sunday afternoon, by a good friend, Mr. Frank Watson, of Chatham. Later they were received into fellowship in the Merlin assembly.

> Living a life so soon to end,
> Dying — and then all Eternity spend
> In hell or in Heaven above.
> The Saviour is calling, Oh now hear His voice,
> Calling to thee, Oh make Him thy choice;
> Thou shalt be saved, all Heaven shall rejoice
> And sing of His wonderful love.

> G. L. S.

1940

The year 1940 commenced with nine weeks of gospel meetings at St. Catharines, Ont., with Mr. Fred Nugent.

Then in April, Mr. Shivas had four weeks of meetings at Fenwick, Ont., with Mr. Robert Booth.

In November, Mr. Shivas attended the Chicago, Illinois Conference, which is noteworthy because of brother Leonard E. Linsted's letter, describing Mr. Shivas' message given at that Conference.

Sat. Jan. 20 Cold and stormy. F. Nugent came at 6 for supper and went on to St.Catharines.
Sun. Jan. 21 Drove alone to St.C., 11 am. Our first mtg on Hill.
Mon. Jan. 22 To St.C. Made calls on Hill. V. McIntee's for S. Mtg.
Wed. Jan. 24 Fred, Bob Booth & I at houses with cards. Mtg.
Thu. Jan. 25 To St.C. At houses. Children's meeting. I opened.
Wed. Jan. 31 Making children's objects. Made calls. Mtg alone.
Fri. Feb. 02 Stormy snowy am. At James', Jones', Roberts'. Mtg.
Thu. Feb. 08 Called at Childs', James', Notley's. Children's mtg.
Wed. Feb. 14 Leonard Piper saved last night and over here this am. Seems real. God grant it. Very stormy day. Fred & I at mtg.
Fri. Feb. 16 L. Piper over. Hurt my back some, pushing cars. Mtg.
Sun. Feb. 18 MB&I to St.C. Good gospel mtg. Good number out.
Fri. Feb. 23 At Tempest's. Mtg. C. Low professed to be saved.
Sun. Feb. 25 MB&I to St.C. Large gospel mtg, Fred & I.
Tue. Feb. 27 Tempest's all night. Booth's for dinner. Made calls and at LeFay's for supper. Good meeting at night.
Thu. Feb. 29 Mild and dull today. Tempest's for dinner. Making calls in aft. McIntee's for supper. Children's mtg, Fred spoke.
Fri. Mar. 01 Testimony mtg. Ten took part.
Sun. Mar. 03 MB&I to St.C. Good gospel mtg. Some saved.
Thu. Mar. 07 Howard Dack professed to be saved last night. God grant it may be real. Children's meeting - B B chart.
Fri. Mar. 08 At Low's, H. Chard's, and Colsell's. Testimony mtg.
Sun. Mar. 10 MB&I to St.C. at 9.30. Mtg in Old People's Home. Mtg.
Mon. Mar. 11 D. Hodgkins saved. Flagg's for supper. Mtg, Fred & I.
Tue. Mar. 12 Fred & I made calls. Hagarman's for tea. Meeting.
Wed. Mar. 13 Very icy but nice few out. Meeting.

The Grass Never Grew Greener!

Thu. Mar. 14 Three boys professed to be saved last night, Beattie and Buddy Campbell, and Edward Lake. Children's meeting.
Fri. Mar. 15 Two professed last night. Good mtg tonight, Job 40.
Sun. Mar. 17 MB&I to St.C. Large gospel meeting.
Thu. Mar. 21 Mtg at H.S. Children's meeting.
Sun. Mar. 24 Left at 5.20 for St.C. Last mtg on Hill, Fred & I.

Sun. Apr. 14 Grimsby. All out in am. Bob Booth and I had meeting at Fenwick.
Mon. Apr. 15 Mrs. Bonham went with us to Fenwick. Mtg - Dayspring.
Tue. Apr. 16 Klager's for supper. Meeting in Pelham.
Wed. Apr. 17 Bob and I visiting at Fenwick. Supper in Hall. Mtg.
Sun. Apr. 21 MB&I to Port Dover. Mtg at Fenwick - God is light.
Tue. Apr. 23 All of us to Fenwick for mtg, Luke 18 - Trusted.
Wed. Apr. 24 All of us to N. Falls. Fenwick for mtg, Bob & I.
Thu. Apr. 25 Made calls at Fenwick & Pelham. Hansell's for tea.
Sun. Apr. 28 MB&I to Straffordville. McQuiggan's for the day. Fenwick for gospel meeting at night.
Mon. Apr. 29 Crawford - Pinches wedding today, F. G. Watson. W. Parnell with me to Fenwick. Meeting.
Tue. Apr. 30 Bob and I to Fenwick and Pelham. Visiting and at Hamler's for tea. Mtg at N. Pelham, Mark 11.
Thu. May 02 To St.C. & Fenwick. Huffman's for tea. Mtg, Luke 10.
Fri. May 03 B&I, Truman's, Mrs. Grasely to Fenwick for mtg.
Sun. May 12 Drove alone to N. Falls. Last mtg at Fenwick at night.

Tue. Nov. 19 Seeing about visa & passport. Johnny Johnson's, Detroit for dinner. At S. McEwen's meeting at night.
Wed. Nov. 20 Went with W. Foster to Chicago. Prayer meeting. Staying at Mill's.
Thu. Nov. 21 Chicago Conference. Over 40 preachers. Large crowds.
Fri. Nov. 22 R. McCrory & I had meeting in the morning. Good spirit in the meetings.
Sat. Nov. 23 Chicago Conference. Large mtg in aft. 26 took part. <u>Preachers</u>. I spoke on fishing, etc. Then to children, Luke 13 - Peanut.
Sun. Nov. 24 At 86 Bishop in am, and at night. Got part of aft. mtg. Spoke at Old People's Home.

The Diaries of George L. Shivas

Galatians 6.9 Witchita, Kansas
6 - 10 - 75

Dear brethren,

While visiting a friend in Iowa I was reading that you were asking for any bits of information about George Shivas.

Here are a couple:

My preaching partner, Tom McCullagh, had just finished speaking at a large conference in the east, and since the crowd was so large, there were no seats nearby. So brother McCullagh had to go almost to the door to sit down, but brother Shivas thought Tom had preached his message and was going to leave, and so, taking the platform as the next speaker, he remarked as only he could do, —

"I have no time for HIT and RUN preachers!"

The other incident I well remember as a young brother just starting out in the Lord's work. It was at the Chicago Conference in either 1939 or 1940. All the "Pioneer preachers" were gathered on the platform for their "3 Minute" report. It was then I heard brother Shivas for the first time. He was talking about fishing. As he spoke he acted it out, as though his line were tangled in a tree. I thought to myself, "This man is a clown!" We laughed until we nearly fell off our chairs. The vast audience was in stitches over his antics.

Then suddenly he stopped, and pointing his finger at the laughing crowd, he said, "There are three ways to catch fish — with a net, a silver troll, or with a worm. With the net and troll, you can use them again. With the worm, you catch only one once." Then lowering his voice, in the hush-filled auditorium, he cried out, "Some of you have never caught a fish in your life for the Lord." Then, with silence so dense it was painful, he shouted, "You could be a worm and catch one, couldn't you?"

The years have come and gone since then and I can't remember one word from the rest of the conference. But I can still hear that cry, as it cut the stillness of that large, hushed audience, "You can be a worm, and catch one, can't you?"

And many a time since then, the principle of the sacrificial worm in Christ's service has gripped my heart afresh, to drive me on after souls.

Sincerely yours in Christ.
(sgd) Leonard E. Linsted

The Grass Never Grew Greener!

Toronto, Ontario
January 27, 1976

Dear brother Ross,

Here are a few remembrances of Mr. Shivas.

At a conference, there were twenty minutes left. Of course, nobody wanted that 20 minutes, especially the theologians. Bro. Shivas got up and said, "Now I don't intend to be very long, and there will be room for two others." He spoke for seven minutes, and two others did follow, taking the same amount of time.

He gave a New Year's message. Can't recall whether it was 1934 or 1935. Anyway, we'll say it was 1935. He read four portions from the Word. They were all Chapter 19, Verse 35. Just fitted in perfectly and was an excellent message for the coming year. (Diary shows it was Tillsonburg Conference, 1934.)

Heard him refer to an expert giving a 40 minute talk on the air, on Economics. The announcer finally came on and said, "Now what the speaker you have just been listening to has been trying to get across for the past 40 minutes is just simply this. If your outgo exceeds your income, then your upkeep will be your downfall."

Then he made the application that the same thing was true spiritually.

One time he read in John 1 about Andrew bringing Peter to Christ. "Now," he said, "I want to read a portion in the book of Amos." Then he said, "I would like to speak on Amos and Andy." At that time Amos and Andy were all the go on the radio. The younger folk won't get the connection on this one.

He was at a Christian's home for supper. Standing looking out the living room window, he noticed a Jew going by, on his wagon. In those days it was common for Jews to go around collecting rags, bottles, etc. The brother noticed the tears on Mr. Shivas' cheeks, and asked him, "Are you all right, brother Shivas?" He replied, "Just think, he was cut off, that I might be brought in." This in reference to Romans 11. So there's something of a different nature.

Trust the above will contribute something to the book.

Sincerely in Him,
(Sgd) Frank Pearcey

1941

The year began with seven weeks of meetings with brother Robert Booth in Grimsby, Ontario, using the Egypt to Caanan chart.

Sat. Feb. 01 Bob Booth came for dinner. He & I put up sign at Hall. MB&I up mtn, Grassie, Smithville in aft.

Sun. Feb. 02 Grimsby. All at the feast. Our first mtg on chart, Bob Booth and I. God grant mercy, Neh. 2 - Journeys.

Mon. Feb. 03 Bob & I called at houses, Ex. 3 & 12 - Blood on door.

Tue. Feb. 04 Bob & I at houses. Saw Jarvis, baker. Nice few out to meeting, Ex. 12. God grant mercy.

Wed. Feb. 05 Bob & I up mtn. Made many calls. Good meeting and attendance.

Thu. Feb. 06 Made letters for object lesson - W.H.R.D. Bob & I out in aft. Looking up children especially for Fri. night.

Fri. Feb. 07 Wet snowy day. Poor night. Thank God for His mercy. Bob & I to houses. Got benches from library. Mrs. Hanson saved? Children's meeting - Bread.

Tue. Feb. 11 Bob & I made calls on Oak St. Exodus - Manna.

Tue. Feb. 18 More snow & colder. Bob & I up Robinson St. Meeting not so large - Gate of Tabernacle.

Wed. Feb. 19 Made a few calls. Large meeting - Gate of Tabernacle.

Fri. Feb. 21 Bob & I out at houses, 'Stirring up the people.' Good Children's meeting, Luke 15.

Mon. Feb. 24 M&I up to Smithville. Bob & I made calls. Good number from Hamilton and St.C. and others. Mtg, Ex. 30 - Laver.

Mon. Mar. 03 Cutting up brush in cellar. Bob and I made calls in aft. Home for supper. Good meeting, Exodus, Hebrews - Vail.

Thu. Mar. 06 Bob Booth and I made calls. Good mtg. H. Hurst professed to be saved. Mtg, Ex. 30.1 - Golden altar.

Fri. Mar. 07 M&I up to Grassie in am, at Black's, Blanchard's, Cowan's. Bob & I made calls and for supper. Children's meeting.

Sun. Mar. 16 Grimsby. All at the feast. Booths there. They here for dinner and supper. Gospel hall full - Rahab.

Mon. Mar. 17 Cold, stormy day. Visited alone, Sniders and Whittakers. 22 to mtg. Very cold & stormy. Spoke from Numbers 20 - Moses smiting rock.

Wed. Mar. 19 Bob & I made calls. Got benches from library. Testimony meeting, 11 spoke.

Thu. Mar. 20 Bob & I made calls, Grasely's, Rooker's, and others. Nice few in to mtg, Josh. 3 & 4 - Crossing the Jordan.

Sun. Mar. 23 Grimsby. Read Ex. 16.16. Trumans & R. Scott for the day. S.S. at 3. Large mtg at 7, Luke 14 - Supper. Last meeting.

Mr. Shivas was alone for five weeks of gospel meetings at Port Dover, Ontario, near the end of the year.

Sun. Nov. 09 Drove alone to Port Dover, for the day.

Mon. Nov. 10 J. Young and I made calls in aft. Mtg at night. God is faithful. He will guide. Made calls. Jeffrey's for supper. Meeting, Isa. 63.1 - Mighty to save.

Wed. Nov. 12 Feeling better from lemon juice. Misener's for supper. Meeting, Acts 4 - Must be saved.

Wed. Nov. 19 Making calls. Bro. Seabrook helped in meeting.

Fri. Nov. 21 At canning factory. Making calls. At Jeffrey's. Mtg.

Sun. Nov. 23 At Port Dover. E. Marks helped at gospel mtg.

Tue. Nov. 25 Out with J. Young. Called on F. Lees & C. Jacksons. E. Jackson professed to be saved. God grant it may be real. Mtg.

Wed. Nov. 26 Made calls. Jackson's for supper. Testimony meeting.

Sun. Nov. 30 Port Dover. Mr. Young helped me in gospel mtg.

Tue. Dec. 02 Made many calls. F. Lampkin's for supper. Good mtg.

Wed. Dec. 10 Made calls. At Milton Porter's. Testimony meeting. Brethren from EastEnd, Hamilton. Mtg, Prov. 26 - Seven men.

Sun. Dec. 14 Port Dover. Lit fire in Hall. Corbett's for supper. Last gospel meeting.

Thu. Dec. 25 Christmas Day. "God is good, and doeth good." "Thanks be unto God for His unspeakable Gift." MB&I at home alone with God's blessing.

Sat. Dec. 27 Tillsonburg Conference. McCrory, Gilchrist, Simpson, A. Douglas, T. Wilkie, F. Nugent, W. Pell, Downey, McMullen, Brown, McConkie, Blackwood, E. Sprunt, Touzeau, Shivas, 15 preachers. Good weather, crowds, and meetings.

Wed. Dec. 31 The last day of the year. Deut. 11.12. Thank God for all His mercy. Saw old year out. God is faithful.

1942

Gospel meetings were held for the month of February at Kensington Ave., Gospel Hall, Hamilton, Ontario.

Sun. Feb. 01 Up to Kensington alone. Thornycroft's for dinner. Crompton's for supper. A. Douglas opened gospel mtg for me.

Mon. Feb. 02 Made calls at houses on Kensington. Gospel mtgs.

Thu. Feb. 05 At W. Booth's. Meeting, Luke 15 - Prodigal.

Fri. Feb. 06 At Sheldrake's. Meeting, Math. 7.

Sat. Feb. 07 Heavy snowfall. Put chains on car.

Sun. Feb. 08 Stormy night, snow and drifts. At Grimsby in am. Left on 3.05 bus for Hamilton. Crompton's for supper & all night. Meeting.

Mon. Feb. 09 Crompton's all night. At J. Rickard's. Mtg, Luke 18.

Tue. Feb. 10 At A. Petrie's. Mtg, John 11 - This man.

Wed. Feb. 11 At Thompson's. Mtg, 1 John - Take away.

Thu. Feb. 12 At Ralph Baxter's. Mtg, Luke 14 - Gospel Supper.

Fri. Feb. 13 Not feeling good with cold. Jones' for supper.

Tue. Feb. 17 A. Roberts' for supper. Mtg larger, Acts 16.

Fri. Feb. 20 Very cold. Made quite a few calls. At F. Sheldrake's for supper. Children's meeting - Abraham & Isaac.

Tue. Feb. 24 Made many calls. At Saynor's. Meeting, Ex. 8.

Thu. Feb. 26 Called on Wagners, Douglas'. Meeting, Josh. 20.

Sun. Mar. 01 Kensington, Hamilton. Last meeting, 2 Kings 5.

Mr. Fred Nugent joined him a week later for six weeks at Watford, Ontario.

Sun. Mar. 08 To Watford. At Jarriott's. Fred Nugent and I in gospel.

Mon. Mar. 09 At Richardson's barber shop and Steel's for supper. Very stormy. 10 at meeting.

Tue. Mar. 10 Fred and I at houses in aft. Nice few out to mtg.

Wed. Mar. 11 At Hayward's. Meeting, Luke 18 - Trusted.

Fri. Mar. 13 Fred & I at school seeing children and homes. C. Mtg.

Sat. Mar. 14 Came home with McIntoshs last night. Visiting today and with George to Inwood, and other place doing chores. At Metcalf Sr's. and George Metcalf's.

Fri. Mar. 20 In to Watford with Mr J. at school, and other calls. Prayer in Hall. Steel's for supper. Children's meeting.

Tue. Mar. 24 Lovely morning. Out at barn in am with Mr. J. Fred & I at Fuller's for dinner. Made many calls, good visits. Meeting.

Sun. Mar. 29 Watford. Visit at Harrower's. Meeting. Some saved.

Mon. Mar. 30 To McIntosh's, Fred and I. Four souls professed to be saved last night. At Mrs. Jas. Johnston's funeral, Dr. Cameron and Tom Wilkie. Meeting, Ex. 8 - Tomorrow.

Tue. Mar. 31 McIntosh's for supper. Meeting, Ex. 17 - Rock.

Thu. Apr. 09 Jarriott's all night. Had talk with Wilbert in am. Mander's for supper. Good meeting, John 5 - Place.

Fri. Apr. 10 Snow and storming. Wilbert Jarriott may have gotten saved last night.

Mon. Apr. 13 Went to Sarnia with Wilbert J. Steele's for dinner. Called at Kember's. Meeting.

Wed. Apr. 15 Hume's for supper. Nice lot out to meeting.

Thu. Apr. 16 36 years in Christ today! Ebenezer! Jehovah Jireh! Lovely day. Newman's for supper. Meeting.

Sun. Apr. 19 At Wilbert's, Mrs. Tanner's, and Hume's. Last mtg.

The two preachers were together again at Embro, Ontario, for June and July.

Wed. June 10 Staying at Mrs. Dent's, Embro. F. Nugent & I went to Galt. At Geo. Riddle's for dinner and Cochrane's for supper. Mrs. Sodman's funeral. Prayed. Meeting at Embro, Heb. 12 - Joy.

Sun. June 14 Embro. At Patterson's for day. Large mtg at 7.30.

Tue. June 16 Load from Clyde - St. Clairs and Reeves. Meeting at Embro.

Wed. June 17 At Lorne St.Clair's for supper. Good meeting.

Thu. June 18 Fred & I changed tires on car. At S. McDonald's for dinner. Meeting, John 11 - Calls.

Fri. June 19 Fixed door hinge for Mrs. Dent. Children's meeting.

Sun. June 21 Embro for the day. Had prayer mtg in aft. Good gospel mtg and large. Street meeting and a good hearing.

Sun. June 28 Embro. Had dinner with Nugents and Marshs in Hall. Supper by mill pond. Prayer mtg at 3.30. Gospel with street meeting after.

1943

Mr. Tom Wilkie joined Mr. Shivas early in the new year at Galt, Ontario for seven weeks of gospel meetings.

Wed. Jan. 13 Cold night. Rested some. Maude pressing clothes, etc. Getting ready to go to Galt. All at Prayer mtg.

Thu. Jan. 14 Carried out ashes. Put oil in car & added water to battery. Left at 2.30 for Galt. No trouble, though stormy. Sunday School Treat, Luke 2 - Stable.

Fri. Jan. 15 At W. Turley's, 13 Ball Ave. Wrote Maude. Called on L. Cochrane, A. Turley, Mrs. Champ in aft and Riddell's for supper. Prayer meeting, Luke 5.

Sat. Jan. 16 Wilburn & I got bed at Mrs. Champ's. G. Ralston's for supper. Tom Wilkie came at 7. Young people's cottage meeting.

Sun. Jan. 17 Galt. Full Hall, Luke 1 - Dayspring.

Tue. Jan. 19 More snow & stormy. Mrs. Champ's for dinner. At Hall and up to S. Gammon's for supper. Cold & stormy. Meeting.

Fri. Jan. 22 Sore throat through night. Some better. "Hope thou in God!" Lovely bright day. Made some calls and at F. Cottrill's for supper. Good meeting, 2 Sam. 14 - Must needs.

Sun. Jan. 24 Galt. At the feast. Tom ministered. At John Windross'. B. Class, Gen. 40. Good turn out and Hall full at gospel meeting,

Tue. Jan. 26 Crossman's for dinner, and two young sailors. Made calls. Wright's (A. Sage), Jardine's for supper. Meeting.

Wed. Jan. 27 Nice morning. Frost on trees. At Mrs. Champ Sr's., and Fairchild's. Made a few calls. Good meeting.

Thu. Jan. 28 Nice morning. Out to sanatorium in aft by streetcar, and at C. Lapsley's for supper. Good meeting, Prov. 5.1 - Place.

Fri. Jan. 29 Nice morning. Got car out in am and made some calls.

Mon. Feb. 01 Windy through night but nice day. Lapsley's for dinner. Made few calls, Latimer's, etc. Stormy. Opened Children's meeting for Tom.

Sat. Feb. 06 Mild day. Bert Bryant's, Preston, for dinner, and Frank Phillip's for supper. Prayer & testimony meeting at 8.

Sun. Feb. 07 Galt. With Frank Phillips for the day. S.S. in his home, Math. 13 - Earth. Large and good meeting at 7.

Thu. Feb. 11 Dull & threatening storm. To Hall in aft. Ralston's for supper. Large gospel meeting.

Mon. Feb. 15 Very cold night and morning. Made calls and had walk. At Hall for supper with G. Jackson & G. Fuller. Children's mtg.

Wed. Feb. 17 Sailor boys at mtg last night. Visited Sanatorium. Cochrane's for supper. Meeting, Ps. 51.57 - Behold.

Thu. Feb. 18 Nice day again. Not so cold. G. Ralston's for dinner. To Hall and back up to Gammon's. Good meeting, two saved.

Sun. Feb. 21 Packed Hall, good meeting at night, Ps. 19 - Voices.

Tue. Feb. 23 Mild and dull. Up to Hospital visiting and Cochrane's. Up to Crossman's for supper. Meeting.

Wed. Feb. 24 Nice day again. Little colder. Called on Chestermans and others. Windross' for supper. Meeting.

Thu. Feb. 25 Lovely morning. At Gammon Sr's., and J. Fairchild's for supper. Meeting.

Sat. Feb. 27 Lovely day. Drove W. L. T. to Hespeler, and us to Bryant's, Preston, and at Gowing's for supper. Testimony meeting, 20 took part.

Sun. Feb. 28 Galt. Dinner and supper in Hall. Hall full at night. Good meeting, Rev. - Lamb.

Tue. Mar. 02 Had visit last night with Mrs J. Spreeman at C. Lapsley's. Lovely day. Also at Riddell's. At hospital. Mtg.

Thu. Mar. 04 Milder somewhat today. Champ Sr's., for dinner alone. Both of us at Mackay's for supper. Mtg, Josh. 20 - Declaration.

Fri. Mar. 05 Lovely morning, thank God. Tom & I made some calls in aft., and to Francis Cottrill's. Meeting.

Sat. Mar. 06 I went alone to B. Bryant's for dinner. Ed Dick and Bob Gowing called for me. Very stormy. Williamson's for supper. Good testimony meeting.

Mon. Mar. 08 Leaving Galt. Had funeral service alone at 2.30 for Mrs. McQueen Sr. Read John 3 - Even so.

The Diaries of George L. Shivas

Quotes from brother G. Shivas.

"With the world, it's an 'up and down' experience, but with the Christian, it's 'down and up!'"
Regarding holiness — "Your neighbour should believe that you live without sin."
Concerning trials in a Christian's life — "All sunshine makes a desert."
"One result of a conference should be that a stirred heart makes a willing spirit."
"Some of us are grasshopper Christians, we only go when we're prodded."
"I don't close my Bible after reading a chapter until I see Jesus in it."
His personal application of Hebrews 9.28 was, "Unto them that look for Him (in the Scriptures) shall He appear (in the Scriptures)."

About 1940 in Brock Ave. Hall basement, he found me alone, just a few years saved, picking up my small Bible bag. "I see you have a bag, brother," he intoned deeply. "Yes," I said, rather quietly. "Reminds me," said he, "of when I was a young man and starting to carry a Bible bag, and a big older preacher said to me, 'George, I see you have a bag.' I said, 'Yes.' He said by way of censor, 'Another man had a bag,' meaning Judas Iscariot. I replied, 'Yes, that's so, but another man carried a bag, David, and five smooth stones in it, too.'" Mr. Shivas was always ready for an attacker, and ready to encourage younger Christians.

In later years I always enjoyed visiting brother Shivas and his wife in their home. If it was vegetable season, he or she always saw to it that you didn't get away without a basketful from their garden.

One day visiting their home, I was exercised about giving him a little gift of fellowship in the Lord's work, hand to hand, when we were leaving. As our hands met in a farewell handshake, here he was giving me fellowship at the same time, and thanking me for dropping in for a visit. Then his dear wife was pressing some bills into my hand the next moment from her "Lord's portion!"

I say, God bless all such folk who are like they were while here below. They knew a "giving God."

(Sgd) Albert Grainger

The Grass Never Grew Greener!

North Bay, Ontario.
May 1, 1991.

Dear brother Murray,

It is surely something that you should ask of our dear brother and sister Shivas. For the past week or two we have been talking of them a good number of times.

First of all, he knew how to stay happy in the Lord. He never forgot the day of his deliverance.

Most of the basic principles of the Word of God we know today, we learned from him and Stan Simms. What they taught us has been a guideline for us for over 30 years, and gave us a good solid foundation on which to build.

We can honestly say they never passed our door without stopping. Many times they did not have the time to come in, but would blow the horn and call to us some encouraging word to help us on our way.

When I first started to preach, it was with Mr. Shivas or Stan for a partner. I think of the number of times they so graciously covered up my mistakes and finished my message for me, before going on with their own.

Although they were never great expounders of the Word of God, I believe with all my heart they knew the God of the Bible. We would surely give them the credit for starting us having confidence in the One who loved us and gave Himself for us.

I trust God will help me to pass on to others some of what these dear brethren have left for us. We revere their names and memories. God is good to us.

Your brother by grace,
(sgd) Ken Moore

1944

Thu. Oct. 05 Eli Davis brought 3 ton coal in am.

This one line in the diary of 1944 speaks of a brother in the Grimsby assembly who was saved in 1928, when Mr. Shivas and Mr. Ed Steen had gospel meetings in the Orange Hall, in Grimsby.

He was a native Indian with a real interest in getting the gospel to his relatives who lived on nearby reserves.

He had three sons, Alex, Russel, and Elijah, and one daughter, Frieda. We recall with genuine pleasure attending Saturday night ministry meetings at Kensington Ave. Hall, Hamilton, and listening to the harmonious singing. Mr. Davis, Russel, and Elijah provided the rich, full bass tones.

Mr. Davis and his family were stedfast friends of the Shivas' and it is appropriate to record an article which appeared in the Grimsby newspaper. It reveals the character of the man, and the good testimony he had in the town.

How Many Thousand Tons of Coal Has He Shovelled?

For 26 years, Eli Davis, with his ready smile, delivered fuel to citizens of this district — a full blooded Indian with a strong desire to succeed.

This is the story of a man who was born to Oneida Indian parents, on the Oneida Reserve in western Ontario, and who settled in the town of Grimsby, where he lived a simple life, worked hard, and turned to Jesus Christ for companionship.

The only boy of a family of ten, Eli spent his youth working on his father's farm on the Reserve. He married when 19 years of age, and had four sons. The fourth boy predeceased his mother by some years. Mrs. Davis died in January of 1948. Eli has 14 grandchildren and 1 great grandchild.

He recalls that he came to Grimsby in April of 1921, and obtained employment with the old G. L. Eaton Coal Company.

How many thousands of tons of coal this man has shovelled just cannot be ascertained, but Eli can tell you of the days when he would empty a railway carload single handed, without the use of such things as conveyor belts and the like. He can tell you of the Model T Ford truck that could transport a ton of coal to a customer if no hills were encountered on the way. The maximum weight of coal for this truck if delivered up the mountain was half a ton.

Life went on for Eli Davis. He was healthy, he had a home, a fine wife and family, but something was lacking until one day he and his wife attended a meeting in the old Orange Hall. It was a religious gathering, and from that assembly came the present day Gospel Hall. Eli was not a Christian, but he kept attending those meetings, and the teachings of Christ caused Eli to wonder. He thought he had everything, but now here was something else. To this day, trusting Christ as his Saviour stands out in his memory as the greatest of all privileges. He was baptized soon after.

He sadly relates how his fellow men and women on the Reserve know little or nothing of the teachings of Christ, and Eli has taken to giving little talks on religion to groups on the Reserve, and his fine, strong features shine radiantly at the thought of helping others as he was once helped.

In the meantime, Niagara Packers had bought out the Eaton coal business, and it was only natural that Eli went with the deal. To say that he has been a great asset to the Packers is a gross understatement. As a customer once said, "It's not that your coal is any better, we just like to see Eli's smile."

Eli has only two years to go before receiving a pension from the firm he has served so faithfully. To the people who know him, all that we have written is merely a tribute to a man whom they know is a fine man. To those who haven't met Eli Davis, we can only say that to meet him is an experience you will not soon forget. The best tribute that we can pay to him, is to say that it is WE who are privileged to be able to write about Eli Davis.

1945

This year saw the end of World War 2, with great relief from the burden of war. Tires were very scarce and it was hard to keep a car in operating order. Some of these difficulties are noted in the diary.

January saw the commencement of six weeks of gospel meetings in Windsor, Ontario, with Mr. Fred Nugent. Blessing accompanied them.

Mon. Jan. 01 Windsor Conf. Govan, Pell, Ferguson, Nugent.

Thu. Jan. 04 Seeing about cards and signs for meetings.

Fri. Jan. 05 Made calls. Put up sign at Hall. At Lever's. Children's meeting.

Sun. Jan. 07 Windsor. At McMurdo's and Ferguson's. Meeting.

Wed. Jan. 10 Mtg in High School. Lancaster's for supper. Mtg.

Thu. Jan. 11 Made calls. At Art Young's. Nice lot out.

Fri. Jan. 12 Lever's for dinner. S.S. Treat night.

Sat. Jan. 13 Made calls on boat at river. At D. Fryday's. Read a Psalm at Shepley's.

Sun. Jan. 14 Windsor. Tom Hutchinson's for dinner. Mtg at 4. Supper in Hall. Hall full at night. Mtg - Seek and save.

Thu. Jan. 18 Made calls and at Bodaly's for supper. Good mtg.

Fri. Jan. 19 Meeting in school, and gospel at night.

Sat. Jan. 20 Walked downtown. Spring Gardens S.S. Treat.

Sun. Jan. 21 Meeting at 4. Supper in Hall. Good gospel meeting.

Mon. Jan. 22 Mtg in Tee school at 3. Dean's for supper. Mtg.

Wed. Jan. 24 Mtg in school at 4.15. Armstrong's for supper. Mtg.

Fri. Jan. 26 Had walk. At Miles' for supper. Children's mtg.

Sun. Jan. 28 Windsor. At Duncan Ferguson's. Supper at Hall. Hall full for gospel meeting.

Mon. Jan. 29 Mtg in school at 3. At W. Reid's for supper. Mtg.

Wed. Jan. 31 Mtg in school at 9 am, and 4 pm. At Gorling's. Mtg.

Sun. Feb. 04 Windsor. Mtg at 4. Supper in Hall. Souls saved.

Wed. Feb. 07 P. Ritchie's for lunch. Art Young's for supper. Mtg.

Fri. Feb. 09 Wrote L. Russell (soldier.) Hoping in God for Salvation!

Sun. Feb. 11 Windsor. Mtg at 4. Supper in Hall. Regis' there and many more. Hall full. 5 saved. Meeting, Mark 8.37 - Gave.

Wed. Mar. 21 Sent off "A" gas ration form. Prayer meeting.

Thu. Mar. 22 To St. C. Saw about tire rations. Home by 5.

Thu. Apr. 12 President F. D. Roosevelt, U.S.A., died.

Fri. May 04 News of German surrender in Denmark and Holland.

Mon. May 07 Germany capitulated today. Prayer & thanksgiving mtg.

Tue. May 08 Public Holiday, "V E" day. Hearing the King speak on radio, also Churchill and McKenzie King.

Sun. June 10 Victoria Road Conference. Frank Pearcey and George Clark had Children's meeting. Frank and I to Orillia for gospel meeting.

Six weeks of tent meetings began in July at Mimico, Ontario, with Mr. Fred G. Watson.

Sun. July 08 To Toronto, Brock Ave. Agnew's for the day. First meeting in tent with F. G. Watson.

Mon. July 09 Mimico. Made calls at houses with F. G. Watson. Mtg.

Thu. July 12 Tent at 3. FGW & I at houses. At Longhurst's. Mtg.

Fri. July 13 McDonald's for supper. Meeting.

Sun. July 15 To Toronto. Hamilton's for dinner. S.S. in tent. Mtg.

Tue. July 17 Seeing baker about bread. "Advertiser." Meeting.

Wed. July 18 F. G .Watson and I at houses. Meeting.

Thu. July 19 Made calls at houses. T. Robinson's for supper. Mtg.

Sun. July 22 Brock Ave. S.S. at tent, 3pm. At Ken Beasley's.

Tue. July 24 Looking up children for mtg. Moffatt's for supper.

Thu. July 26 Called on W. Bennett & O. Sprunt. Put ad in paper.

Fri. July 27 At greenhouses. Potter's for supper. Mtg.

Sun. July 29 To Brock Ave. At Watson's. S.S. in tent. Large mtg.

Mon. July 30 At houses. T. Robinson's for supper. Meeting.

Tue. July 31 Day's for supper. Children's mtg and gospel meeting.

Mon. Aug. 06 Civic holiday. Mtg in tent at 3. Watson, Henderson, McMullen, T. Robinson, and I. Moffatt's for supper. Testimony mtg.

Fri. Aug. 10 At W. Stubb's and C. Steven's. Herb Day's for supper.

Wed. Aug. 15 Public holiday, "V J" day. Mtg in Junction at 3. Tent at 8.

Sun. Aug. 19 R. Hamilton's for dinner. S.S. in tent. Tent full. Last meeting in tent.

Mon. Aug. 20 Helped take down tent. Home to Grimsby.

Fri. Sep. 28 M&I left Grimsby at 7.30 for Detroit Conference. Congestion on bridge at Windsor, 2 hour delay. At Prayer mtg.

Wed. Oct. 03 Donald Clark and Gills came yesterday pm. 3 of us worked all day on roof. Lovely weather. Thank God. All went to the Falls at night and saw illuminations.

Sat. Oct. 13 M&I to Toronto. Two blowouts and taxi from Oakville, $5.50, to Toronto.

Thu. Nov. 22 To Toronto. Got tire fixed at Radford's. Paid fine $10. at City Hall, speed, 43 mph.

At the end of the year the gospel was proclaimed for four weeks in Guelph, Ontario, with Mr. Tom Wilkie.

Sun. Nov. 25 Alone to Guelph. Tom Erwin's for day. Had first meeting, Tom Wilkie and I.

Mon. Nov. 26 To Kitchener for pencils. At school. Children's mtg.

Tue. Nov. 27 Made calls. Stewart's for supper. Meeting.

Thu. Nov. 29 Some snow. At J. Ritchie's. Meeting.

Sun. Dec. 02 Left home 9.30. Frozen radiator and missed the feast. Sought to be "in the Spirit." At W. Turney's (Helen Dobbin). Mtg.

Mon. Dec. 03 Got Prestone in am. At school seeing children. Martin's for supper. Chldren's meeting.

Mon. Dec. 10 Tom & I made calls. Lit fire in Hall. At Buckley's for supper. Children's meeting. I opened - Peanut.

Tue. Dec. 11 Much talk re car insurance. "O Thou preserver of men!" Made calls and at Barron's for supper. Meeting, John 5.

Fri. Dec. 14 Made calls. At Roughley's and Stewart Sr's.

Sat. Dec. 15 Waxed floors. Put tracts in cars. Erwin's for supper.

Wed. Dec. 19 Made calls. At Norman Foster's and Burnham's. Mtg.

Fri. Dec. 21 Some strangers in to gospel meeting.

Sun. Dec. 23 T. Erwin's for the day. Last meeting.

April 16, 1946

And thou shalt remember all the way which the Lord thy God led thee these forty years in the wilderness, to humble thee, and to prove thee, to know what was in thine heart, whether thou wouldest keep his commandments, or no.   Deuteronomy 8.2.

With thankful heart and joyous tears, afresh I start;
'Tis forty years since that first step towards heaven,
With sin to part, my doubts and fears gone from my heart.
The glory nears, my sins are all forgiven.

It scarce seems it can be so long - the sky so blue,
That happy song I first began to sing;
Sun's brightest hue, birds sang among the sparkling dew,
A happy throng, the heavens with joy did ring.

What shall I say of that dear Friend? Through all the way
His love no end, His faithfulness and grace
Have power to stay; His help He sends for every day.
His wealth I spend, until I see His face.

He'll keep me still till days are done: to do His will,
Yea, His alone, this sure is always best;
O'er dale and hill, my race to run, nor stay until
The Victory's won. I then with Him shall rest.

G. L. S.

1946

Meetings for six weeks at Niagara Falls, Ont. with Mr. James Smith of Detroit, Mich., began the year.

Sun. Feb. 24 To Niagara Falls. Jas. Smith Detroit there. Pinches'for dinner. Mattice's for supper. Meeting in S. End Hall.

Mon. Feb. 25 Put up sign for meetings.

Wed. Feb. 27 Back to N. Falls. Smith & I made calls. Meeting.

Thu. Feb. 28 J. Smith & I at houses with cards. At Pinches'. Mtg.

Tue. Mar. 05 Winston Churchill spoke tonight, 10.30.

Fri. Mar. 08 Mtgs all week. Took J. Lawson & R. Davis to N.F.

Sun. Mar. 10 To N.F. Bailey's all day. Large mtg. God helped.

Thu. Mar. 14 J. Smith & I made calls. Hartley's for supper. Mtg.

Tue. Mar. 19 To N.F. at 3. At Ralph's and Fisher's. Meeting.

Fri. Mar. 22 To St.C. Saw Gordon Reager. At Sherriff's. Mtg.

Sun. Mar. 24 To N.F. At Mattice's for day. Adams' there too. Mtg.

Sun. Mar. 31 Drove alone to N.F. Picked up young Indian man. Dinner at Bailey's, supper at Pinches'. Gospel mtg.

Wed. Apr. 03 Called on Smythes, Dobsons, Petries, and McLeans.

Fri. Apr. 05 Called on Blacks, Millers, at Killough's for supper.

Sun. Apr. 07 To N. Falls. At Bailey's and Pinches'. Last mtg.

Tue. Apr. 16 Forty years saved. Thank God. Wrote some verses.

During May of 1946, Mr. Shivas and Mr. Robert Booth conducted four weeks of meetings in Campden, Ontario.

Sat. May 04 R. Booth, A. King & I called on houses in Campden.

Sun. May 05 Grimsby. R. Booth & I had our first mtg in Campden.

Mon. May 06 To Campden in aft. Made calls. Meeting.

Thu. May 09 Mtg in Old People's Home & school in aft. Mtg.

Fri. May 10 To Campden, M&I, to Children's meeting.

Mon. May 13 Bob & I making calls at Campden. Took Davis' to mtg.

Fri. May 17 At Campden school. Took Quinns to Children's meeting. Heard of 3 generations saved.

Tue. May 21 Bob & I visiting at Rockway and Gordon Byes. Mtg.

Mon. May 27 Up to Campden in aft. Bob & I visiting. M&I to mtg.

Wed. May 29 Bob & I at Campden at Lyne's and D. Pitchkos'. Mtg.

Fri. May 31 Had mtg in school at Campden. Children's meeting.

December 31st, 1947

Today is the last day of the year, my dear,
And the moments are passing away;
At times in our eye was a tear, my dear,
But thank God, it was not there to stay.

For the days were seldom drear, my dear,
And the most of them filled with a song;
God was better than all our fear, my dear,
And the dark days have never been long.

Today I say, be of good cheer, my dear,
As a fresh "Ebenezer" we raise;
His "goodness and mercy" is clear my dear,
So we offer our tribute of praise.

The New Year is coming quite near, my dear,
But still we can trust in His grace;
For soon will our Saviour be here, my dear,
'Twill be glory to look on His face.

The sound of His voice we can hear, my dear,
To sweeten the days that may come,
May we serve Him with listening ear, my dear,
For the call that shall gather us home.

To Maude, G. L. S.

1947 - 1957

In the year 1947 a new cloud appeared on the horizon for Mr. Shivas. I began keeping company with his daughter Elizabeth, who was nursing at Toronto General Hospital. I have already given my testimony in this book in connection with gospel meetings at Merlin, Ontario, in the spring of 1939.

We were both attending Brock Ave. Gospel Hall. I was boarding with Marguerite Robertson and her mother. Marguerite enlisted me to drive Mr. and Mrs. Bob Steen to and from meetings. Uncle Bob, as we called him, had a dark green Chrysler sedan, with 'Fluid Drive.' His eyesight was failing and he needed someone to drive for him and his wife. Mrs. Hattie Steen was a sister of Mrs. Shivas.

Needless to say, I jumped at the opportunity, and even volunteered to teach Uncle Bob's niece to drive. The rest, as they say, is history! Betty and I were married in Toronto, on January 10th, 1948, with Mr. Shivas officiating.

Mrs. Shivas' family was raised in South River, as you will recall from the first of the book, and several of them had built cottages on nearby Eagle Lake.

In 1935 Mr. Shivas obtained a lot on the lake, and with the help of brother Roly Peacock, built a genuine log cottage from the logs on the property. This meant that Mrs. Shivas would have the company of some of her family in the summer months, and would allow Mr. Shivas to get around to the northern assemblies, where he had laboured for many years.

It was a fortuitous arrangement, and gave many of the Lord's people a few day's rest when they visited the Shivas'. It was also an attractive place for the Shivas' grandchildren. Many a comment in the diary reads, "Dinner and supper with the dear children at the lake."

It also afforded an opportunity when our family was on vacation for Mr. Shivas and me to explore some nearby creeks and fish for speckled trout.

He wasn't what you would call an ardent fisherman, yet he was an ardent "fisher of men." I had to begin fishing quickly when we went out together, because after he tried a few holes, he would call, "Yoohoo, Murray, come on, let's go, there's nothing here." I wouldn't answer, because I'd be squatted down underneath the brush at the water's edge, quietly fishing. He would come looking for me, and go right by me within a few feet without seeing me!

One incident stands out in my memory. We had tried fishing in the Distress River, south west of Eagle Lake, at a beautiful waterfall, without much success, and had made our way along the side of a field of oats back to the road.

Away down the road, at a brisk rate of speed and in a great cloud of dust, came a black pickup truck. Mr. Shivas moved to the centre of the road, and swinging both arms, hailed down the truck. The young driver had no choice but to stop, and accomplished it in a shower of gravel and sand. Mr. Shivas went up to the driver's door and started a very pleasant conversation with the driver, who was looking us over warily.

Finally Mr. Shivas said, "Well, we'd better let you go." Then he put his foot on the running board, his hand on the door latch, and leaning up close to the man, he said, "You know, you're very fortunate that this pair of rascals is letting you away this easy. The truth is, my mother was a common thief, and my father was a receiver of stolen goods! And worse than that, my older brother was a murderer!!" Each statement was made with his usual emphasis.

With this, I saw the man gently ease the truck into first gear, quite prepared to extricate himself at a moment's notice. Meanwhile, I stood at the edge of the road, with my fishing rod in one hand, and a big smile on my face, trying to look as innocent as possible.

Mr. Shivas backed off to arm's length and began to chuckle. "Do you know what I mean?" he asked. "Do you remember from Sunday School, how Eve took of the forbidden fruit, and how Adam took it from her, and how Cain slew Abel?"

The man agreed that he knew, and Mr. Shivas went on to remind him that we were all sinners, descendants of Adam, and in need of a Saviour. He told him of God's love in sending His Son to die in our place on the Cross of Calvary.

Finally, Mr. Shivas told him who we were, thanked him for his time, and he went on his way, perhaps not rejoicing, but certainly impressed.

Mr. Shivas said to me, as we watched the truck go around the first bend in the road, "I love my fellow man."

Then we headed down the road to the car, and came upon a small weather-beaten church building, which obviously hadn't been used for many years. He managed to get the door open and we stepped inside.

There was a rough pulpit, and a few wooden pews. We took off our caps and sat down for a few minutes, then both had a word of prayer, and went on our way.

Such a "fishing" trip is not easily forgotten!

Another such "fish" story is told concerning a conversation Mr. Shivas had with a local minister in Grimsby.

It is in connection with the following diary entries.

1949 Sat. Jun. 11 Got new hose connection put on gas tank pipe at Slades, $1. Some work in garden. Phoned Clyde.

Sun. Jun. 12 M&I to **Clyde**. Mansell Willmott's for supper and all night. Gospel meeting.

Mrs. Willmott asked Mr. Bob Reeve over to their place after meeting for a visit with Mr. Shivas, knowing that Bob was concerned about his soul's welfare.

Mon. Jun. 13 Bob Reeve saved last night. God grant it. Made calls in am at Reeve's and Paul's, and at M&B's, Drumbo, for dinner. At Brantford and Ham. on way home by about 5. Thank God for all.

On Tuesday, June 14th, Mr. Shivas met this minister downtown in Grimsby, and the gentleman told Mr. Shivas about the fish he had caught the previous Saturday.

Mr. Shivas replied that he had been fishing on Sunday. This was a shock to the minister, but not as great a shock as when Mr. Shivas told him that he had caught a fish over six feet long!

All who know how tall brother Bob Reeve is, will appreciate this story.

During the years 1950 to 1962, Mr. and Mrs. Shivas were able to make a yearly trip to the Conference at Garnavillo, Iowa. They stayed in a cabin during the conference, and thoroughly enjoyed the weekend. The 1956 diary gives a sample year's expedition to Iowa.

1956 Mon. May 28 Up 6am. M&I left before 8 and came on to Echo Bay, 3.15pm. Lost Teddy and hunting for him before and after supper. Gave away tracts and spoke with some. Thank God for all. *(Losing the dog just provided more opportunities!)*

Tue. May 29 Hurley's all night. Teddy back in am. Came to Clark's, Soo, for the day. Over river for mtg. Cabin at night. Thank God.

Wed. May 30 Good night in motel, $5. Ate lunch at Manistique, by the lake as last year. Came by 28-98-2-41-35 to White Front Cabins, No.1, $4., 10 miles north of Green Bay. Had walk by road and river after supper. Lovely evening and good day indeed. The glory all to God.

Thu. May 31 Left cabin 8 am. Dinner at Madison, Wis., Dubuque, and on to **Manchester** Prayer meeting. Read Isa. 53 - Pleased God. Came on to Garnavillo. Thank God.

Fri. June 01 **Garnavillo**. Kuenzels Cabins all night. Comfortable, but cool night. Good day and good Prayer meeting. F. G. Watson spoke.

Sat. June 02 Spoke in am mtg on Luke 17 - Returning, and read verses "Go back". Good weather and crowds. Maude & I at all meetings. Staying in cabin. Thank God for all His mercy.

Sun. June 03 Garnavillo Conference. At Bible Reading, after breakfast in cabin, John 20, good. Good morning meeting. Sunday School, Paul Elliott opened. I spoke on "Blacker." Left after 4. Cabin at Sycamore at night. Thank God.

Mon. June 04 Drove all day via Chicago, and to Glencoe, Ont. by 10 pm. *(Where his daughter and family were then living.)* Thank God for all His mercies.

Tue. June 05 Nice visit with the dear children. David Calderhead for supper. Went with him and helped in meeting at Newbury.

Wed. June 06 Left Glencoe 9 am. Via No.3 and got new cultivator at Becketts. Hwy 400 to Orillia. Clark's for supper & home, 9.30.

Thu. June 07 M&I assembling new garden tractor and using same in garden. Got load of wood from Andersons. Saw Roly at hospital. To Chapman Valley prayer meeting. God is good.

The Diaries of George L. Shivas

In 1954 the urge to get back to "home territory" became irresistable. This urge was expedited by the challenge of tearing down the old 2 story family frame home in South River, and rebuilding a bungalow type home on the original stone foundation, using the available lumber.

He and I measured the foundation and drew a set of plans for the house. There was no need to skimp, the foundation was eighteen inches wide.

There was an ample supply of 12" to 16" wide pine boards, a full inch or more thick, with which the newly built house was sheeted, both inside and outside the framed walls.

Anything Mr. Shivas built was constructed sturdily!

A few years later he built a covered driveway from the house to the street. This meant no snow shovelling over that distance in the wintertime. It also provided a place to walk and exercise in inclement weather.

Mr. Jim Hicks, stone mason, of the Chapman Valley assembly, and now with the Lord, built the fireplace and chimney. To this day, both are masterpieces of stone work.

1954 Fri. Sep. 17 Clearing up old lean-to foundation today.

This entry is noteworthy. Mrs. Shivas was born in that lean-to when the original house was being built in 1885. Her parents and family were moving by wagon from Magnetawan to South River. As they were coming over Bunker Hill near Eagle Lake, a wheel came off and Mrs. Holditch fell out of the wagon. Maude Robena was born that night in the lean-to of the new house while the nurse held an umbrella over her mother. The lean-to had sheeting on the roof, but no shingles yet, and the rain leaked through freely.

Mr. and Mrs. Shivas lived in this home in South River from 1954, until he moved to his eternal home in 1963.

Our Fortieth Wedding Anniversary

It's forty years today, my dear,
Since we began our journey here
As man and wife together.
The skies have not been always clear,
But love and joy have kept us near,
In bright and cloudy weather.

Our Ebenezer now we raise,
A tribute to Jehovah's praise,
As we His care remember.
His faithfulness through all the days
Is keeping us in all our ways,
In June or dark November.

So by His grace we onward press,
Our love and joy are none the less
Than when we first began, dear,
For Jesus' sake, God still will bless,
And keep us safe in strain or stress,
As loving wife and man, dear.

G.L.S. April 8, 1949

1958

The last 5 years of his life, Mr. Shivas fulfilled two of his own sermons, "Going on still," and "A little farther."

Wed. Jan. 01 New Year = New Mercies!!! SNOW. Maybe 6". Shovelled same, broke driveway with car. M&I had walk. "O give thanks unto the Lord for He is good!"

Thu. Jan. 02 Took light wood for kindling to Hall in car.

Fri. Jan. 03 Up town with car in am and got candies, oranges & nuts for S.S. Treat. At Hall in aft. Cut wood, lit fire, put lesson on blackboard for S.S. Treat at 7.30. 32 children, 10 adults.

Sat. Jan. 04 M&I to Sundridge. Got this diary, 95c. Fixed Hall for the Lord's Day. Thank God.

Sun. Jan. 05 **South River**. Good gospel meeting, 29 out.

Mon. Jan. 06 Very dizzy all am. Some better in late aft.

Sun. Jan. 12 S.R. M&I out in am, 7. 12 at night mtg but help.

Thu. Jan. 16 Talk with J. Murdock. To Chapman Valley meeting.

Fri. Jan. 17 Stormy day - blizzard. Uptown in aft. Saw Dave P.

Tue. Jan. 21 Mild. Cut some wood. 13 out to meeting.

Wed. Jan. 22 Walked Teddy. Gave tracts to R.R. engine. Good day.

Sun. Jan. 26 S.R. 8 out in am. Gospel alone, 17. Took Dick home.

Tue. Jan. 28 Mild and snowy. Visited H. Loney in aft. 16 at mtg.

Wed. Jan. 29 More snow. Paid car Ins. $23. "Oh to trust Him then more fully!" Thank God.

Thu. Jan. 30 More snow. Shovelled our own and at the Hall. Called on King's and down to Novar to see Mrs. Haggart. At Simms' for supper. At C.V. mtg. Thank God for all.

Fri. Jan. 31 Dave & Ena up a while. Got hymn books at station.

Sun. Oct. 26 South River. First gospel meeting, Stan Simms & I.

Fri. Oct. 31 Very good meeting, 26 out. Thank God.

Sun. Nov. 02 Two Roads chart up. Nice few out.

Fri. Nov. 21 Elmer Merrick professed Tuesday. Meetings continue.

Wed. Nov. 26 Snowy day. Had walk and fall. God grant mercy. 16 at meeting.

Tue. Dec. 09 Our last meeting. God is good.

Wed. Dec. 31 "Surely goodness and mercy ..... all the days."

Fifty Years in Christ Jesus!

I've journeyed on along life's way
With strength from Heaven each passing day,
Through this dark vale of tears,
Since first I learned to sing and pray,
And all my cares on Jesus lay,
And now it's fifty years.

The road has led o'er many a hill,
By waters rough and waters still,
Midst hopes and doubts and fears;
His paths are right and sweet His will,
Goodness and mercy follow still,
And have for fifty years.

April sixteen, that happy date,
Nineteen o' six - the time seems late,
Our cries still reach His ears;
He still regards our low estate,
And leads us on to Heaven's gate,
And has for fifty years.

Our God is good, He doeth good,
And near my soul has ever stood;
His love His Name endears;
To please Him, serve Him, this we would,
To love us more He never could
Than through these fifty years.

And now our heart and voice we raise,
A song of gratitude and praise,
As clear the Glory nears;
To keep His Word in all our ways,
To spend for Him a few more days,
Who knows no end of years.

G. L. S., April 16, 1956.

1960

Four weeks of gospel meetings in Dunchurch, Ontario, with bro. Stan Simms, in January of this year, proved to be Mr. Shivas' last series. There were souls saved at that time, including brother Ken Moore.

Wed. Jan. 06 Shovelled snow. (Much snow in am.) and cut wood, and some chinks in shed. Stan Simms and I to Dunchurch. Made calls re Orange Hall. Simms' for supper. 23 at meeting, Robertson's home. Thank God.

Fri. Jan. 08 Very cold day and some drifting. More snow through night. Shovelled back and front. Cut some wood. M&I to Dunchurch. Spoke from Luke 14. Thank God for all.

Mon. Jan. 11 Another cold night. Snow and wood! M&I to Chapman Valley Hall and got 4 tent seats. Took E. & B. Alexander and Roy to Dunchurch. Spoke from John 9 - Altogether. Thank God.

Wed. Jan. 13 Took W. Walker and Paul, also Sam & Vi Patterson to Dunchurch, Mark 11 - Colt.

Thu. Jan. 14 M&I took Ed M. and his mother to Dunchurch, Josh. 2.

Fri. Jan. 15 M&I to Dunchurch alone. Called at Roly's. Large mtg.

Sun. Jan. 17 M&I to Dunchurch, took 4 from Merrick's. Nice few in.

Mon. Jan. 18 M&I to Dunchurch. Mtg, 2 Kings 6. Much snow! Home safe.

Mon. Jan. 25 Very stormy. Small mtg. Heard of 3 souls saved! To God be all the Glory.

Mon. Feb. 15 Milder. Cut some wood. Shovelled some snow. M&I to Dunchurch in evening. Further blessing! Thank God for all.

Thu. Feb. 25 M&I to Chapman Valley mtg. Gas at Swan's, and at King's. Ken Moore and wife at meeting, from Dunchurch. Good. Thank God for all.

A Little _____.

For yet **a little while,** and he that shall come
will come, and will not tarry.   Heb. 10.37.

"A little while" - to watch and wait,
To walk the way, so plain and straight,
And soon we'll reach the Golden Gate,
Then we shall see His face!

_____

And as for me, when I came from Padan, Rachel died
by me in the land of Canaan in the way, when yet
there was but **a little way** to come unto Ephrath.
                                            Genesis 48.7.

"A little way" - it can't be long,
The way He leads is never wrong;
The Lord's own joy will keep us strong
To run life's little race!

_____

I know thy works: behold, I have set before thee
an open door, and no man can shut it: for thou
hast **a little strength,** and hast kept my word,
and hast not denied my name.   Rev. 3.8

"A little strength" - to keep His Word,
To sow the seed, to wield the sword,
And then to share His own reward,
"We'll praise Him for His grace!"

                                            G. L. S.

1963

Mr. Shivas faithfully supported the local assembly, and as well rarely missed going to the Chapman Valley assembly prayer meeting on Thursday evening, spring, summer, fall, or winter.

I recall brother Stan Simms imitating Mr. Shivas calling him on the phone, and saying, "Hello Stanley, don't think we'll make it down tonight. No, not feeling too well, and the weather looks bad." Mr. Simms would reply, "That's fine, Mr. Shivas, we'll be praying for you." But when Mr. Simms would arrive at meeting, the Shivas' would be there, almost every time.

He put everything he had into everything he did; in his preaching, in his praying, in splitting wood, in lighting the Hall fire, in shovelling the walks, in gathering up children, and in never failing to drop a word for the Lord to the perishing at every opportunity.

He took ill on Friday, August 23rd, and departed this life early the next morning. The last entry in his diary was on Thursday, August 22nd, 1963.

Thu. Aug. 22 Jim Clark called. Picked some corn and took to lake for Ren Fletcher and Martin Kerr. Nice visit. More work on floor, washed car, walk in bush. Lovely day. Thank God for all.

Brother Albert Joyce and brother Stanley Simms shared the funeral service. Brother Joyce summed up his life accurately with the words, "He loved the people of God, the assembly of God, and the truth of God, which he sought to maintain to the end."

He was laid to rest in the South River cemetery where his tomb-stone is inscribed with the verse John 3.16 in full.

George and Maude Shivas

Epilogue

A fitting way to end this book is to add the following letter written by brother John Vance, of Toronto, who was with Mr. Shivas when he passed into the presence of his Lord.

Willowdale, Ontario.
June 23, 1975.

Dear brother,

The first time I heard Mr. Shivas speak was at the Creemore conference in 1958 at Thanksgiving time. He read from Nehemiah and asked the audience to stand up as he read the Word. He said, "I can give you Scripture for doing that," and he referred to Nehemiah 8.5, "And Ezra opened the book in the sight of all the people, (for he was above all the people) and when he opened it, all the people stood up."

On other occasions he impressed me with the reverence he had for the Word of God. At Christmas in 1958 I spent five days in South River at the home of Ed Miller. We were at the Shivas' home for supper one night and I placed my Bible on the table with the hymnbook on top. A little later he spotted it and in a voice no one could take offence at, commented, "Who put this book on top of the Bible?" He then put the Bible on top, saying, "The Word of God must always have first place."

At the Breaking of Bread, in South River, the next Lord's Day, was the first time that I, a young believer, ever took part in a morning meeting. I believe it was due to Mr. Shivas' whole attitude as the "leading brother" there, that one felt free to do so. He helped to give an informality to the meeting, a simple remembrance, without any hint of ritual, that made it easy to take part.

The Grass Never Grew Greener!

On another occasion, in June 1960, he took Ed Miller and me to a cottage meeting in Dunchurch. We assumed the meeting had all been arranged, but just before we got there, he said, "Which of you brethren is going first?" After a little word himself, he had us give our testimonies, and have a little preach. It was so informal, with his occasional comments about us, and what our plans were for the summer. It was in Dunchurch, but it was by no means a churchy service.

Concerning giving to the Lord, he spoke of the devil tempting him to give less. "Don't forget, you have quite a few expenses this week, and the car seems to be giving a bit of trouble," and so on, until Mr. Shivas told him, "If you don't stop bothering me, I'll give the Lord the whole thing!"

Indeed, on the matter of money, I believe that many a person in the South River area received help quietly from him, when they were in need, and these were often unsaved folk as well.

What comes most vividly to mind, is the time that dear Mr. Shivas was called home.

I had been staying with Mr. Stan Simms in Magnetawan, and had decided to go to North Bay to see Ed and Milly Miller. On the way I called in to see Mr. and Mrs. Shivas, and found them getting ready to go to the New Carlow conference. While Mr. Shivas was in the bedroom dressing, Mrs. Shivas said that she thought he was not as well as usual. She was very keen that I should go with them and do the driving. Before I left, Mr. Shivas went out to the garden to get some corn and other items, for me to take to the Millers.

I left then, but since the Hall in South River had recently been renovated, I stopped the car there to have a look. It was just down the street from their home. Moments before I drove off, Mrs. Shivas came running down the street to say Mr. Shivas had taken sick. Rushing back, I found him lying on the couch, his face ashen. I raised him up, and after a few minutes he came around a bit, but was very weak. The doctor came, and advised taking him to the hospital in North Bay for further examination. Mrs. Shivas was reluctant, due to the difficulty of visiting him, so the doctor agreed to leave him for the night and return in the morning. I agreed to stay with them.

The Diaries of George L. Shivas

That evening Mr. Shivas spoke of people in Bracondale, and as I mentioned some who were no longer there, but had passed on, he remarked, "Frail mortal man." During the night he took another attack of breathlessness, but he revived. About 7am, with Mrs. Shivas kneeling beside him, he had another attack, and though I raised him up, and we both tried to revive him, he died in my arms, and his spirit returned unto God who gave it.

That was Saturday, August 24th, 1963. The undertaker made a remark to me in the hallway which I never forgot. "Well, Mr. Shivas has gone to the place that he tried to tell everyone else about." No doubt this man had heard more than one word of gospel from Mr. Shivas.

So the mortal frame by which we remembered him was laid in the grave a few days later, and as was said at the cemetery, "If I could die with a testimony like Mr. Shivas', I would be happy."

The words, quoted so often of the passing of a loved one, were very true to me, in this case. "Thou shalt be missed, because thy seat will be empty."

Yours sincerely,
(Sgd) John P. Vance

"The time is brief —
Soon He shall come
— To bring relief,
To take us home.

This is our day —
To keep His word
To watch, to pray, —
Use shield + sword.

— To sow the seed,
The lost to seek
The lambs to feed —
To spend, to speak.

To live for Him,
Who for us died.
Our Camp to trim,
To shine world-wide.

One brief short life,
'Twill soon be gone
Past storm & strife
To share the throne."

G.L.S.

Tune. "Beulah Land"

Grimsby Mar 10/41.

The Grass Never Grew Greener!

Series

Series of meetings held by Mr. Shivas, of 2 or more week's duration.

YEAR	MONTH	WEEKS	PLACE	WITH
No diaries until 1912				
1912	MAR	3	Hartfell, Ont.	Ed Steen
1913			Strongville, Ont.	John Silvester
1915	AUG	2	Arnstein, Ont.	Ed Steen
	SEP	2	Deer Lake, Ont.	John McCartney
	OCT	4	South River, Ont.	Ed Steen
1916	FEB	4	Chapman Valley, Ont.	Ed Steen
	MAR	3	Sault Ste. Marie, Ont.	Ed Steen
	AUG	5	Chapman Valley, Ont.	Ed Steen
	NOV	4	Duluth, Minn.	Alone
1917	JAN	14	Cheboygan, Mich.	Leo Sheldrake
	NOV	3	Pickford, Mich.	Leo Sheldrake
1918	MAR	3	Victoria Road, Ont.	R. McClintock
	APR	4	Collingwood, Ont.	John Silvester
	JUL	6	Pickford, Mich.	Leo Sheldrake
1919	FEB	6	Arnstein, Ont.	Ed Steen
	MAY	13	Chapman Valley, Ont.	Ed Steen
	SEP	2	Deer Lake, Ont.	Ormer Sprunt
	NOV	6	Orillia, Ont.	Alone
1920	JAN	3	Victoria Road, Ont.	R. McClintock
	JUN	4	Chapman Valley, Ont.	Ed Steen
	JUL	6	Cambray, Ont.	EdSteen
	SEP	2	Orillia, Ont.	John Silvester
	NOV	5	Sault Ste. Marie, Ont.	Ed Steen
	DEC	5	Sault Ste. Marie, Mich.	Leo Sheldrake

YEAR	MONTH	WEEKS	PLACE	WITH
1922	MAR	3	Collingwood, Ont.	George Gould Sr.
	MAY	3	Victoria Road, Ont.	Alone
	JUN	10	Udney, Ont.	Herb Harris
	NOV	4	Toronto, Ont. Lansing.	Alone
1923	AUG	5	Montreal, Que.	Hugh Walker
	NOV	5	Owen Sound, Ont.	John Silvester
1924	MAR	3	Orillia, Ont.	John Silvester
	MAY	4	Midland, Ont.	Alone
	JUL	7	Orillia, Ont.(Tent, Gill St.) Alone	
	SEP	2	Strongville, Ont.	Alone
	OCT	3	Strongville, Ont.	J. Pearson
1925	JAN	6	South River, Ont.	Ben Widdifield
	MAR	2	Chapman Valley, Ont.	Alone
	JUL	7	Montreal, Que.	Mr. Livingstone
	OCT	2	Niagara Falls, Ont.	Alone
1926	FEB	4	Cheboygan, Mich.	Alone
	APR	3	Orillia, Ont.	Alone
	JUL	7	Eldon, Ont.	John Gilchrist
	NOV	5	Collingwood, Ont.	Ben Widdifield
1927	JAN	8	Midland, Ont.	John Silvester
	OCT	5	Earlton, Ont.	Alone
1928	JAN	4	Grimsby, Ont.	Ed Steen
	JUL	7	Bracebridge, Ont.	Robert Bruce
	OCT	2	Chicago, Ill. Avondale.	Alone
1929	JUL	6	Manitoulin Island.	Alone
	NOV	2	Houston, Texas.	Alone
	DEC	7	Long Beach, Cal.	R. A. Barr

YEAR	MONTH	WEEKS	PLACE	WITH
1930	FEB	3	Los Angeles, Cal.	R. A. Barr
	MAR	5	Monrovia, Cal.	R. A. Barr
	MAY	6	Vancouver, B.C.	Alone
1931	FEB	5	Sault Ste. Marie, Ont.	Leo Sheldrake
	MAR	3	Sault Ste. Marie, Mich.	Leo Sheldrake
	JUL	8	Dunnville, Ont.	Tom Wilkie
	OCT	2	Grimsby, Ont.	Tom Wilkie
1932	MAY	5	Sundridge, Ont.	Ed Steen
1933	JAN	6	Grimsby, Ont.	George Gould Jr.
1934	JAN	4	Straffordville, Ont.	John Govan
	FEB	3	Grimsby, Ont.	John Govan
	JUL	6	Port Dover, Ont.	Fred Nugent
	SEP	3	Sault Ste. Marie, Ont.	Lorne McBain
	OCT	2	Duluth, Minn.	Lorne McBain
	NOV	4	Grimsby, Ont.	Fred Nugent
1935	FEB	9	Beamsville, Ont.	Alone
	NOV	4	Burlington, Ont.	John Gilchrist
1937	FEB	4	Grimsby, Ont.	G. G. Johnston
	AUG	4	Arnstein, Ont.	Alone
	NOV	3	Grassie, Ont.	Tom Wilkie
1938	JAN	6	Grassie, Ont.	Tom Wilkie
	MAR	7	St. Catharines, Ont.	Tom Wilkie
	NOV	5	Niagara Falls, Ont.	Alone
1939	JAN	4	Niagara Falls, Ont.	Tom Wilkie
	FEB	7	Toronto, Ont. Pape Ave.	Alone
	MAY	6	Merlin, Ont.	Fred Nugent
	OCT	7	Toronto, Ont. Bracondale Hall	Alone

YEAR	MONTH	WEEKS	PLACE	WITH
1940	JAN	9	St. Catharines, Ont.	Fred Nugent
	APR	4	Fenwick, Ont.	Robert Booth
	JUL	5	Duluth, Minn.	Alone
1941	FEB	7	Grimsby, Ont.	Robert Booth
	NOV	5	Port Dover, Ont.	Alone
1942	FEB	4	Hamilton, Ont. Kensington Ave.	Alone
	MAR	6	Watford, Ont.	Fred Nugent
	JUN	3	Embro, Ont.	Fred Nugent
	JUL	3	Embro, Ont.	Fred Nugent
1943	FEB	7	Galt, Ont.	Tom Wilkie
1945	JAN	6	Windsor, Ont.	Alone
	JUL	6	Mimico, Ont.	Fred G. Watson
	NOV	3	Guelph, Ont.	Tom Wilkie
1946	FEB	6	Niagara Falls, Ont.	James Smith Detroit
	MAY	5	Campden, Ont.	Robert Booth
1947	JAN	4	Oshawa, Ont.	Fred Nugent
1949	FEB	5	Grimsby, Ont.	A. Philip
1953	JAN	4	Grimsby, Ont.	Tom Wilkie
1958	OCT	6	South River, Ont.	Stan Simms
1960	JAN	4	Dunchurch, Ont.	Stan Simms

Contemporaries

The following list is of servants of the Lord who were contemporaries of Mr. Shivas, during the different decades of his life. The list may not be complete, but contains the names, gleaned from the diaries, of older brethren with whom he shared ministry.

Some readers will note the names of brethren they knew in younger days. The memory of these beloved men who served their Lord faithfully, and are now in His Presence, may inspire fresh confidence in the words of the Lord Jesus found in Mark 12.27,

" He is not the God of the dead, but the God of the living."

1907 to 1910	Beattie	J. C.
	Douglas	W. P.
	Lyon	James
	Morrison	A.
	Stack	Edward
	Steen	Edmund
	Telfer	Robert
	Watson	Fred G.
During the 1910's	Barker	Mr.
	Binch	S.
	Bradford	Ben
	Bruce	Robert
	Butcher	Mr.
	Cameron	Dr.
	Crone	H.
	Dempsey	H.
	Dickson	J. T.
	Dobbin	Thomas
	Duncan	George
	Ferguson	John
	Fletcher	Henry
	Gill	John
	Goodfellow	John
	Greaves	J.
	Harris	Herb
	Harris	Russell

1910's continued	Hicks	George T.
	Hogg	Mr.
	Johnston	Gordon G.
	Johnson	W. B.
	Keller	Charles
	Keller	Sam
	Kendrick	B. W.
	Livingstone	Alexander
	Livingstone	D.
	Martin	Dr.
	Matthews	William
	McCartney	John
	McClintock	R.
	McCracken	R.
	McCrory	Robert
	McDonald	Alex
	McGeachy	Dan
	McMullen	James
	Muir	T. D. W.
	Munro	Donald
	Oliver	David H.
	Paul	J. G.
	Pearson	Joe
	Pinches	George
	Rouse	J. J.
	Roy	D.
	Scott	D. R.
	Sheldrake	Leo
	Silvester	John
	Sykes	S.
	Touzeau	Thomas
	Waugh	James
	Widdifield	Ben
	Williams	W.
During the 1920's	Baillie	William
	Barr	R. A.
	Bernard	John
	Black	Thomas
	Conaway	J.

1920's continued....................Crocker   A. R.

Garratt	George
Gilchrist	John
Gillespie	William
Gould Sr.	George
Govan	John
Gunn	James
Gunn	John
Joyce	Albert
Kerr	Mr.
Marshall	James
Mehl	F. W.
Mick	Steve
Miller	David
Milnes	Mr.
McBain	Lorne
McClure	W. J.
McEwen	Hugh
McEwen	John Knox
McEwen	Sam
Nugent	Fred
Pinches	William
Rae	Sam
Schwartz	F.
Stewart	Archie
Thorpe	Mr.
Warke	William
Wilkie	Tom

During the 1930's...................Adams   Arnold

Alves	Hector
Blackwood	James
Bousefield	William
Brandt	Louis
Davies	Vincent
Dickson	R. J.
Douglas	Andrew
Downey	H. K.
Draper	Charles

1930's continued	Elliott	Paul
	Foster	Wm.
	Gould Jr.	George
	Greer	Sam
	Hamilton	Sam
	Hatherly	Mr.
	Innes	Charles
	Klabunda	Albert
	McConkey	Ross
	McCracken	C.
	Moneypenny	J.
	Paul	Mervin
	Pell	Peter
	Pell	Will
	Simpson	Mr.
	Smith	George
	Smith	Oswold
	Smith	W. G.
	Spink	James F.
	Stenhouse	Andrew
	Summers	Charles
	Taylor	G. P.
	Willoughby	C. H.
	Winemiller	Mr.

Postscript

If anyone is interested in a certain series of meetings or a particular place or time, please feel free to write for details. Only portions of the diaries are included in the book, but all the diaries are available on disk. The records of any particular place or time can be readily copied, and will be sent to you free of charge.

Or if anyone has more details of any time or event,

I would be pleased to add them to the records.

Just write to:

Murray D. Regis,
80 Ontario Street North,
Apt. 809,
MILTON, Ontario. L9T 4Z6